What is Modern Israel?

Yakov M. Rabkin

Translated by Fred A. Reed

First published in 2014 by Les Éditions Écosociété, Montréal, under the title Comprendre l'État d'Israël. Idéologie, religion et société.

First English edition published 2016 by Pluto Press

345 Archway Road, London N6 5AA

www.plutobooks.com

Copyright © Les Éditions Écosociété 2012; English translation © Fred A. Reed 2016

The right of Yakov M. Rabkin to be identified as the author of this work has been asserted by him in accordance with the Copyright, Designs and Patents Act 1988.

British Library Cataloguing in Publication Data
A catalogue record for this book is available from the British Library

ISBN 978 0 7453 3582 7 Hardback
ISBN 978 0 7453 3581 0 Paperback
ISBN 978 1 7837 1782 8 PDF eBook
ISBN 978 1 7837 1784 2 Kindle eBook
ISBN 978 1 7837 1783 5 EPUB eBook

The publishers and author are grateful to the SODEC for their help in the translation of this book.

Typeset by Curran Publishing Services, Norwich

Printed and bound by CPI Group (UK) Ltd, Croydon, CR0 4YY

'A key text in the search for a sustainable and just approach to the future of Israel and Palestine, and should be read and reflected upon by anyone concerned with the wellbeing of these two peoples.'
– Richard Falk, former UN Special Rapporteur on Human Rights, author of *Palestine: The Legitimacy of Hope*

'Insightful and useful to all concerned about the future of Israel.'
– Ronnie Kasrils, former Minister of Intelligence Services, South Africa

'A precise and empathic account that will benefit all involved. A must-read.'
– Professor Gil Anidjar, Columbia University, author of *The Jew, the Arab: A History of the Enemy*

'A bold and thought-provoking work.'
– Professor Richard Foltz, Concordia University, author of *Iran in World History*

Contents

Acknowledgments

I would like to thank Mr. M. Billis, Mr. F. Derbesse, Ms. D. Glup, Professor K. Kanno, Mr. A. Kurganov and Rabbi G. Shuster-Bouskila for their corrections to a text for which I remain solely responsible. However, I cannot be responsible for the content of quotes, pro- and anti-Zionist, that some readers may find objectionable.

In view of the rapidly changing events in and around Israel, I have updated and slightly modified the English translation of the original text. In the process of preparing this book, I have benefited from exchanges of views with colleagues, as well as with audiences, around the world who have heard me speak on the state of Israel and on Zionism. The questions asked by journalists, especially in Japan where this book was published in a first version, broadened my horizons and helped me clarify my thoughts. All the members of my family, along with numerous guests at our Sabbath table, have listened with good grace to repeated and detailed discussions on the subject. Their participation and their benevolence are extremely dear to me, particularly as each one of them has his or her own views on the subject of this book.

Glossary

Most terms, except those identified as or clearly belonging to another language, are derived from the Hebrew. The Hebrew letters "het" and "he" are transliterated as English "h."

Agudat Israel, or **Aguda** (short form): Association of Israel, an Orthodox movement and political party founded in 1912.

Aliya: going up, meaning immigration to Israel; olim: immigrants to Israel.

Ashkenazis: Central and Eastern European Jews.

Betar: acronym for Brit Yosef Trumpeldor (Josef Trumpeldor Alliance), a militarist youth organization founded by Jabotinsky in 1923.

Bund (Yiddish), lit. alliance: the General Alliance of Jewish Workers of Russia and Poland, founded 1897.

Emancipation: ongoing process begun at the end of the 18th century, which granted Jews equality before the law and abolished the political, social, and professional restrictions under which they had suffered in most Christian countries for centuries.

Eretz Israel: the land of Israel. The term appears for the first time in Samuel I 13:9; not to be confused with the state of Israel, which has existed since 1948, or the kingdom of Israel, founded in the 10th century before the modern era.

Goyim, pl. of **goy**: nation, people; used today to refer to non-Jews; the Pentateuch also uses the term with reference to the children of Israel, particularly in the precept: "You shall be for me a kingdom of priests and a holy nation."

Haggadah: corpus of Biblical and other texts relating the flight out of Egypt recited at the Passover holiday.

Haganah, lit. defense: a military organization founded in 1920 by the Zionist Labor Movement in Palestine; integrated into the regular army of the state of Israel in 1948.

Halakhah, lit. step, progression: the corpus of Jewish law based primarily on the Mishna and the Talmud.

Halukah, lit. sharing: a system for sharing gifts among the Haredi communities in the Holy Land.

Haredi, pl. **Haredim**, lit. strictly observant: common appellation of all traditional Jewish groups; visually distinguishable by a two-color dress code, black and white; referred to in the media as "ultra-Orthodox."

Haskalah, lit. the act of making intelligent: the Jewish version of the Enlightenment, which reached its high point in the 19th century; maskilim: those who follow this doctrine.

Hassid, pl. **Hassidim**, adj: Hassidic, followers of the mystical Jewish renewal movement begun in 18th-century Russia.

Hibbat Tzion, Hovevei Tzion (Hebrew), lit. love of Zion, lover of Zion: Jewish settler movement in Palestine, founded in Russia in 1881; joined the Zionist movement after 1896.

Ketuba, lit. inscription: a Jewish marriage contract.

Kibbutz, pl. **kibbutzim**: collectivist community or village developed in Palestine by socialist Zionists in the early 20th century. Many kibbutz members were members of the Zionist and later the Israeli elite, until the late 1970s.

Knesset, lit. assembly: part of the traditional expression "bet ha-knesset" (synagogue); used since 1948 to designate the Parliament of Israel.

Leshon ha-kodesh (in Yiddish "loshn koydesh"), "language of holiness": refers to Hebrew before its modernization and secularization in the 19th century.

Liberalism: political ideology that promotes individual (as opposed to collective or community) freedoms and equality of all before the law.

Midrash (adj. **midrashic**), commentary: corpus of rabbinical commentaries written at the beginning of the common era; part of the oral Torah.

Mishna (adj. **mishnaic**), repetition, study: basis of the oral Torah written by Judas the Prince in the 2nd century; used as a basis for the Talmud, which draws from it guidance in the formulation of Jewish law and moral teaching.

Mitzvah, precept: corpus of 613 commandments that should guide a Jew's behavior, in conformity with the written and oral Torah.

Mizrahi, oriental: allusion to the land of Israel; also an acronym for merkaz ruhani, or "spiritual center"; name of the religious Zionist movement founded in 1904 by Rabbi Isaac Jacob Reines.

Moshav: cooperative agricultural settlement.

National Judaism: movement formed in the early 20th century in the

Russian Empire to protect the religious way of life of Jewish settlers in Palestine; played a key role in the settlement of the territories conquered following the Israeli victory in 1967, interpreted within the movement in messianic terms.

Neturei Karta (Aramaic), Guardians of the City: anti-Zionist movement founded in Jerusalem, 1938.

New Historians: Israeli historians and journalists that have published, since the 1980s, research that cast doubts on the founding myths of the state of Israel.

Olim, see *aliya*.

Rav, Hebrew for the title rabbi.

Rebbe, version of the title rabbi: designates a Hassidic leader who exercises both social and intellectual authority, as well as being a source of inspiration and comfort for the members of his Hassidic group.

Responsa (Latin: plural of **responsum**, answer): a body of written decisions and rulings given by legal scholars in response to questions addressed to them.

Sages (Hazal, an acronym for Hakhameinu Zikhronam Liv'rakha, or "Our Sages, may their memory be blessed"): a general term that refers to prominent Jewish scholars of the period 250 BCE–c. 650 CE.

Satmar (Sathmar, Szatmar): today a region in eastern Hungary, former center of a Hassidic dynasty.

Shas, acronym of shomrei torah sefaradim, Sephardic Guardians of the Torah, alluding to one of the common designations of the Talmud; name of an Israeli Sephardic religious party.

Shoah, lit. calamity: the usual reference in Modern Hebrew to the Nazi genocide of Jews during Second World War.

Talmud, lit. study: corpus of commentaries of the Mishna, which draws upon its conclusions in the formulation of Jewish law and elements of moral teaching.

Torah, lit. teaching: corpus of normative texts; includes the written Torah (Pentateuch, Prophets, and Hagiographa) and the oral Torah (Mishna, Talmud, Midrash, as well as commentaries and practical applications).

Yeshiva: noun derived from the verb to sit; Talmudic academy attended only by boys and young men.

Yevsektzia (Russian), Jewish section: Jewish section of the Bolshevik Party, responsible for the persecution of Judaism in the USSR.

Yishuv, colony, settlement: term designating Jewish settlements in the land of Israel; the Old Yishuv consisted of the Jewish population before the arrival of the Zionists, in the 1880s.

Yom ha-shoah, Day of the Shoah: day of Israeli state commemoration of the Shoah.

Zionism: ideology of protestant Christian origin that propounds the assembly of the Jews in Palestine. At the end of the 19th century, a group of activists of Jewish origin in Central Europe established the Zionist political movement that led to the proclamation of the state of Israel in 1948.

Preface

Taking time out from the painstaking editing of this book, I went for a stroll along my favorite streets of Jerusalem. Friends warned me against it: several knifings had occurred there in recent weeks. The perpetrators were disgruntled Palestinians, disappointed with the "peace process" which has led them to a dead end of despair. These attacks seem spontaneous and uncoordinated, and they bring the otherwise oblivious Israeli majority back to the awareness that right next to them, and under their control, live millions of Palestinians, mostly relegated to inhabit another world and another epoch.

My previous book was about Jews who rejected Zionism, from the very religious to the very assimilated. That rejection is not a relic of the past. The Israeli edition of my book is titled *Jewish Opposition to Zionism: A Continuing Struggle*. When I was in Israel to promote it over a year ago, several hundred thousand devout Jews demonstrated against the induction of their young men into the Israeli military. These Jews did not want to join the country's secular mainstream and its Zionist worldview. The demonstrators (whom the media usually call "ultra-orthodox") were a diverse group, whose attitude to the Zionist state varied from indifference to mistrust and all the way to principled opposition. Yet outside of Israel that opposition often appears incongruous, almost like the idea of boiling snow. The apparently paradoxical character of Jewish opposition to Zionism may explain why that book has been published in over a dozen languages around the world.

This book is different, even though it naturally relies on my earlier work. The reader is invited to look at modern Israel from a variety of perspectives, political, social, religious but also personal. For me, the story of Israel is not only a political drama and a historical narrative; it is also a deeply personal experience. At the same time, I have tried to treat Israel as I would any other country, without prejudice or partiality. In the course of over four decades, I have accumulated an intimate knowledge of the country, have learned to speak its main language and to listen to people of different walks of life and ethnic origin. My native Russian has also turned out to be an asset, since over a million Israelis continue to use it in everyday life. My book reflects this intimacy and, I hope, benefits from it. It is written with a hope that walking in Jerusalem will one day be safe for everyone.

Yakov M. Rabkin
Jerusalem, February 2016

Introduction

An inescapable presence on the international political scene, the state of Israel plays a role out of all proportion to its size. The estimated 7 million inhabitants of this tiny country in Western Asia account for barely 0.1 percent of the world's population, smaller in fact than any mid-size city in China. But for all its imposing economic and political status, Israel remains a state that is frequently ill understood. Indeed, the origins and the legitimacy of Israel, as well as the ideology upon which it was founded, raise fundamental questions, including that of political rationality.

The founding ideology of the state of Israel has emerged from a complex relationship with the heritage of the Enlightenment. On the one hand, Zionism would have been impossible without the emancipation of the Jews of Europe, founded upon the principle of equality that underlies the Enlightenment ideal. But on the other hand, Zionism marks a clear break with the Enlightenment by postulating the eternal character of anti-Semitism and affirming ethnic exclusiveness. Furthermore, many of the challenges Israel faces arise from the uneasy encounter between politics and religion. The lessons that the relatively short history of this state offers can assist us in better understanding today's world, whatever the distance that separates us from Western Asia.

One of the particularities of Israel has been the reticence of the leaders of the Zionist movement, and later of the Zionist state, to define its borders: a peculiarity that can be traced back to the beginnings of the Zionist project, and that made it possible to negotiate the existence of a state with the Great Powers of the day. The tactic proved effective, and led to the unilateral declaration of independence in May 1948, under which no borders were established. Territorial expansion is thus one of the distinguishing characteristics of the history of Israel. In place of well-defined borders, we witness the Zionist equivalent of the continuously expanding American frontier. Acting "in the name of the Jewish people," formally transnational organizations such as the Jewish National Fund (JNF), which enjoy non-profit status in many countries including Canada, are full-fledged participants in the administration of the state. It is in this fashion that Israel, since its founding, has conquered and colonized increasingly greater territory without ever seeking to define its eventual borders. The colonization by over half a million Israeli citizens of the territories occupied in 1967 has unfolded, in a strictly segregated manner, on lands inhabited by a Palestinian majority who, though now living in an Israeli-run administrative and economic space, are not citizens.

Israel today is a prosperous country with a per-capita gross national product (GNP) estimated at nearly US$40,620 in 2014.[1] This places it far above its neighbors. It attracts substantial direct foreign investment. In 2013 the total investment was close to $12 billion, but it dropped by nearly half the following year.[2] Israel's economy is often described as "a transplant economy,"[3] that is, insulated from the economy of Arab Palestine and the surrounding countries, and based primarily on high-tech industry, particularly in the military and security sectors. By comparison, the per-capita GNP in the Palestinian territories under Israeli control since 1967 is considerably lower ($3,060).[4]

For all its prosperity, Israel displays a high level of socio-economic inequality among the industrialized countries, even within its 1949 borders, putting it in second place just behind the United States. Once a relatively egalitarian society, Israel today exhibits a poverty level of 21 percent, the highest among members of the Organisation for Co-operation and Economic Development (OECD). Extremes of wealth are particularly pronounced between Arab and non-Arab citizens, the income of the latter being three times higher than that of the former. Although Israel ranks 22nd among 177 countries on the Human Development Index (HDI), the position held by the Arab population would relegate it to 66th place.[5] While they account for 20 percent of the population of Israel, its Arab citizens own less than 3 percent of the land.[6] Inequalities are particularly pronounced in educational expenditure: $192 annually for each Arab student as against $1,100 for each non-Arab student. Similar disproportions may be observed in public health indicators: infant mortality is twice as high among Arab babies, while cervical cancer is diagnosed five times less among Arab women than among non-Arab women.[7]

At the same time a powerful military-industrial complex, which produces and maintains sophisticated weapons both nuclear and conventional, ensures that for the moment no regional army or coalition of armies can be taken as a credible threat to Israel's dominant position. The country occupies the tenth place in the world arms trade,[8] rather disproportionate to its modest size. Israel also exports its expertise in security-related matters, a sector overwhelmingly staffed by former members of the intelligence services and the IDF.

Politically, Israel can rely on the solid support of the elites of Western nations. For example, only a few months after the Israeli attack on Gaza in the winter of 2008–09 ended with more than 1,400 people killed by the IDF and nine by Palestinian forces,[9] the diplomats of the wealthiest countries voted unanimously to admit Israel into the OECD. Condemnation of the human rights violations, not to mention the war crimes committed during the offensive, by eminent UN experts—Richard Falk and Richard Goldstone, both Jews—did not appear to have the slightest impact on the outcome of the vote within the OECD. Israel also sought and obtained the cooperation of all the Western nations in turning away pro-Palestinian pacifist demonstrators who attempted to travel by sea or air to Gaza and the Occupied Territories as part of a solidarity campaign in the summer of 2011.

The essentially European character of this recently established settler colony, which resembles in many ways the United Kingdom's former colonies throughout the world, also explains Western support of Israel. Its self-ascribed identity as a "Jewish state" brings *de facto* legitimacy to the renewal of ethnicity as the criterion for belonging. The congenital and organic links that the Zionist state possesses and cultivates with the West go far to explain the impunity it enjoys in the eyes of the European powers, or those whose majority population is of European descent, such as the United States, Canada, and Australia. These links have acquired even greater influence within the increasingly accepted ideological construct of the "clash of civilizations," which has enabled Israel to position itself as the West's protective rampart against the hypothetical threat from the East.

Guilt over the Nazi genocide, to which some attribute this preferential treatment, appears today less significant than Israel's service to Western interests in the region. These interests, reinforced by Evangelical "end-times" beliefs, form the bedrock of non-Jewish Zionism, which well antedates Jewish Zionism, and whose history is discussed in the pages that follow. In our day, Western partiality toward Israel suffers from a democratic deficit: contrary to their elites, the majority of the citizens of the Western nations consider the state of Israel as a threat to world peace.[10]

All nationalisms are based on "imagined communities,"[11] but some of these communities appear to be more imagined than others. Most European nationalisms were constructed around regional identities that had to be transformed into national ones. In this sense, political Zionism is at once typical and exceptional.[12]

Political Zionism is typical in that it is part and parcel of the history of late-19th-century ethnic nationalisms. The nationalism that led to the creation of Israel is essentially and profoundly European, drawn up by Europeans to solve the "Jewish question," itself strictly European in nature. But the Zionists were obliged to mobilize considerable energies in order to be able, within a single century, to transfer almost half of the world's Jews to Palestine, a transfer that involved not only people but also their fears. The nightmare of the pogroms of Tsarist Russia were projected upon the previously largely peaceful reality of Ottoman Palestine, a mosaic of different religious, ethnic, and linguistic groups. The sequels of the Nazi genocide, conceived and perpetrated in Europe by Europeans against other Europeans, were also projected onto existing Palestinian society, and contributed to the transformation of that territory into a nation-state on the European model, complete with European aspirations and Western allegiances.

Long ill at ease with minorities, Europe at the turn of the 20th century became particularly intolerant with the rise of ethnic nationalism, which often took the form of "scientific racism." The collapse of multinational empires in the wake of the First World War released powerful nationalist feelings, with new states being established in Central and Eastern Europe at the war's end. The United Kingdom, which not only kept its empire but also sought to extend it to the Middle East, expressed in 1917 by way of the Balfour Declaration its support for the idea of a "Jewish national home in Palestine."[13] In this sense, Zionism is an integral part of the European colonial history. Colonialism at the time had no negative connotation: the principal financial arm of the Zionist movement was then officially known as the Jewish Colonial Trust.

What made Zionism exceptional was the imperative of creating a single people out of disparate religious groups scattered throughout the world. As we will soon see, the Zionists did not simply have to shape and propagate a sense of national belonging of the European variety among Jews who were utter strangers to it, but also to provide them with a common language. Unlike other European nationalisms, it was vital to create prospective settlers from these diverse populations in such a way as to facilitate the establishment of Zionist settler colonies in West Asia, on the model of European colonies in Africa, Australia, and the Americas. But at the turn of the 20th century most Jews did not consider themselves as belonging to a distinct race or nation, in the European sense of the term, a conception that then possessed a pronounced odor of anti-Semitism.

In fact, the Christian motivation for the restoration of the Jews in the Promised Land lent a powerful practical impetus to the Judaic hope of return, which had been traditionally characterized by an entirely different sensibility and ultimate goal. As we will see in these pages, Jewish tradition holds that this return must be a part of a messianic project rather than the human initiative of migration to the Holy Land. It then becomes much easier to understand why the Zionist enterprise, reflecting as it did Christian motifs, was rejected by an overwhelming majority of Jews at the turn of the 20th century. There was little room for Jewish tradition in the Zionist scheme, which not only originated among Protestants but was also sustained by individuals of Jewish origin who were atheists or agnostics.

This book accords particular weight to this rejection, which may appear paradoxical in our day when Jews and Zionists, Judaism and Zionism, the millennia-old Jewish tradition and 20th-century National Judaism,[14] Israeli state interests and those of the Jewish citizens of other countries, are often conflated and confused. To understand Israel, it is necessary to distinguish between religion, ethnicity, and nationalism, precisely because the Zionist ideology has created a fusion of the three. By way of example, the Centre for Israel and Jewish Affairs established in Canada in 2004 embodies this fusion and illustrates how the public perception of Jews and Israel is manipulated.

Both the Zionists and their adversaries are well aware of the ideological fragility of the Zionist project. While many Israelis affirm that Zionism constitutes the principal obstacle to peace between Israel and Palestine, and thus to the integration of Israel into the region, the current Israeli government insists on the acceptance of the country as a "Jewish and democratic state" by the international community and by the Palestinians who are its primary victims. Even though its principal function is to obstruct any possible peace settlement, the demand testifies to the fragility of the Israeli state, for all its power and prosperity, as felt by many Zionists.

The Russian novelist Fyodor Dostoevsky (1821–81) described St. Petersburg as the "most abstract and premeditated city in the whole wide world."[15] Built as an act of will by Peter the Great upon the 60th parallel and perpetually threatened by flooding, the city remains at the mercy of the elements, precarious and even illusory in the midst of the surrounding

marshlands. A mere nine years after its founding, the new city was proclaimed capital of a vast empire, even though it was closer to New York
City than to the empire's easternmost reaches. Russia's greatest authors
saw that city of majestic elegance as an incongruous intruder, both foreign
and strange, prophesying a dreadful end in the form of nature's revenge.
When one day the mirage would vanish—wrote the Russian poet Mikhail
Dmitriev (1796–1866)—only the highest tower of the Peter and Paul
Fortress would protrude above the waters that had engulfed the proud
and haughty city:[16]

> A small boy, taken fishing by an aged companion, hears from the old fisherman
> the story of a proud city, now submerged, with only a thin spire still breaking
> through the water's surface to mark the spot. Mesmerized and horrified by the
> story, the lad asks the name of the drowned city, and hears in reply:
>> Its name was—well, not one of ours,
>> One I have not recalled for years.
>> Its sound was not one we would know,
>> And so 'twas lost long, long ago.[17]

Some fear that the state of Israel, foreign and incongruous in its region,
will suffer a similar fate, becoming a desert in whose midst, among the
shifting sands, will stand the ruins of City Gate, the 200 m high Tel-Aviv
skyscraper that once symbolized the material success of Israel.

The association with St. Petersburg does not end there. It can be found
as well in the cost in human lives of the Zionist enterprise. The Israeli
poet and author Benjamin Harshav, who found refuge in the Soviet Union
during the Second World War, compared the two ambitious projects in
these (translated) words:

> Peter the Great did build
> His capital St. Petersburg
> Atop the northern marshes
> And atop peasant bones
> David Ben-Gurion[18]
> Paved a road
> To his capital Jerusalem
> With the bones of adolescents from the Shoah
>
> …
>
> Ben-Gurion gathered in rags

To deceive his enemy.
Atop the bone-yard of youths from the Shoah
We paved the bypass
That leads to Jerusalem.[19]

This book examines the origins and the nature of the state of Israel, as well as its place in Jewish and European history, from several angles. It reminds us that the founders of Zionism saw their movement as a clean break with Jewish history; the pioneers of the colonization of Palestine were proud to have carried out "the Zionist revolution." But paradoxically, if the status of the land of Israel was indeed central to Jewish tradition, Christians were the ones who sought the actual ingathering of the Jews in the Holy Land to bring about the Second Coming of Christ. Its deep and intimate connivance with Christianity goes far to explain the powerful support the state of Israel enjoys in the United States, where evangelical Protestant groups are numerous and influential.

At the same time, this book provides the reader with access to the essential sources of Jewish opposition to Zionism, and in particular to rabbinical writings that may appear almost impenetrable to the uninitiated.

The work also sketches the context of the emancipation that made it possible for the Jews of Central and Western Europe to integrate into their societies, and examines why the choice between integration and separate development remains even today, for the Jews, a crucial issue defining attitudes toward the policies and the very nature of the state of Israel. It goes on to detail the major identity shifts that placed the state of Israel at the center of the concerns of most of the world's Jews, ranging from unconditional support for Israeli policies to condemnation and even outright rejection of the Zionist—that is, nationalist—concept of the Jew. It demonstrates why the state of Israel divides Jews far more than any other political, social, or religious question. It follows that the widely accepted idea that all Jews are necessarily Zionists and thus fierce defenders of the state of Israel appears as what it is: a myth that fuels anti-Semitism.

Any book about Israel must necessarily take up the question of anti-Semitism. Zionism, however, cannot be reduced simply to Jewish reaction to persecution, threats and anti-Semitic attitudes. The Zionists proved adept at benefitting from anti-Semitism, even on occasion by collaborating with its adherents. This troubled page of Zionist history is largely unknown to the general public.

The Nazi genocide is another major theme of contemporary Jewish history. The approach adopted here, far from being content to state the obvious, is one of integrating this 20th-century tragedy into the theology developed through centuries of Jewish thought. In the event, this tragedy has been transformed into a vector for national unity in Israel, and for Zionist allegiance in the diaspora. It is a transformation that has given rise to a serious critique, particularly among Israeli intellectuals, of which this volume presents an overview.

Another crucial question is the critical role that has been—and continues to be—played by Jews of Russian origin in the Zionist enterprise. It is essential to take into account the discrimination that they suffered under the Russian Empire and their official transformation into a nationality among many others (Ukrainian, Uzbek, and so on) during the Soviet period. The book also attributes the reliance on the use of force that has marked Israeli society since its beginnings, setting it apart from the majority of the Jewish communities of the diaspora, to the lessons that Russian Jews derived from the violence of the pogroms and later of the Nazi genocide.

Above and beyond the still-contested legitimacy of the state of Israel, the question of Jewish identity remains the primary stumbling block. Certainly, Zionism has succeeded in creating a New Hebrew, speaking a new language, Modern Hebrew; but the attempt to graft this new identity onto the traditional, historic Jewish identity has not been a complete success. Jewish communities around the world have been able to protect certain specific characteristics, and the term "the Jewish people" covers, as it always has, diverse populations guided by interests different from, if not opposed to, those of the state of Israel.

While bringing to light certain aspects of history that are often, whether deliberately or not, left in the shadows, this work explains the achievements of the Zionist movement, and later of the state of Israel, which has risen to the rank of a world scientific, technological, and military power. At the same time, it provides an historical background to the apparently paradoxical enthusiasm that the Israeli experience has stimulated among Europe's extreme right-wing parties.

Although there exists an abundant literature on Israel and Zionism, many of these writings are actually works of historical concealment. This book therefore intends to bring into focus some of the elements that are essential to understanding the nature of political Zionism and the history of the state of Israel. To expose certain facts, to make visible aspects of history that have been cast into oblivion, is to invite you, the reader, to participate in the lively debate about Israel, and the reverberations the Zionist state's creation has touched off around the world. In these pages you will find food for thought and a challenge to the clichés, mantras, and stereotypes that make it difficult to have a clear view of this fascinating and controversial state.

Chapter One

The Land of Israel and Its Place in Jewish Tradition

The relationship of the Jews with the land of Israel may at first appear paradoxical.[1] Although it occupies a privileged place in Jewish identity, never in their pre-Zionist two-millennia-long history did the Jews attempt to settle there en masse. It should come as no surprise that the Judaic sources speak with anything but one voice when it comes to geographical boundaries. The divine promise given to Abraham in no way implies a claim to possession of the Promised Land, as clearly illustrated by Abraham's insistence on paying for the plot in which he would bury his wife Sarah (Genesis 23: 6–13). "Promised land" means, in fact, that it belongs not to the one to whom the promise was made, but to the one who made the promise.

According to Jehiel Jacob Weinberg (1884–1966), a rabbinical authority who developed a creative synthesis of Lithuanian Judaism and German Orthodoxy:

> Jewish nationality is different from that of all nations in the sense that it is uniquely spiritual, and that its spirituality is nothing but the Torah. … In this respect we are different from all other nations, and whoever does not recognize it, denies the fundamental principle of Judaism.[2]

The founding event of Jewish identity is the epiphany at Mount Sinai. It was the instant of the gift of the Torah, written or inspired by God, that tradition celebrates as the "birth of the people of Israel." The Judaic sources trace the origins of the Jews to their shared experience during the exodus from Egypt and the reception of the Torah on Mount Sinai. As a group, the Jews were distinguished by their commitment to the precepts of the Torah. Although it contains abundant episodes of transgression and forgetfulness on the part of the children of Israel, its defining, normative relationship with them continues to this day.

More than a geographic identity, it is this relationship and the obligation to follow the commandments of the Torah that have traditionally been the hallmark of the Jews and that makes them a "chosen people," a concept that implies moral and ritual responsibilities rather than intrinsic superiority. Understandably, this concept can readily be deformed to justify attitudes of superiority, and even racism. As in every religion, the status of "chosen," whose meaning lies in the fulfillment of Judaic precepts, can give rise to a sense of ontological supremacy, particularly in our day, when the bonds between Jews and their spiritual tradition has been weakened.

In a broader sense, Jewish tradition administers a powerful antidote to racism by speaking of the origins of a personality as central as the Messiah. The sages concur that the Messiah will arise from the lineage of King David, which would appear to confer upon him a superior ascendancy. However, the same sages trace the Messiah's origin to three quite daring female initiatives, those of Ruth, Tamar, and Lot's daughters.

Ruth was a Moabite widow, the issue of a people whose origins, according to the biblical account, can be traced to Lot's daughters. For fear that the world was ending, they inebriated their father and became pregnant by him, and gave birth to Moav, the ancestor of Ruth (Genesis 19: 30–38). Ruth is she who takes her destiny into her own hands in approaching Boaz: "and she went over stealthily and uncovered his feet and lay down. In the middle of the night, the man gave a start and pulled back – there was a woman lying at his feet." (Ruth 3:7-8)[3] The origins of Boaz, in turn, can be traced to the story of Tamar (Genesis 38: 1–30). Successively married to two of the three sons of Judah, son of Jacob, Tamar witnessed the death of her two husbands. The third brother, according to Levirate law, would then have been obliged to marry her, but Judah sent her back to her parents on the pretext that his son was a minor. Even when he reached the age of majority, Judah remained undecided for fear that his youngest son would die as his brothers had. Tamar could wait no longer, disguised herself as a prostitute, slept with Judah and gave birth to twins, one of whom became the ancestor of Boaz.

In each of the three cases the fatality of death is overcome by women affirming life through their own initiative to conceive and give birth. But above all Jewish tradition emphasizes the humble origins of the Messiah, the savior of the world meant to return the Jews to the Promised Land, which tempers any temptation to claim superiority for the Messiah's lineage.

The biblical texts put emphasis not only on the divine origin of the

Torah, but also on the fact that it was granted outside the land of Israel. According to the Pentateuch, the Jews, or more precisely the children of Israel, did not originate in the land of Israel. As a group, they emerged in Egypt, having been consecrated as a distinct people near Mount Sinai only by their acceptance of the Torah. Spiritual purification, essential for entry into the Promised Land, took place—obviously—outside that land, during 40 years of wandering in the desert. As many commentators have underlined, the Holy Land cannot sanctify the Jews,[4] but their transgressions can profane the land, which in turn will "spew" them out (Leviticus 18: 28).

Tradition defines the relation with the Holy Land in explicitly conditional terms:

> Take care not to be lured away to serve other gods and bow to them. For the Lord's anger will flare up against you, and He will shut up the skies so that there will be no rain and the ground will not yield its produce; and you will soon perish from the good land that the Lord is giving you.
>
> (Deuteronomy 11: 16–17)

This conditional possession is often compared with a married couple: their relationship lasts only as long as the two spouses obey certain rules and regulations. If not, divorce ensues. Significantly, when the granting of the Torah (*Shavuot* or Pentecost) is celebrated in some synagogues, the scroll of the *ketubah* (marriage contract) that seals the relationship between the Torah (the fiancée) and her chosen one (the people of Israel) is read, one of the leitmotifs of the ceremony being the consecration of the Jews' relationship with the land of Israel.

Tradition also underlines the grave danger of living in the Holy Land, by comparing the land of Israel to a royal palace in which any transgression immediately assumes enormous proportions. Rabbi Israel Meir Kagan (1838–1933), better known as Hafetz Haim (the title of his book dealing with the laws against derogatory speech), points to the grave risk of living in the Holy Land while casting aside the Torah and its commandments. The very specific fear of transgressing the Torah in the Holy Land discouraged simple Jews, those believed most likely to sin, from seeking residence in Israel. The relationship between the Jew and the land of Israel is qualitatively different from that of a Frenchman with France, or a Russian with Russia.

Jewish tradition tends to attribute all calamities, and even the most minor of accidents, to moral failure. According to this tradition, the land of Israel could only be acquired through the universal impact of good deeds as part of a messianic project, unlike the two other acquisitions, that of Joshua, and that which followed the return from Babylon, both of which were brought about by earthly power. It would thus be permanent, brought about directly by God.

Furthermore, only a minority of Babylonian Jews returned to the land of Israel with Ezra and Nehemiah, who restored political autonomy following the destruction of the First Temple. That is why the destruction of the Second Temple, which took place several centuries later, reinforced the status of exiles accepted by the majority of the Jews rather than causing a thorough transformation of their identities. Thus the Jews experienced only a few instances of "political crystallization": the Hasmonean Dynasty, the Khazar Khanate, and the Jewish principalities established in Yemen and Morocco (founded to a great extent on conversion).[5] Here again we observe the notable marginality of the Jews to world political history and their centrality to its religious development. In the Jewish tradition exile, whatever its historical circumstances, is above all a state of spiritual incompleteness, a loss of contact with divine presence, rather than expatriation from an actual physical location.

For many pious Jews the refusal to be associated with political power in the land of Israel thus constitutes an integral part of Judaism. Their attitude has little to do with a transcendental principle of passivity. It should instead be seen as an act of resistance, often difficult and courageous, against the sentiment of national solidarity, which some Jewish thinkers consider a particularly great temptation. Two attitudes, active each in its own way, are locked in confrontation. Those who adhere to Jewish tradition insist that:

> We did not go into Galut because we did not possess a Hagganah [pre-1948 Zionist militia] and because we had no political leaders of the Herzl and Ben-Gurion type to guide us along the same path. But we are exiled because we did possess them and did follow their lead. And certainly Jewish salvation will not come through such agencies.[6]

The miraculous nature of salvation is a classical concept of Judaism shared by both traditionalists and the followers of National Judaism, a movement that originated a century ago in the Russian Empire and took the name Mizrahi ("oriental," as well as an abbreviation for *merkaz ruhani*, "spiritual center"). Quite contrary to the warnings issued by Mizrahi's founders, the devotees of National Judaism today affirm that the Zionist enterprise is nothing less than the realization of divine will, "the finger of God" that was made manifest during the flight from Egypt. Both agree that total destruction will precede redemption but they disagree on what constitutes such destruction.

While the ideology of National Judaism maintains that the destruction came to an end in 1945 and that the massacres of the Jews by the Nazi regime provided a springboard to redemption, the theoreticians of rabbinical anti-Zionism affirm, on the contrary, that the tragedy in Europe was merely the beginning of a long process of destruction that the existence of the state of Israel continues to aggravate. In their view, all the achievements of the Zionist enterprise will be annihilated before the arrival of the Messiah, who would find the Holy Land in a state of total desolation. From this perspective, which categorically denies any form of Zionist messianism, the state of Israel appears as an obstacle on the path toward redemption. To concentrate millions of Jews in such a dangerous place, according to this way of thinking, borders on suicidal folly. The physical reconstruction of the Holy Land by the impious will also bring about spiritual destruction. The Zionist will then stand guilty of inflicting upon the people of Israel an exile even more appalling and cruel than the two preceding ones. This warning is frequently reiterated in rabbinical discourse.[7]

While Jewish tradition postulates that salvation can only be the result of messianic action, it remains prudent and forbids "forcing the end": that is, accelerating the process of redemption. The sign for liberation can come from God alone, and only God can bring an end to exile.

On this subject, the Talmud[8] reports three oaths sworn to God on the eve of the dispersal of the rest of the Jews to the four corners of the earth: the Jews vowed not to return en masse and by force to the land of Israel, and not to rebel against the nations, while "the nations" were sworn not to subjugate the Jews excessively. The three oaths stand at the center of discussions on the admissibility in Judaism of the use of force (an issue that this volume will explore). In the aftermath of the Nazi genocide, the argument that the three oaths are now invalid is often heard. The violation by the Nazis of the third oath, the argument runs, cancelled the first two. But an oath sworn to God is not the same as an agreement between two parties, the Jews and the non-Jews.

The classical commentator Moses Nahmanides (1194–1270) touched off a great furor among his colleagues in Catalonia, the Kabbalists of Girona, when he took up residence in the Holy Land a few years before his death. They protested, insisting on the full application of the Talmudic oaths, and raised other arguments, primarily of a mystical nature, the better to reinforce the prohibition against settling there. According to the Orthodox Jewish thinker and professor at the Hebrew University of Jerusalem Yeshayahu Leibowitz (1903–1994), "Nahmanides is undoubtedly alone among the masters who lends practical significance to the commandment to settle in the Land of Israel and to conquer it in the current sense of the terms. But his opinion on this question was hardly echoed in rabbinical *responsa*."[9] A recent edition of the Babylonian Talmud, examining the controversy that continues to swirl around this question, reports numerous sources that challenge the assertion that Jews are commanded to settle in the land of Israel.[10]

Historians of Judaism agree that the fear of attempting to accelerate redemption cannot be considered an anti-Zionist innovation on the part of any particular school of thought.[11] It is not something that has been called into service for the cause, but forms an integral part of Jewish continuity, with deep roots in classical Jewish literature. For generations, well before the emergence of Zionism, the Judaic authorities enjoined the Jews to accept the yoke of exile. Even if the oaths are invoked when emigration to and settlement in the land of Israel has become a viable social option, the strictly Jewish use of the three oaths precedes the emergence of political Zionism by many centuries and thus cannot be seen as an anti-Zionist innovation.[12] The three oaths underlay the warnings issued in Spain during the 15th century in the context of Christian reconquest of the Iberian Peninsula and the subsequent expulsion of the Spanish Jews. An extremely limited number of Spanish exiles took up residence in the land of Israel, even though it was then a part of the Ottoman Empire, which extended to them a generous welcome.

The German rabbi Jacob Emden (1697–1776), an authority whose impact has been felt in jurisprudence down to the present day, also refers to the three oaths in his critique of the messianic movement of Sabbatai Zevi. The story of Zevi (1626–1676), the false messiah born in Izmir, who aroused entire Jewish communities with the prospect of immediate deliverance but ultimately converted to Islam, is often cited as a warning. This story, and its sequels in Europe and elsewhere, traumatized the Jewish world and sharpened its sense of prudence toward all manifestations of messianic expectation. In underlining the fact that those were propitious times for a redemption that seemed so imminent, Rabbi Emden accuses the false messiah of having attempted to hasten the process and thus of causing a great tragedy for the Jews. The oaths are also frequently invoked even in the writings of those whom the Zionists consider their own spiritual predecessors, such as Rabbi Zevi Hirsch Kalisher (1795–1874), and Yehuda Alkalai (1798–1878), who lent their support to the colonization of the Holy Land but discouraged all messianic activism.

Alkalai was only one of several Sephardic thinkers who sought to calm this kind of enthusiasm. Rabbi Yosef Haim of Baghdad, better known as Ben Ish Hai (1834–1909), an eminent authority in Judaic law, also cites the three oaths in a preemptive attempt to dampen any form of messianic activism.[13] A broad consensus seems to exist that a return to the land of Israel by political means does not correspond with the idea of salvation in Jewish tradition.

From this perspective, which might appear absolutist, unrealistic, and even anti-existential, messianic aspiration must remain intact and free of all compromise, until the arrival of the Messiah, the redeemer of Israel. Exile would thus have a therapeutic, and even a cathartic function. A parable attributed to Rabbi Joseph Haim Sonnenfeld (1848–1932), one of the pillars of the community of pious Palestinian Jews, explains the logic underlying the longing for messianic salvation:

> God has exiled us on account of our sins, and exile is as a hospital for the Jewish people. It is inconceivable that we take control of our land before we are completely cured. God keeps and protects us, and administers to us His "medicinal" trials in perfect measurement and dosage. We are certain that when we are completely healed of our sins, God will not hesitate for a moment, and will deliver us to Him. How could we be in such haste to leave hospital in the face of mortal danger? What we seek of deliverance is that our cure be complete; we seek not to return in ill health to the royal palace, God forefend.[14]

By way of affirming their confidence in divine mercy, these thinkers made every effort to bring their day-to-day conduct into line with the precepts of the Torah, for Jewish tradition holds that every positive action has an effect on the world as a whole. The importance of positive actions, as prescribed in the Torah, would be all the greater if every Jew were obliged to view the world as though they were half-guilty and half-meritorious, hence each action, no matter how slight, would be weighed in the balance of divine justice and for ultimate redemption.

The story of the repeated destruction of the Temple of Jerusalem provides the most telling narrative framework for the teaching of Judaic morality. The Zionists also make use of the same story, the better to promote rebels like the Maccabees or Bar Kokhba, who are then upheld as romantic heroes of the resistance against foreign invaders. Such use of history rejects the rabbinical interpretation and draws a conclusion contrary to that offered by Jewish tradition: the rebels should have fought on, and fought better.

A yawning chasm thus opened between the historic sensibilities of Jewish tradition and those of the Zionists, who drew their inspiration primarily from European romantic nationalism. It should come as no surprise that the rabbinical authorities in Palestine attempted to conclude separate agreements with Arab leaders during the 1920s and 1930s, and organized demonstrations under the white flag during the fierce battles that raged in Jerusalem following the unilateral declaration of independence by the founder of the state of Israel, David Ben-Gurion (1886–1973) in May 1948. The Zionists of the day denounced their behavior as treachery, calling it a vestige of exile. Insofar as the notion of exile remained central to Judaic sensibilities and tradition, those accusations were certainly justified.

The text of the prayer recited by all practicing Jews thrice daily refers to it repeatedly: "Blessed are You, the Lord, Who gathered in the dispersed of His people Israel. Restore our judges as in earliest times and our counselors as at first."[15] Grace after meals, another text recited each time a practicing Jew eats bread, also contains powerful passages that speak of the return to the Holy Land. They end with an ardent supplication: "Rebuild Jerusalem your city[16] … Blessed are You, the Lord, Who rebuilds Jerusalem in His mercy."[17]

Some enumerate the references to Jerusalem in order to legitimize Israeli control over the holy city. But for those who follow Jewish tradition they mean the abandonment of all pretense to earthly power and the appeal for divine mercy, which alone can bring about redemption. Interpreting texts as a call to national liberation would appear to distort their explicit content and would constitute an anachronistic extrapolation.

Even though the range of images of redemption is quite broad, messianism makes up its central core. This is not unique to one particular school of thought but reflects a constant in Jewish tradition. That these usages are wielded for polemical purposes in the critique of Zionism and of the state of Israel diminishes not at all their central position in Jewish continuity. It is understandable that the emergence and rapid growth of Zionism would, in the 19th and 20th centuries, have favored the increasing frequency of references to sources that deal with the characteristics of salvation. But the presence of clear warnings against messianic impatience is constant, and the warnings become more and more frequent as the possibility of settling in the land of Israel appears, or as messianic enthusiasm gains sway among the masses.

Among those who point to the paradoxical nature of the Jewish relationship to the land of Israel is political analyst Shlomo Avineri. He draws attention to the privileged place this relationship enjoys in Jewish identity, but recognizes that never in their pre-Zionist history did the Jews make the slightest effort to settle there en masse:

> for all its emotional, cultural and religious intensity, this link with Palestine did not change the praxis of Jewish life in the diaspora: Jews might pray three times a day for the deliverance that would transform the world and transport them to Jerusalem, but they did not emigrate there; they could annually mourn the destruction of the Temple on Tishah be-Av [the ninth day of the month of Av according to the Jewish calendar] and leave a brick over their door panel bare as a constant reminder of the desolation of Zion, but they did not move there.[18]

One of the prayers recited in the festival ritual observed by practicing Jews throws light on the place held by the Land of Israel in Jewish continuity. On the occasion of the festivals of Pilgrimage—Passover, Shavuot, and Sukkot, those festivals celebrated by the Jews of Jerusalem during the era of the Temple—the Jews of Israel, like their coreligionists throughout the world, proclaim:

> O God, God of our fathers, because of our sins we have been exiled from our land and sent far from our soil .... Draw our scattered ones near, from among the nations, and bring in our dispersions from the ends of the earth. Bring us to Zion, Your City, in glad song, and to Jerusalem, home of Your sanctuary, in eternal joy.[19]

Even though nearly half of the world's Jews now live in Israel, no adjustments have been made to the Orthodox prayer books, which has disturbed some modernizers within this stream of Judaism.[20] Messianic hope thus remains intact, and is not in the slightest affected by the physical concentration of millions of Jews in Israel. When practicing Jews recite this prayer, their feelings may range from joy in the founding of the state of Israel, a miraculous event that foreshadows the advent of ultimate redemption, to the keenly felt premonition that the Zionist revolt will one day bring about a terrible punishment. What is at stake is not simply the practice or the abandonment of Judaism, but the entire theological interpretation of Jewish history; in other words, the understanding of what it means to be a Jew.

Who Are the Jews? History and Collective Memory

A trenchant comment by the British Jewish philosopher Leon Roth can best provide the background for discussion of this theme: "Judaism has always been greater than the sum of its adherents. Judaism created the Jew, not the other way round. ... Judaism comes first. It is not a product but a program, and the Jews are the instrument of its fulfillment."[21]

In order to grasp the complexity that underlies any discussion about the Jews since the 19th century, we must first look closely at the phenomenon of secularization: that is, the abandonment of the "yoke of the Torah and its commandments"[22] that marks the break between "Jewishness" and "Judaism." In describing a Jew before the 19th century, people referred to a normative connotation: a Jew is someone whose conduct must follow a certain number of principles that flow from Judaism; Judaism is thus the common denominator. Even though Jews might transgress the Torah, they do not reject the validity of the framework it provides. "You shall be unto Me a kingdom of priests and a holy nation" (Exodus 19:6) stands as a precept, a vocation and an aspiration. However, the biblical passage cannot be taken to mean that the Jews are by their nature "a holy nation," or that the Holy Land can confer upon them any holiness whatsoever.

The German-American rabbi Simon Schwab (1908–1994) depicted traditional Jewish life thus:

> The Jewish people on every continent lived its own life, devoted to its divine culture, set apart from the political history of the world around it, which had bestowed on it alternatively grudging love and boundless hatred ... There was within Judaism only one interpretation of Jewish purpose, history and future that was considered authentic. Loyalty to the Law of God was life's

ultimate purpose for every individual. It was also basic for the ethnic existence, the national unity of Israel, which survived the collapse of all Jewish political independence. ... Then, there was the ardent desire for the coming of God's Messiah, a fervent hope, an impassioned aspiration for a still-veiled future.[23]

Unlike the movements in Central and Western Europe such as that of the Reform synagogue that modified Judaism without abolishing it, Jewish revolutionary movements in Eastern Europe were designed to eliminate any notion of religious responsibility. The process of secularization that swept over Europe beginning in the early 19th century radically altered Jewish identity, which then, for many Jews, lost its normative significance and became little more than a descriptive identity. Traditional Jews could be distinguished by what they did or what they should do; the new, secular Jews could be distinguished only by their origins, with no sense of obligation with regard to God. This new meaning of the word "Jew" was not far removed from that utilized by modern anti-Semites, for whom the Jews constitute a separate nation, or a distinct race.

As early as the 19th century it became difficult to define the Jew, for the majority of Jews had begun to abandon the complex of shared traits that had long constituted their primary identity. The practice of the precepts of the Torah can be observed in the daily life of the pious Jew, unlike faith, which is a profoundly internal matter and therefore remains concealed from view. For example, in order to respect Judaic dietary laws, the pious Jew is obliged to abstain from consuming food that is not kosher, an act that can be easily recognized by all. The concrete nature of the practice of many precepts provides positive feedback and reinforces allegiance to the Torah. According to the terms of the Pirkei Avot, a collection of Jewish maxims drawn from oral tradition, "... a mitzvah [commandment] brings another mitzvah, and a transgression brings another transgression."[24] Other precepts are equally concrete: for example, fasting on certain days, or respecting the Sabbath, which shapes the Jew's relationship with time.

Taken together, these precepts make up the traditional framework of Jewish identity, but the assimilation of a large number of Jews has meant that these same precepts tend nowadays to create divisions. Assimilation is not a phenomenon restricted to Jews. Michel Brunet, a historian who has analyzed the behavior of French-Canadians, defines it as:

To assimilate is to become like the others. He who assimilates forgets who he is and attempts to imitate those whom he wants to be like. For assimilation is always the result of the desire or the necessity to imitate others. ... Such a person aspires to be accepted.[25]

The assimilation of the Jews into the surrounding society reflects a certain discomfort with being Jewish, and implies the abandonment of Jewish practice, especially in the context of the emancipation proclaimed in several European countries in the 19th century. The following question thus arises: do the Jews constitute a "people"? To help us answer the question, let us turn once more to Leibowitz:

> The historical Jewish people was defined neither as a race, nor as a people of this country or that, or this political system or that, nor as a people that speaks the same language, but as the people of Torah Judaism and its commandments. ... The words spoken by the celebrated Arab philosopher and Rabbi Saadia Gaon (882–942) more than a thousand years ago: "Our nation exists only within the Torah" have not only a normative, but also an empirical meaning. They testified to a historical reality whose power could be felt up until the nineteenth century. It was then that the fracture, which has not ceased to widen with time, first occurred: the fissure between Jewishness and Judaism. ... The majority of Jews—while sincerely conscious of their Jewishness—not only do not accept Judaism, but abhor it.[26]

In fact, a mere handful of assimilated Jews in Central Europe invented Jewish nationalism in the second half of the 19th century. Frustrated, despite their best efforts as individuals to assimilate, these Jews did not feel entirely accepted by their non-Jewish environment. As a remedy to their frustration they sought collective assimilation: to become a nation like all other nations. It is hardly surprising that as we shall soon see, their movement, which took the name of Zionism, touched off a profound sense of rejection among the vast majority of Jews.

The better to understand the extent of the shift brought about by Zionism in Jewish life, let us take heed of the words of the American academic and rabbi Jacob Neusner, one of the most prolific interpreters of Judaism, with regard to the shift in the meaning of the word "Israel": "Today 'Israel' in Jewish synagogue worship speaks of that holy community, but 'Israel' in Jewish community affairs means 'the State of Israel.'"[27] By positing that "the state has become more important than the Jews" he clearly distinguishes Jews from Judaism, and explains this shift in identity as the transformation of a community of faith into a community of fate:

> If the Jews as a group grow few in numbers, the life of the religion, Judaism, may yet flourish among those that practice it. And if the Jews as a group grow numerous and influential, but do not practice the religion, Judaism (or any other religion), or practice a religion other than Judaism, then the religion, Judaism, will lose its voice, even while the Jews as a group flourish. The upshot is simple. A book (that is, a set of religious ideas, divorced from a social entity) is not Judaism, but the opinions on any given subject of every individual Jew also do not add up to Judaism.[28]

History is omnipresent in the Jewish tradition. It reflects the imperative found in the Torah: "Remember the days of old, consider the years of ages past" (Deuteronomy 32:7). But the Jewish tradition sees the past as a backdrop, a vision of the world, rather than a source of specific information. Yosef Hayim Yerushalmi (1932–2002), a former professor at Columbia University, affirms that the sole act of memory prescribed by the Torah is that of divine intervention in history, and not of historical exploits. The objective is to prevent the Jews from succumbing to the temptation to replace God, and to attribute to themselves the role of exclusive actors in history. Jewish tradition underscores moral conclusions rather than the onward march of history:

> The comings and goings of Roman procurators, the dynastic affairs of Roman emperors, the wars and conquests of Parthians and Sassanians, seemed to yield no new or useful insights beyond what was already known. Even the convolutions of the Hasmonean dynasty or the intrigues of Herodians—Jewish history after all—revealed nothing relevant and were largely ignored.[29]

The oral Torah is quite laconic with regard to the details of the military activity of the Roman troops besieging Jerusalem in the 1st century. Instead, it dwells on the moral lessons to be learned: the Temple was destroyed because of the sins of the Jews, and principally because of "gratuitous hatred" among the Jews.[30] The Talmud relates how a petty quarrel over honor between two self-important Jewish notables led to a national—in fact, universal—tragedy.[31] The teaching derived by Jewish tradition could not be clearer: people must remain both prudent and circumspect in their actions, whose long-term consequences are impossible to foresee.

A vital corollary of this story is that the Jews themselves were responsible for the destruction of the Temple, and for their exile from the Land of Israel.

History, from the perspective of Jewish tradition, must teach, and it is in the Torah that these teachings must be found:

> Ironically, the very absence of historical writing among the rabbis may itself have been due in good part to their total and unqualified absorption of the biblical interpretation of history. No fundamentally new conception of history had to be forged in order to accommodate Rome, nor, for that matter, any of the empires that would arise subsequently.[32]

Jewish destiny is therefore a function of the covenant with God. The tragedies from which the Jews have suffered, and particularly their exile from the Promised Land, stand as punishments by which tradition deems their sins expiated. This interpretative framework recurs constantly in Jewish history; it was only with assimilation in Europe, inspired by the secularization of mentalities in the surrounding society, that many Jews would come to reject it.

Beneath the radical nature of the shift in Jewish life following the emancipation of the 19th and 20th centuries lay an interest for history in the European sense of the word, most of all among those Jews who had distanced themselves from tradition. Yerushalmi notes that:

> The modern effort to reconstruct the Jewish past begins at a time that witnesses a sharp break in the continuity of Jewish living and hence also an ever-growing decay of Jewish group memory. In this sense, if for no other, history becomes what it had never been before—**the faith of fallen Jews**.[33]

History, in other words, became a substitute for Jewish tradition, which, for many Jews, had ceased to have meaning.

Christians believed that Jews have exited history by refusing to accept Jesus and remaining in exile. They could return to history only by the acceptance of Christ. These two steps should complement each other: although the "ingathering of the exiled Jews" is meant to accelerate the Second Coming of Christ and constitutes an important motif in Anglo-Saxon Protestant thinking, particularly from the early 19th century onwards,[34] pious Jews reject the claim that their exit from political history has excluded them from all history.

Echoes of this Christian world view continue to influence historical thinking despite its apparent secularity. In an era when history had come to mean above all political history, and that of states, it became apparent that "an end had been put to the history of Israel with the collapse of the Jewish state" in the 1st century.[35] The British historian Lionel Kochan (1922–2005) argued that the Jewish intellectuals of the late 19th century associated the Jews with other "ahistoric" peoples, the Ukrainians, the Rumanians, and the Lithuanians, who, unlike such "historical" peoples as the Hungarians, the Germans, or the Italians, did not possess a national state of their own. Many, including the Zionists, concluded that in the words of Karl Marx (1818–1883), it was necessary not only to understand history, but to change it. For Zionists this meant to create their own state and to return to history.

This idea, however, was categorically rejected by the rabbis at the turn of the 20th century. While the Zionists maintained that the history was essentially the work of non-Jews, pious Jews affirmed that quite the contrary, the Jews had always played an active role in their history. They had found a sense of responsibility in their relationship with God, whose attributes—justice, compassion, and mercy—determine the fate not only of an individual Jew or a Jewish collectivity, but that of the world in its entirety. The mechanisms of this relationship remain imponderable, and Jewish philosophy provides a range of differing and contrasting interpretations of the effects of human conduct on Jewish history and human history writ large.[36] From the standpoint of the traditional Jewish sensibility, in its break with modern Jewish perceptions, everything that happens to the Jews can be attributed to the actions of the Jews themselves, in both individual and collective terms.

Moreover, the idea that the Jews are absent from history because of their "rootlessness" is by no means unanimously accepted even among intellectuals remote from tradition. Franz Rosenzweig (1886–1929) and Simon Dubnow (1860–1941), to name but two, viewed Zionism with disdain and described the organic link with exile as one of the essential elements that had assured the survival of the Jews down through the centuries. This happened, in the words of Rosenzweig:

> because Jewish history from the beginning moves from exile to exile and because therefore the spirit of exile, the alienation from the land [*Erdfremdheit*], the struggle for the higher life against decline into the limitations of soil and time, is implanted in this history from its beginning.[37]

Many committed works present Jewish history in teleological terms, as leading to its Zionist culmination. First-generation Israeli historians— for example Benzion Dinur (1884–1973), who was born in the Russian Empire and served as Israeli minister of culture between 1951 and 1955— contributed abundantly to the imposition of this interpretation: their Zionist allegiance came first and foremost. Their teleological reading of history, often described as "tearful" or "victimized," lays emphasis on the persecutions and expulsions suffered by the Jews through the centuries. A new perception of Jewish history, emptied of the traditional Judaic explanation of suffering, bred despair and frustration that only collective liberation could assuage. Zionist historiography postulates that the history of the Jews has been a constant and ineluctable progression toward the establishment of the state of Israel.

In the 1980s, several Israeli historians and journalists (who would later be dubbed the "New Historians"[38]) started to publish research in which they called directly into question the founding myths of the Israeli state. They denounced a massive "Zionization" of historical writing published previously in Israel,[39] including even a teleological deformation of the history of Jewish messianic movements.[40] History writing of this kind, which in pushing Jewish tradition aside had contributed for several decades to the training of patriotic and highly motivated soldiers, has increasingly come under critical scrutiny in Israel and beyond, as Michel Abitbol notes:

> Rejecting the positivist determinism of their elders, the new historians, specialists in Jewish history, carried out a double revision: the rehabilitation of the diaspora, on the one hand, and the—downward—re-evaluation of the role of the nationalist trends of thought in the evolution of Jewish history. This history can henceforth be seen as more polyphonic, more polycentric, and above all more open to global society, be it Christian or Muslim.[41]

The demystification of Zionist history that continues in the work of Israel's "New Historians" has been echoed among those Jews who find it hard to accept Zionism. Narratives of the "New Historians" and the observations of religious anti-Zionists sometimes converge. For example, both denounce the Zionist leaders' alleged indifference, bordering on complicity, to the Nazi genocide (see Chapter 5). Together with other post-Zionist intellectuals they decry the "cultural genocide" of immigrants to Israel, such as Yemenite Jews,[42] and more generally the Zionists' colonialist attitudes to the Arabs, whether Jewish, Christian, or Muslim.[43] Their investigative work, based on military archives and the personal papers and writings of the fathers of Zionism, have caused an outcry. The New Historians are accused of undermining Zionist ideology by turning a significant part of Israeli youth away from the principal theses of Zionism. The historiographical trend identified with the New Historians, raising as it did serious doubts about the founding myths of Israel, led to serious criticism, including accusations of undermining the Zionist state from within.[44]

In other words, "it is the totality of composite parts of Israeli national conscience as it has been 'invented' by a century of Zionism that has been called into question. ... As a result, we are far, very far indeed from the time when the country spoke in a single voice."[45] In truth the country has never spoken in a single voice, but dissenting voices, especially those of the Judaic adversaries of Zionism, have been barely audible, as their language and their conceptual framework have excluded them from mainstream debate. Several legislative measures adopted by the Israeli parliament in recent years have had the effect of limiting public access to dissenting historical narratives, particularly concerning al-nakba—the catastrophe—the term used by Palestinians to describe the events of 1947–49. Municipalities and schools that commemorate the Palestinian tragedy now risk being fined.[46]

Yet in the enthusiasm of reconciliation on the occasion of the Oslo Accords in the early 1990s, Israeli schoolchildren became briefly aware of the Palestinian interpretations of history, which cast doubt on the Jews' exclusive rights to the land of Israel. Moreover, as early as the late 1970s, well before the New Historians appeared on the scene, several studies and memoirs written and published in Israel began to recognize that expulsions of Palestinians had indeed taken place in 1947–49.[47] Today, almost half the non-Arab Israelis acknowledge that the Israeli armed forces terrorized the Palestinian Arabs by carrying out the ethnic cleansing considered indispensable to the foundation of the state of Israel.[48]

While recent museum exhibits openly refer to the expulsion of Arabs,[49] the window opened onto Palestinian suffering is rapidly closing. Zionist collective memory remains strongly categorical: "We—Jews—are the good people; the Palestinians, the Arabs, and the Muslims are bad." For what is inculcated in Israeli children are above all valor, bravery, courage, and the quality of intrepidity,[50] precisely those qualities that were said to have vanished from Jewish life as a result of exile. Haredi schools,[51] on the other hand, teach that these same character traits, such as arrogance and intransigence, were the root cause of exile. The two viewpoints remain deeply opposed, and shape the lessons that each group draws from Jewish history, which remains of capital importance:

> Today Jewry lives a bifurcated life. As a result of emancipation in the diaspora and national sovereignty in Israel, Jews have fully re-entered the mainstream of history, and yet their perception of how they got there and where they are is most often more mythical than real. Myth and memory condition action. There are myths that are life-sustaining and deserve to be reinterpreted for our age. There are some that lead people astray and must be redefined. Others are dangerous and must be exposed.[52]

The secular romanticism of the first Zionist decades, which had gone to extraordinary lengths to demonstrate the material connection of the Jews with the land of Israel, has been replaced by National Judaism, which attempts to anchor Zionism in Jewish continuity. This movement has been successful in justifying the Zionist settlement of the territories occupied in 1967 among a significant segment of Israeli Jews, most of whom do not share the political commitment and even less the faith of the followers of National Judaism. In fact, the ideological impact of National Judaism remains limited to its own adherents and certain recent immigrants. In its attempt to "normalize the Jews," nationalism can only defy the historical continuity that expresses itself in terms of the dichotomy between reward and punishment, exile, and redemption.

It was in this way that Jewish secular identity acquired a socio-cultural dimension: those who consciously rejected Judaism could preserve, at least for a while, a specific language (Yiddish) and a few cultural markers. This new identity was conjugated in a wide range of political options, often of socialist or nationalist inspiration.[53] By consummating the break with tradition, the concept of the secular Jew, at variance with the traditional Jewish vision, made it possible to redefine the Jews as a "normal people" and thus became the cornerstone of Zionism. The term "secular" does not quite correspond with the Hebrew *hiloni*, its usual equivalent, which is used to designate those Jews who, since the 19th century, had abandoned all Judaic practice. In the Israeli usage *hiloni* has taken on more militant connotations, drawing nearer to the term "anti-Judaic," or even, on occasion, "anti-Semitic."

The concept of the secular Jew continues to cause controversy, particularly with regard to the often assumed common biblical origin of the Jews.[54] The prominent Israeli historian Israel Bartal, in criticizing the concept of "an invention of the Jewish people," admits that "Although the myth of an exile from the Jewish homeland [Palestine] does exist in popular culture, it is negligible in serious Jewish historical discussions."[55] It was essentially in Europe that this popular myth of a common geographic origin, under the double impact of the emancipation and of secularization, would acquire the political connotations that fostered the emergence of Zionism.

Chapter Two

The Jews of Europe: Between Equality and Extermination

Jews have been living in Europe since Roman times. In fact, their presence often predates that of populations such as the Hungarians who deem themselves "original," even though the Jews' seniority did little to protect them against persecution by the Christian majority. Anti-Jewish sentiments were encouraged by the teachings of the Church, which claimed to replace the Jews with the Christians as a chosen people, or even accused them of deicide. Some Jewish communities prospered; others lingered in poverty. From time to time, down through the centuries, Jews were accused of ritual murder, of poisoning wells, and other imaginary crimes. They were then dispossessed, exiled, and even massacred.

Great diversity existed then, and still exists, among European Jews. Large communities lived under Muslim regimes in the Iberian peninsula between the 8th and 15th centuries. This era of relative tolerance, when Jews, Christians, and Muslims enjoyed *la convivencia*, particularly in Andalusia, came to an end with the Christian reconquest of the peninsula. The Jews, like the Muslims, were then given the choice: exile or conversion to Christianity; by the hundreds of thousands they were expelled to other lands. Those who remained in Europe found refuge in the Ottoman Empire, or in Protestant countries like the Netherlands and England. Some emigrated as far as Catholic Poland, where the Jews were welcomed as skilled intermediaries between nobility and peasantry. The divisions of Poland that took place during the last half of the 18th century placed nearly 1 million Jews under Russian suzerainty.

As the concept of equality was foreign to existing social structures, it was not until the French Revolution that after some hesitation, the Jews acquired all the rights of citizens in France. These same rights were extended to them in other European countries in the wake of the Napoleonic conquests. Elsewhere on the continent, the Austro-Hungarian Empire, the United Kingdom, and some Germanic states were to confer equality before the law to their Jewish subjects in the course of the 19th century.

Many Jews interpreted the emancipation as the advent of messianic times. Entire communities, from the Netherlands to Poland, welcomed the French troops as the Redeemer who would free them and lead them to the Promised Land of "Liberté, Égalité, Fraternité." Jews even composed messianic hymns to the honor of their liberators.[1] But hardly the same enthusiasm welcomed Napoleon's call in the midst of his military campaign in the Levant in 1799, inviting "all Jews ... to rally under his banner," to re-establish a Jewish state in Palestine and to rebuild the Temple.[2] The transfer of the concept of redemption from the exclusive dominion of God to the field of politics marked a break with tradition (as was shown in Chapter 1) that would later become a key element of Zionist ideology.

Messianic longing had repeatedly manifested itself in Jewish history, but in a radically different way. When it flared up, the rabbinical authorities would attempt to moderate those upsurges of enthusiasm which, they argued, might well lead to disappointment and end up by completely alienating the faithful, as in the rise and fall of Sabbatai Zevi (see Chapter 1).

The emancipation of the European Jews has been a continuous process that began at the end of the 18th century, but suffered a tragic setback under the Nazis. It offered Jews equality before the law, and abolished the political, social, and professional restrictions under which most of them had been living in most Christian countries for centuries. Emancipation theoretically allowed the Jews to enter the modern world as fully fledged citizens. Nonetheless, the fact of their entry appeared, and continues to appear, dangerous to a large number of non-Jews. The freedoms brought and bestowed by Napoleon's armies were to transform European societies, but their impact was far less drastic on the Christian population than it was upon the Jews. Emancipated Jews had to change their language (from Yiddish to the national tongue: French, German, or Hungarian), their dress (adopting European-style clothes), even their trades. Without rejecting emancipation in its broad lines, a substantial number of Judaic thinkers and rabbinical authorities expressed serious doubts regarding the breadth and depth of the changes that confronted the Jews of Europe as the 19th century dawned. Zionism, which took shape at the end of the century, must be seen as the direct result of the modernization of consciousness that the Jews had begun to experience under the influence of the Enlightenment and the French Revolution.[3]

But though the upsurge of ethnic nationalism in late 19th-century Europe weakened political liberalism, it did not pose a serious threat to the advantages it had brought to the Jews of Western Europe. In Central and Eastern Europe, however, where Zionism drew its main support, the organic nationalism that was on the upswing at the turn of the 20th century tended to be intolerant, exclusivist, and bellicose. In these regions of Europe, national renewal called for sacrifices, above all by those who did not belong to the "titular nation," an obligation that seemed quite natural at the time.[4]

The internationalism of the Bolsheviks and the promise of a new world to come once again awakened the messianic expectations of the Jews, as had the emancipation in Western Europe. Many of them participated enthusiastically in the building of socialism in the Soviet Union and elsewhere. But the longing for political redemption that inspired secularized Jews in the late 19th and early 20th centuries could only increase the skepticism of the rabbinical authorities, some of who warned against the inevitable disenchantment that must follow political projects with messianic overtones. Zionism was only one of many of the revolutionary programs that were to inspire millions throughout Europe in the 20th century.

In the Western European countries, where Jews began to identify with the state following the emancipation, Jewish identity remained primarily religious, even though it had become diluted under the impact of secularization. Emancipation held out to Jews a national identity they could share with their non-Jewish neighbors (French, German, or Italian), a step that was made easier by the fact that the Jewish concepts of "nation" and "people" had little in common with those same concepts in the societies of Christian origin in which the Jews of Europe lived. Jews could thus feel fully French in the European sense of the word, all the while integrating their Judaism into an unconditional allegiance to the French state.

Rabbi Samson Raphael Hirsch (1808–1888), leader of modern Orthodoxy in Germany, encouraged the Jews to integrate into the surrounding society, to appreciate German and more generally Western culture, while at the same time reinforcing the personal discipline typical of the Orthodox Jew. In Hirsch's view, Jewish nationalism could only be a transcendent idea, contingent neither on possession of land, nor upon political sovereignty.[5] "The Torah does not exist for the state but the state for the Torah."[6] In the midst of Europe rife with all sorts of nationalism Hirsch was simply restating the classic concept: the Torah, and only the Torah, makes of the Jews a collective entity:

Not in order to shine as a nation among nations do we raise our prayers and hopes for a reunion in our land, but in order to find a soil for the better fulfillment of our spiritual vocation in that reunion and in the land, which was promised, and given, and again promised for our observance of the Torah. But this very vocation obliges us, until God shall call us back to the Holy Land, to live and to work as patriots wherever He has placed us, to collect all the physical, material and spiritual forces and all that is noble in Israel to further the wealth of nations which have given us shelter. It obliges us, further, to allow our longing for the far-off land to express itself only in mourning, in wishing and in hoping; and through the honest fulfillment of all Jewish duties to await the realization of this hope. But it forbids us to strive for the reunion or the possession of the land by any but spiritual means.[7]

Rabbi Jehiel Jacob Weinberg, an influential 20th-century rabbinical authority, affirmed that:

Jewish nationality is different from that of all nations in the sense that it is uniquely spiritual, and that its spirituality is nothing but the Torah .... In this respect we are different from all other nations, and whoever does not recognize it, denies the fundamental principle of Judaism. Jews should thus be viewed as a unique people that shuns political reality the better to flourish in the practice of Judaism, "the four cubits of Jewish law, all that is left to God since the destruction of the Temple."[8]

The emancipation spread eastward, but came to a stop at the Russian border. Inspired by developments in Europe, a theoretician of cultural Zionism, one of the many variants of Zionism, Ahad Ha-Am (pseudonym of Asher Hirsch Ginzberg, 1856–1927), a tea merchant from Odessa, insisted that Judaism was nothing more than an optional aspect of Jewish national identity. But when adapted to the situation of the Jews of the Russian Empire, where emancipation had been slow in coming and where Jews lived in relatively homogenous and compact communities, the idea of an "optional Jewish religion" produced an entirely different effect.

Thus crystallized the concept of the "secular Jew." The new concept, which quickly gained popularity in Eastern Europe, and particularly in the Russian Empire, eliminated the religious—and thus normative— dimension of Jewish identity and retained only its biological and cultural dimensions. At the same time, most Jews had become estranged from the imperial regime, particularly following the assassination of Tsar Alexander II in 1881. The impact of pogroms and socialist doctrine forced the secular Jews of Russia to define themselves in radically different ways, in relation to both Judaism and the Russian Empire, where Jews were officially one group among other *inovertsy* (those of different faith, heterodox), and thus had religious minority status conferred upon them, as in Western Europe.

Paradoxically, the history of the last decades of the Romanov dynasty was to have a greater impact on that of Israel than on the history of Russia itself. While many of the Russian Empire's Jews were attempting to integrate into Russian culture, this largely literate population experienced frustration at finding only limited opportunities for advancement. It was a frustration that led to the radicalization of a significant number of Russian Jews, who embraced the idea of political violence. In this regard, the history of the Jews in Tsarist Russia was exceptional: hardly any other Jewish group welcomed the use of force in defense against its non-Jewish neighbors. But sequels of radicalization would continue to affect political realities in Israel, whose founding and structures reflect the concepts and realities of Eastern Europe of a bygone era.[9]

It was only under Stalin that the Jews ceased to be defined by Judaism and became a "Jewish nationality," marked in their identity cards, quite like the Armenians, the Uzbeks, or the Russians. Within a few generations, this line entry, the notorious "fifth point" of the Soviet internal passport, had become the only remaining factor that preserved the distinctive "national" identity of the Soviet Jews, an identity that was largely devoid of any positive content and as such became both a burden and an obstacle to social and professional advancement. So it was that secular Jews in Russia acquired an objective identity free of normative content: that is, free of any connection to Judaism. At the same time, the Jews integrated quite rapidly into Soviet society, and played a significant role in the country's political, scientific, cultural, and artistic life.[10]

The secularization of Russian Jews was striking in that it carried with it a transformation more radical than that of other nations, the majority of whose characteristics remained unchanged whatever their level of religious practice. A Russian Christian remained a Russian in spite of the extremely brutal secularization suffered in the 20th century under the influence of a militantly atheist state. While in the Soviet Union Jews acquired national minority status, in Central and Western Europe they were seen as a confessional grouping that, in legal terms, enjoyed in principle all the rights of citizens. Reality, however, proved more complex. The surrounding society often remained hesitant if not resistant to the integration of the Jews, and above all to their upward social mobility. The same rejection was directed at Jews converted to Christianity, for the new form of anti-Jewish sentiment was now formally detached from the issue of religious confession and proudly proclaimed itself "anti-Semitism."[11]

The introduction of the term "anti-Semite" is generally attributed to the Austrian Jewish intellectual Moritz Steinschneider (1816–1907), who in 1860 protested against "anti-Semitic prejudice": that is, attacks against "Semitic peoples" that he found in literature and in the press, among which were the writings of Ernest Renan.[12] In the 19th century it was common practice to identify peoples or races with linguistic families; the term "Semite" was used to designate those who used Semitic languages, primarily the Arabs and to a lesser extent those literate Jews who used Biblical and rabbinical Hebrew for religious purposes. Because of all the "Semites" only the Jews happened to find themselves in Europe, the term rapidly took on the meaning of "anti-Jewish" (even though in our day, all "enemies of the West," and above all the Arabs, acquire anti-Semitic traits in the collective imagination. "Anything than could be said of the Jews could also be said of the Arabs.")[13]

The anti-Semitic movement took shape in 1879 in Germany, with the creation of the Anti-Semitic League, whose objective was to struggle against the "Jewish takeover." The "de-theologized" Jew was thus associated with race, an extremely fashionable concept at the turn of the 20th century. (Conversely, today's Arabs are often "theologized" in order to fabricate the figure of the threatening Muslim.) Historians tend to agree that the concept of "Semitic peoples" does not refer to a verifiable reality, and appears to be of recent construction. But that did not stop anti-Semitism from becoming a popular movement in more than a few European countries and former European colonies. Anti-Semitism was to provide the foundations of German National Socialism, which led to the creation of a system of bureaucratic discrimination, exclusion, and finally of extermination. Seen in this light, the 12 years of the Nazi regime in Europe can be best understood as a tragic interruption of the emancipation and the integration of the Jews.

Racialist anti-Semitism was to act as a catalyst at the end of the 19th century to rally a handful of Central European Jewish intellectuals to the Protestant notion of the physical ingathering of exiled Jews in the Holy Land. In such a form, Jewish nationalism proved to be conceptually compatible with anti-Semitic principles, for it also postulates the impossibility for a Jew to become a full member of European society. History has shown that the attractiveness of Zionism increases with the intensity of anti-Semitism or economic hardship, which explains the fact that relatively few British, American, or Swedish Jews hastened to accept the Zionist project at first, and up to the present day most are reluctant to leave their countries to take up residence in Israel.

It is also the reason that both Christian and Jewish Zionists consider a liberal, multicultural society as a major obstacle to the expansion of a Jewish national conscience. They remain skeptical about the trust in equality and tolerance shown by more than half the world's Jews, who prefer to reside in the diaspora rather than settle in Israel. But as Israeli political commentator Zeev Sternhell notes, "To accept the liberal concept of society would mean [for the Jewish nationalist intelligentsia] the end of the Jewish people as an autonomous unit."[14] The main threat to Zionism is European liberalism, which offers Jews an individual choice but, according to many Zionists, denies them the opportunity to live a true national life.

In contrast to Western Europe, however, the Jews of Eastern Europe faced intense and widespread anti-Jewish sentiments. Situations varied, of course, but as an extreme indicator, the survival rate of Jews during the genocide was much lower in Eastern Europe than in the rest of the continent, including Nazi Germany itself.[15] It should come as no surprise that Zionism and the perspective of immigration to Palestine attracted more Eastern European Jews. As we shall soon see, the great majority of the early colonists and almost all the Zionist leadership in Palestine originated in that part of the world.

The Zionist transformation of Jewish identity into a modern and particular nationalist identity was no easy task. For Jews who felt or who wished to feel that they were integrated into the Western nations, the new Zionist identity was threatening and unacceptable. Even in the Russian Empire, many Jews who suffered from systematic discrimination by the state were not at all interested in embracing Zionism, and even less in migrating to Palestine. Out of the 1.2 million Jews who emigrated from Russia at the turn of the 20th century, a mere 30,000 made Palestine their destination, and of those, only a quarter remained there.[16]

Shlomo Avineri notes that those Jews who emigrated to America or Australia incarnated the traditional reaction to life's adversities: they moved from one country to another while avoiding what many in our day consider to be the "homeland of the Jewish people." Surprisingly, their attachment to the Jewish tradition of exile turned out to be more ingrained than Judaic practice, surviving the suppression of religious practice and the forced removal by the Soviet regime of every source of traditional Jewish identity. When emigration from the Soviet Union became possible from the 1970s onwards, the great majority of departing Jews preferred to seek residence elsewhere than in the state of Israel, which unlike Ottoman Palestine which had offered so few possibilities to their grandparents, offered the generous services of a modern state to attract and accommodate immigrants. In order to attract more settlers, in the closing years of the 20th century Israel carried out a full-scale diplomatic campaign in an effort to prevail upon its allies (primarily the United States and Germany) to limit immigration to their countries of Soviet Jews.[17] Thus the Israeli government replicated the approach of Lord Balfour who, in his conviction that the Jews belonged in Palestine, was opposed to their immigration to the United Kingdom.

The same tendency can be observed among North African Jews. The majority of those who could settle in France, Canada, or the United States did so, bypassing the inducements offered by Israel. In truth, ideologically motivated *aliya* has from the beginning accounted for only a tiny proportion of those who migrated to Israel. The devotion of most Jews to the tradition of exile underlines once more the radical nature of the metamorphosis that the creation of a new national identity demands. Hence the preservation, however tenuous, of the religious component of Jewish identities in most modern countries: in the 19th century Jews become French Israelites, Americans of Hebrew persuasion, or Germans of the Mosaic Faith. Only the state of Israel offers the Jews the ultimate freedom to reject totally their spiritual heritage and become a "normal people." The new Israeli identity appears to facilitate collective assimilation while sparing those who adopt it the feeling of guilt often linked to assimilation on an individual basis, and above all to conversion to Christianity. Language and territory are the fundamental markers of the new identity, which is radically distinct from the traditional Jewish identity anchored in a religious consciousness and bereft of a common either language or territory.

Such a shift in identity is all the more difficult in that it entails the assimilation of Judaic notions into European conceptual frameworks. The distinction between the religious and the secular (unlike the sacred and the profane) never arose for the Jews before the late 19th century, and then only in Europe. In fact, what took place has been aptly described as the "Christian secularization" of the Jews.[18]

Such is the transformation that lies at the heart of the Zionist project, which as we have seen and as will be elaborated on in Chapter 3, is deeply rooted in the Christian perception of the Jew. Political Zionism, in calling for the colonization of a country outside of Europe, was intended above all to reintegrate Jews into a strictly European colonial history. Meanwhile, Muslim-majority societies were to remain for nearly a century far removed from the Westernization of the concept of identity, Jewish as well as Muslim.

An assimilated Austrian Jew, Nathan Birnbaum (1864–1937), invented the term "Zionism" at the beginning of the 1890s, inspired by the name of one of Jerusalem's hills, Zion, which in Biblical terms symbolizes the entire Land of Israel. Birnbaum, who was president of the World Zionist Organization, established in 1897, was a prime mover in the propagation of Jewish nationalism. But he later came to reject Zionist ideology and turned into its tireless critic. Ironically, his successor in the position a century later, Avraham Burg, would also come to denounce the very concept of the "Jewish state" and to articulate a radical critique not only of the Zionist movement, but also of the Israeli society of which he is a product:

> When I was a boy I was a Jew. In the language prevalent here: a Jew-boy. I attended a *heder* [religious school]. I was taught by former yeshiva students. After that, for most of my life I was an Israeli. Language, signs, smells, tastes, places. Everything. Today that is not enough for me. In my situation today, I am beyond Israeli. Of the three identities that form me—human, Jewish, and Israeli—I feel that the Israeli element deprives me of the other two.[19]

The elevation by the Zionists of the Volk ("people" in German) as the exclusive subject of Jewish history led rabbis, since the late 19th century, to denounce the cardinal element of Zionist ideology:

> There is no Jewish nation. The Jews form, it is true, a separate stock [*Stamm*], a special religious community. They should cultivate the ancient Hebrew language, study their rich literature, know their history, cherish their faith, and make the greatest sacrifices for it; they should hope and trust in the wisdom of divine providence, the promises of their prophets, and the development of humankind so that the sublime ideas and truths of Judaism may gain the day. But for the rest,

they should amalgamate with the nations whose citizens they are, fight in their battles, and promote their institutions for the welfare of the whole.[20]

The controversy over Zionism is not surprising: to the extent it has any religious origin whatsoever, that origin is Protestant rather than Jewish.

Chapter Three

A Return to the Promised Land
as a Return to History

The Jews came to Zionism long after the Christians. The translation of the Bible into vernacular languages during the Reformation, and primarily into English, encouraged the belief that the concentration of the Jews in the Holy Land should be considered as an event of supreme importance for Christianity. Such an occurrence would bring about the return of Jesus to Earth, precipitating the Apocalypse and the ultimate triumph of Christendom, which would be signaled by the mass conversion of the Jews. It was a notion first promoted in the United Kingdom, even when no Jews had been living in the country for several centuries (they were only authorized to return under Oliver Cromwell in 1656). In 1621 in England there appeared a book entitled *The World's Great Restauration, or Calling of the Jews, and with them of all Nations and Kingdoms of the Earth to the Faith of Christ.* The book was rapidly forbidden, having been pronounced seditious by King James I. But the Puritans were to spread ideas such as these in North America, and it was in the Anglo-Saxon world that "Zionism" (though the term had not yet been invented) was to be articulated and reinforced beginning in the 18th century. By way of example, Joseph Priestley (1733–1804), a prominent scientist and philosopher, attempted to convince British rabbi David Levi (1740–1799) to organize a transfer of Jews to Palestine. The rabbi rejected the idea of reinstating the Jews in the Holy Land by material means and affirmed that the Jews must accomplish their mission in their countries of residence.[1]

The literal reading of the Bible, a practice typical of several fundamentalist Protestant denominations, thus forms the ideological basis of Zionism. Unlike the interpretive reading of the Catholic Church, Protestants are encouraged to establish an immediate and direct connection with the word of God, replacing the tradition developed over time by the Vatican with an autonomous reading of scripture.

An Anglican preacher, John Nelson Darby (1801–1882), launched the Christian 'proto-Zionist' movement, in Plymouth, where he formulated a doctrine that he termed "dispensationalism." Drawing on a literal reading of three biblical verses (Genesis 15, 18–21) he affirmed that the Second Coming of Christ was possible only if the land of Israel belonged exclusively to the Jews. This novel doctrine was favorably received in the United States where, in 1908, the *Scofield Reference Study Bible* was published. The interpretations contained in this edition of the Bible were to acquire a long-lasting popularity.

Drawing on these ideas, the modern-day authors Tim LaHaye and Jerry Jenkins wrote *Left Behind*, of which more than 100 million copies were printed, and which was adapted for the cinema.[2] In it, the state of Israel is clearly presented as the incarnation of Darby's vision. Christian Zionism, which today has become a significant political force, can thus be seen as part of a several centuries' long continuum.

The idea that the Jews belong to the Holy Land would not have startled German philosophers. For Immanuel Kant (1724-1804), the Jews were "Palestinians living among us,"[3] while the rigid anti-Judaism of Johann Gottlieb Fichte (1762-1814) held that "the Holy Land should be conquered and all of them dispatched to it."[4] In France, Napoleon's proclamation inviting the Jews to settle in the Holy Land under the protection of the French army was inspired primarily by geopolitical considerations— which are rarely absent from ostensibly religious projects designed to Judaize Palestine.

Strategic considerations in the region certainly lay behind the United Kingdom's decision to open its first consulate in Jerusalem in 1838. A year later, the Church of Scotland sent a delegation to the Middle East and Central Europe with the aim of encouraging Jewish settlement in Palestine. And in 1841, the *Colonial Times* of London published a "Memorandum to the Protestant Monarchs of Europe"[5] calling for the return of the Jews to Palestine, indicating that the project was more than a pious wish and that in fact it had become a political objective. Emblematic of this new dynamic was Lord Palmerston (1784–1865), British foreign minister then prime minister. Though by no means an assiduous reader of the Bible, he was the man who transformed evangelical activism into a geostrategic program that designated the Jews as the bridgehead for British interests in the Middle East.[6] Palmerston would later address Queen Victoria on precisely this subject,[7] while the Colonial Office had begun, as early as 1845, to draft plans for a British protectorate that would become an independent Hebrew state, even though colonial administrators are not known for encouraging national independence movements. These plans provided as well for the deportation of the local populations to create "living space" for the future immigrants. Drawn up by British statesmen, this European variant of Zionism amply preceded the movement founded by Theodore Herzl (1860–1904) in 1897.

The Balfour Declaration, a typewritten document of less than a page, issued in 1917 on the eve of the British occupation of then-Ottoman Palestine, reflected the already well-established tradition of using Christian beliefs to advance the imperial aspirations of the European powers. It followed a broader agreement between Britain and France (the Sykes–Picot Agreement) to carve up the Middle East. Zionism proved to be a natural part of those colonialist aspirations. The same spirit pervades a work by Laurence Oliphant (1829–1888), a British Christian activist, who called for the removal of the Arab population to reserves on the North American model:

> the Arabs have very little claim to our sympathy. They have laid waste this country, ruined its villages, and plundered its inhabitants, until it has been reduced to its present condition; and if they were driven back to the Arabian deserts from which they came, there is abundant pasture in its oases for their camels and goats. ... In fact, the same system might be pursued which we have adopted with success in Canada with our North American Indian tribes, who are confined to their "reserves," and live peaceably upon them in the midst of the settled agricultural population.[8]

Oliphant's book is dedicated to one of Queen Victoria's daughters, Princess Christian of Schleswig-Holstein, "as a mark of deep gratitude for the warm sympathy and cordial interest manifested by her Royal Highness in the author's efforts to promote Jewish colonization in Palestine."

Oliphant's book was published in 1880, one year before the assassination of Alexander II in St. Petersburg, which touched off an outbreak of violence against the Jews, and two years before the arrival in Palestine of the first Jewish colonists of the Russian movement Hibbat Tzion ("Love of Zion"). In it we encounter for the first time the use of the term "repatriation" to describe the settlement of the Jews in Palestine; the term was to become a widely used Zionist expression, above all in Russian. Oliphant also anticipated the contemptuous attitude of Russian Zionist settlers to religious Jews when he wrote, "It is certainly not among the Jews of Jerusalem that I should look for colonists."[9]

Also well before the Balfour Declaration, a Protestant visionary by the name of William Hechler (1845–1931) befriended Herzl and encouraged him to gather the Jews in the Promised Land. Hechler thus became the "prophet" who inspired Herzl, the "prince," in his project for the salvation of the Jews.[10] As the former vice-mayor of Jerusalem André Chouraqui (1917–2007) has noted, Herzl's program seems to be primarily of Protestant inspiration:

> Thanks to him [Hechler] Herzl was able to anticipate the realities of a certain incarnation of the word and accept the evidence of transcendence. For it was a Christian, the chaplain of the British Embassy in Vienna, who stood at Herzl's side and who, from beginning to end, accompanied him along the Path. They formed a curious couple indeed: a totally de-Judaified journalist whose plays had won a measure of success on the boulevards of the great capitals, whose first impulse had been the massive conversion of all Israel and its entry into the bosom of the Church to bring once and for all an end to the tragedy of anti-Semitism; and a "court Christian", both dreaming of the redemption of Israel and the restoration of Zion. Both were to pursue their path and to enclose us in the belly of the paradox in which Jews and Christians are caught up as history's ultimate confrontation unfolds.[11]

Driven by a messianic Zionism, André Chouraqui added that "without the firm hand of Hechler who recognized him and opened for him the first doors—the most crucial—might not Herzl, like Moses before the burning bush, like Jonas upon hearing the call, have been tempted to flee, to escape his destiny?"[12]

This particular relationship with the Bible, as with history when all else fails, was later to be exploited by the Zionist leadership. "Moreover, the Biblical heritage common to all Jews could be used to cement unity and ultimately transformation."[13] Ben-Gurion, all the while raging against Jewish tradition, was in the habit of quoting the Bible the better to justify the Zionist project. In his memoirs, for example, he connects the origins of the Israel Defense Force (IDF) with the "revelation of the sovereign power of the Hebrews after the royal days of Judah and Israel."[14] For him, the right to establish the Zionist state "derives from the uninterrupted historical link between the Jewish people and their ancestral fatherland, a link which the law of nations has also recognized."[15]

By invoking the "unbroken chain" Ben-Gurion ignored his own writings of 1918, in which he affirmed that the Romans exiled only a few members of the elite, and that the majority of Jews of the era of the Second Temple continued to live in the land while pursuing their economic activities. Furthermore, historians of the Roman era by no means support the thesis of the exile of the entire population of conquered countries. Later, under Byzantine and then Arab influence, this population may have morphed into the group that today identifies itself as Palestinian.[16]

In 1922 Ben-Gurion affirmed that the Palestinian *fellahin* (peasants) were most probably the biological descendants of the Jews of the 1st century.[17] Thirty years later, however, setting an example for all of Israel's future leaders, he categorically refused the right of return to those very Palestinians, who had been driven from their ancestral homes in 1947–49. For him, Jewish settlers from Europe had replaced the local population in the role of legitimate heirs of the biblical Hebrews. In 1952, taking the Biblical story for a historical and legal document, in a Knesset speech on foreign affairs Ben-Gurion declared that his government bore Egypt "no ill will for what she did to our forefathers in the days of Pharaoh."[18] His reference to events described in the Bible illustrates the kind of questions raised by the Zionist character of the state of Israel about the rationality of political discourse.

These questions have by no means disappeared since the era of the founders of the state. In 2010, in an official speech delivered in Washington, the Israeli prime minister Binyamin Netanyahu rejected the claim that "the Jews are foreign colonialists in their own homeland [as] one of the great lies of modern times":

> In my office, I have a signet ring that was loaned to me by Israel's Department of Antiquities. The ring was found next to the Western Wall, but it dates back some 2,800 years ago, two hundred years after King David turned Jerusalem into our capital city.
> The ring is a seal of a Jewish official, and inscribed on it in Hebrew is his name: Netanyahu. Netanyahu Ben-Yoash. That's my last name. My first name, Benjamin, dates back 1,000 years earlier to Benjamin, the son of Jacob.[19]

Many observers noted, however, that the prime minister's original family name was Mileikowsky. His father, born in the Russian Empire in 1910, like many Zionists adopted the pseudonym "Netanyahu" (Gift of God) originally as a pen name.[20] During the 1970s, which he spent in the United States, the future prime minister abridged his family name to "Nitai," another pen name used by his father, one that the Americans would find easier to pronounce. But the substance of the argument, and not the fine detail of name changing, points to the political and ahistorical usage of archeology, as well as of the Bible, in Zionist discourse.

On the same subject, the Israeli intellectual Amnon Raz-Krakozkin reflected, with both precision and concision, the paradox of the position held by the founders of Zionism: "God does not exist, and he promised us this land."[21] But invoking divine promise was and remains effective before audiences of the Protestant persuasion. If Ben-Gurion, by brandishing the Bible, was able to gain the sympathies of the Peel Commission in 1936,[22] Binyamin Netanyahu, by invoking divine promise, was able to draw standing ovations from the two houses of the US Congress in 2011.

The Congressional enthusiasm had much to do with the influence of a variety of pro-Israel forces, including several Protestant evangelical groups located on the far right of the political spectrum that seek to hasten the Second Coming of Christ by gathering the world's Jews in the Holy Land. These Christian Zionists, who number more than an estimated 50 million[23] in the United States alone, far exceeding the world's Jewish population (estimated at 14 million), generously underwrite the most intransigent Zionist factions.

By way of contrast, the traditionalist or "ultra-Orthodox" Jews who call themselves *haredim* ("those who tremble") would not use the official term "the state of Israel." Simply put, Haredi men can be identified by their dress (primarily black and white). It is easy to identify non-Zionist or anti-Zionist Jews: they will avoid pronouncing the words "state of Israel" and even "Israel," using instead the traditional terms, usually with an Ashkenazi pronunciation: *Erets Yisroel* ("land of Israel") or *Erets ha-koidesh* (sometimes *koidesh*, "Holy Land"). The *haredim* approach the question of national security without invoking the Bible. Unlike the Zionist Jews and Christians, they eliminate any consideration of biblical belonging to any particular territory from the decision-making process. A *haredi* parliamentarian puts it clearly:

> The Zionists are wrong. There is no need to foster love of the land of Israel by the political and military rule in the entire land. One can love Hebron even from Tel Aviv ... even if it is under Palestinian rule. The State of Israel is not a value. Only matters of spirituality belong to the family of "values."[24]

Chapter Four

The Zionist Enterprise

Zionism, in the version that ultimately prevailed, represents a nationalist movement with four essential goals:

- to transform the transnational Jewish identity centered on the Torah into a national identity like that of other European nations;
- to develop a new vernacular language, or a national language, based on biblical and rabbinical Hebrew;
- to displace the Jews from their countries of origin to Palestine;
- to establish political and economic control over Palestine.

While the other nationalisms of the era had only to deal with the struggle for political and economic control of their countries, Zionism set itself a much broader challenge, to accomplish its first three objectives simultaneously. It was an idea that, for the majority of Jews, appeared novel and bold.[1]

It also constituted an audacious modernization project. The Zionists articulated an ambitious vision, one of modernizing a land they considered backward and which, they claimed, longed for redemption by settlers from Europe. In this sense, the state of Israel represents a case of imposed modernization typical of Western colonialism, a policy rejected not only by the Arab populations that saw themselves as victims, but also by the traditional Jewish populations. Both groups have known rapid demographic expansion and have been strangers to the definition of the Jew borrowed from European nationalism that lies at the heart of the Zionist enterprise.[2]

Zionism stands today as the last vestige of all the 20th-century movements committed to radical transformation, probably the most ambitious among them. Ben-Gurion was an admirer of Lenin, and we can better understand the strong-willed character of the Zionist project through his admiration for the socialist regime in Russia: "the great revolution, the primordial revolution, which has been called upon to uproot present reality, shaking its foundations to the very depths of this rotten and decadent society."[3]

The Zionist experience raises multiple questions for those Jews who practice Judaism and identify with Jewish tradition. How could the return of the Jews to the land of Israel before messianic times be interpreted? Would their return obliterate the unique nature of Jewish history and its metaphysical dimension? Did political docility constitute a practical accommodation to exile, or was it a religious doctrine characterizing rabbinical Judaism? And finally, what were the Zionists' ultimate goals? Was their rebellion directed solely against Jewish political docility, or did the Zionists intend to eradicate Judaism root and branch: that is, uproot the entire religious tradition that they accused of having engendered submission and political inaction?

Separate Development Against Liberal Society

Zionism had found an echo among certain Jews only by the end of the 19th century. The historians of Zionism point out that the founders of this movement all emerged from among the assimilated Jews. As Shlomo Avineri writes:

> They did not come from the traditional religious background. They were all products of European education, imbued with the current ideas of the European intelligentsia. Their plight was not economic nor religious. ... They were seeking self-determination, identity, liberation within the terms of the post-1789 European culture and their own newly awakened self-consciousness.[4]

Zionism could not have developed before the French Revolution, no matter how violent the anti-Jewish persecutions of earlier centuries.[5] The assimilated Jews of Central Europe suffered from repeated outbreaks of anti-Semitism and felt rejected in their desire to feel a part of the dominant culture, even though they, and often their parents, no longer obeyed the commandments of the Torah and knew nothing of the normative framework of Judaism. In fact, they followed the path of secularization that was sweeping Europe at the turn of the 20th century, and felt a sense of frustration at not being able to enjoy a full and complete acceptance from those around them.

Theirs was a peculiar frustration, one that a non-Jewish German or French citizen would never experience in a lifetime. That frustration, so acute as to resemble suffering, was psychological in nature: they did not suffer economic or physical consequences of that rejection. It was the frustration felt by a small number of Jews who aspired to become members of ambient high society; they saw a failure of the emancipation in their failure to penetrate high society. Indeed, the emancipation failed to deliver them the anticipated social and psychological benefits, particularly the feeling of total acceptance. In other words, "Zionism was an invention of intellectuals and assimilated Jews ... who turned their back on the rabbis and aspired to modernity, seeking desperately for a remedy for their existential anxiety."[6] Zionism thus provided its first promoters with the hope of rejecting individual assimilation in favor of a broader vision of collective assimilation, seen as a "normalization" of the Jews. Virtually none of these assimilated Jews had any misgivings about assimilation, which in their minds constituted an indubitable index of progress. Some of them even opted for conversion to Christianity, either on an individual basis or, as Herzl proposed in 1893, collectively.[7]

No matter the magnitude of individual frustrations, they alone were not enough to propel a mass movement. Such a movement could only take off where anti-Jewish measures had been systematized and where the will to organize politically existed. That is why the true birthplace of practical Zionism must be situated in Eastern Europe, and above all within the Russian Empire, from which almost the entire Zionist—and later Israeli—elite had originated for more than a century. But the Russian Jews were not the only ones that persecution turned toward Zionism. After 1933 many German Jews, who had formerly been either indifferent or hostile to the Zionist movement, sought emigration to Palestine.[8]

The rapid emergence of Zionism raised the issue of the legitimacy of Jewish nationalism and of a specifically Jewish political or military activism. The pretension of Theodore Herzl, the founder of political Zionism and subject of the Austro-Hungarian Empire, to represent the Jews of the world irritated both the rabbinical authorities and community notables. But his pretension reflected the spirit of the times: the Bolsheviks, a tiny group of intellectuals, claimed to represent the entire working class. More generally, there spread in Europe the idea of a vanguard that has grasped the objective processes of history, despite the apathy and even the opposition of the masses whose interests it pretends to represent.

According to the Zionists, the Jews had always used religion as a means to assert their "will to exist." In other words, Judaism was nothing but an instrument of survival. According to this conception, the Torah had been given to the Jews in order to maintain their unity. But once they had returned to their land, they would no longer need to follow its precepts, for their national consciousness, as experienced in the land of Israel, would be sufficient to sustain that unity.[9] Like the expression "will to exist," this explanation originated in those European nationalist movements that proclaimed the will of peoples dispersed throughout the Russian and Austro-Hungarian empires to survive and to form a national state. "Power of the will" is often invoked in interpreting the history of Zionism, which some historians present as exceptional, in defiance of normal social and political circumstances.[10] In an oft-cited phrase Herzl reportedly said, "if you will it, it is no dream."

Zionism, however, remains at root a response to the challenges of liberalism rather than a reaction to ambient anti-Semitism, genuine as it was. In fact, liberalism continues to attract Jews. Despite a rich variety of programs designed to promote *aliya*, far more Israelis take up residence in the world's liberal democracies than citizens of those countries immigrate to Israel. Migration statistics could not be clearer.[11] Most indicators point to a clear preference for liberal democracies over the state of Israel, despite the fact that it is often identified as the "Jewish state." Thus, Zionist leaders and Israeli political figures must often stress the impossibility for Jews to live fully as Jews anywhere else than in Israel. In this regard, they follow in the footsteps of the Christian precursors of the Zionist movement who warned that emancipation threatened the "Jewish nationality" that, for them, was indispensable to the realization of their own project, that of "ingathering the Jews in the Holy Land."[12]

The emancipation was accordingly denigrated the better to promote a national vision; subsequent Nazi persecutions would later provide Zionism with a powerful argument. A constant can therefore be said to exist in Israeli politics, one that considers all Jews as potential Israeli citizens. The habit of claiming for themselves the Jews of the diaspora, especially when the latter are in a state of migration, repeats itself throughout the history of the state of Israel. Thus Israeli governments, whatever the ruling party, attempt to channel Jewish migratory movements toward Israel, trying to stem—for example—the migration of Russian Jews to the United States and Germany (since the 1970s), Argentinian Jews to the United States (between 1970 and 1980), North African Jews to France and Canada (between 1950 and 1970), and so on.[13] The habits of treating the Jews of the diaspora as state property, and of placing the interest of the state above individual freedoms, are evident in the memoirs of the retired head of Israel's intelligence agency Nativ in charge of channeling Jews from the former Soviet bloc to Israel.[14]

While the pretension that it "owns" the Jews has provoked criticism in liberal circles, Israel has also attempted to suborn the memory of the Jews in many countries, many of them Soviet, who died for these countries during the Second World War. The monument raised to their memory in Israel displays, in a manner as anachronistic as it is incongruous, the symbol of the Israeli army, which was established three years after the end of the war.

If the equality of rights that the emancipation granted the Jews is no longer a source of controversy today, in the early years of the 21st century, the question of double loyalty remains, even though it is less an issue given the benevolence of the Western democracies with regard to Israel. Jews' expressions of solidarity with Israel at times edge on rejection and condemnation of their own countries; quite a few diaspora Jews identify with the state of Israel and oppose the policies of their countries of citizenship.[15]

Zionist opposition to open, multicultural societies has had more than negligible effects on Jews, the majority of whom prefer, however, to live outside the state ostensibly created for them nearly 70 years ago:

> Political Zionism teaches Dual Loyalty and, in this dual loyalty, when the occasion arises, greater loyalty to the State of Israel than to the country of one's birth or adoption. Political Zionism is thus not only not consistent with good citizenship, but has in it most fertile seeds for proliferation of anti-Semitism. … Political Zionism intentionally stirs up anti-Semitism. From the very beginning, it has been the policy to deliberately incite hatred of the Jew and, then, in feigned horror, point to it to justify a Jewish state. Machiavellianism raised to the ninth degree.[16]

The insistence of many Jewish community representatives that Israel must be supported unconditionally tends to efface, in public perceptions, any distinction between Zionism and Judaism, between Jew and Israeli. This support in turn raises the question of the legitimacy of those habitually identified as the "representatives of the Jewish community": do they represent their local co-religionists or do they view themselves first and foremost as defenders of the state of Israel? Élie Barnavi, the historian and former Israeli ambassador to France, refers unequivocally to "an Israel-vassalized diaspora."[17] Several observers have noted that some of

Israel's defenders in the diaspora go beyond the official positions of the state of Israel: they become "more Catholic than the Pope."

In the diaspora, support for Israel, particularly in North America, solidified in the wake of the June 1967 war. In large measure it was due to the sense of pride felt by a large number of Jews at Israel's military victories and the breaking-off of diplomatic relations with the Soviet Union, which placed Israel squarely on the Western side of the cold war. The moral transmutation of the meek compromising Jew into a proud combative Zionist can be understood as the principal effect of the state of Israel, for both the critics and the partisans of Zionism.

Identification with the state of Israel has tended to substitute for the value system typical of Judaism (including mercy and humility) the ideals intrinsic to nationalism in its many forms (among them egotism and national pride). For the Zionists in the diaspora, there emerged a vicarious "Israeli" identity, obviously contingent on the perpetuation of the Zionist state. For the critics of this orientation, to mortgage the future of Judaism to the fate of a fragile state would be nearsighted to say the least.

It has been observed that many Zionist community leaders, despite being distinguished citizens of their own countries, display no scruples in presenting an Israeli diplomat as "our consul" or "our ambassador." Now, at the beginning of the 21st century, more than a few observers of Jewish life note the existence of something more than double allegiance, an accusation feared by many opponents of early Zionism; for a substantial number of diaspora Jews, what can be observed is a form of exclusive allegiance to the state of Israel:

> I fear that blind Jewish support of Israel will sooner or later give rise to suspicions of divided loyalty. It may seem absurd (for now), but as a retired US Foreign Service officer, I have nightmarish visions of Jewish Americans being excluded from the Foreign Service and other sensitive government agencies because of doubts about the reliability of their support for American policy in the Middle East. And may Heaven preserve us from another Jonathan Pollard![18]

The case of Jonathan Pollard, a convicted Israeli spy within the American military infrastructure who spent 30 years behind bars, certainly remains exceptional. But the transformation of Pollard into a martyr and of his defense into a Jewish community cause has generated deep concern among American Jews and their friends:

Perhaps the saddest—and most dangerous—aspect of the Pollard case is that demands for his release are an enormous gift to anti-Semites… I beg you: Stop for a moment. Ask yourself how your defense of Pollard looks to your fellow countrymen.[19]

Such are perceptions that, across the Atlantic, fully half of British people believe that the Jews of their country show allegiance to Israel rather than to the United Kingdom.[20]

The Israeli daily *Haaretz* echoes these concerns in its analysis of the situation of French Jews:

Whether this is apathetic ignorance, lack of solidarity, or a cynical world view that regards any increase in immigrant applications as the sole goal to be pursued, Israel, which regards itself as guardian of the world's Jews, may discover it is the source of their troubles.[21]

Indeed, from the very beginnings of their movement, the Zionists have affirmed that all Jews must first and foremost declare allegiance to the state of Israel. After the Israeli attack on Egypt in 1956 (which was immediately condemned by both the United States and the USSR), Ben-Gurion declared, "every Jew, wherever he was, was proud of the Israeli Army and the State."[22]

The unconditional defense of Israel into which certain community leaders have dragooned the Jews tends to expose them to criticism, which in turn justifies Zionism and makes the state of Israel indispensable as an insurance policy. Even proudly secular Israelis find this policy suicidal for the future of the diaspora:

For the Jews, this creates a vicious circle. The actions of [Ariel] Sharon create repulsion and opposition throughout the world. These reinforce anti-Semitism. Faced with this danger, Jewish organizations are pushed into defending Israel and giving it unqualified support. This support enables the anti-Semites to attack not only the government of Israel, but the local Jews too. And so on …. If I were asked for advice, I would counsel the Jewish communities throughout the world as follows: break out of the vicious circle. Disarm the anti-Semites. Break the habit of automatic identification with everything our governments do. Let your conscience speak out. Return to the traditional Jewish values of "Justice, justice you shall pursue" (Deuteronomy 16:20) and "Seek peace and pursue it" (Psalms 34:15). Identify yourselves with the Other Israel, which is struggling to uphold these values at home. All over the world, new Jewish groups that follow this way are multiplying. They break yet another myth: the duty of Jews everywhere to subordinate themselves to the edicts of our government.[23]

Many observers trace a direct link between anti-Jewish incidents in the diaspora and the policies of the Israeli government. "The intensification of local anti-Semitism is a big lie," states a Haredi activist, who accuses Israel of provoking incidents so that it can exploit the consequences to convince Jews to migrate to Israel.[24] In his view, this vicious circle only confirms his conviction that the state of Israel represents the greatest danger for Jews, both in Israel and in the diaspora. This assessment is reflected in the title of an impressive work on Jewish–Israeli relations by a British journalist intimately acquainted with Israel and its past leaders, Alan Hart's *Zionism: The Real Enemy of the Jews*.[25]

But even though more and more Jews are becoming aware that the nature of the state created in 1948 goes against their own moral and political values, they nonetheless feel obliged to support it, given that its existence is now an accomplished fact. Within Reform Judaism, and despite the positions of the American Council for Judaism—heir to the anti-Zionist tradition of the Reform movement—a majority of the members consider themselves Zionists. However, as their number is small in Israel (and their branch of Judaism is not officially recognized, meaning that their rabbis cannot officiate at marriages that the state recognizes), the reality of their lives in the United States and other democratic countries mea ns that they tend to remain for the most part politically liberal (in the American sense of the word) and support Israeli policies only selectively. They also represent a major source of funding for human rights organizations and quite a few centers of political dissidence in Israel.[26]

Concern for Israel hardly ends with the personal fate of its Jewish inhabitants. Several intellectuals have observed that Israel, taken as a political entity, is more important than the well-being of the Jews themselves. According to Shlomo Avineri:

> Other Jewish communities are merely aggregates of individuals, and as such they have no normative standing as a public entity. Israel, on the other hand, is conceived not only as an aggregate of its population, but its very existence has immanent value and normative standing.[27]

The state of Israel, in the eyes of the Zionists, is unlike any other, and above all any other democratic entity, where the political configuration of the state can be debated like any other political question.

The denigration of Jewish life outside of Israel has long been a feature of Zionist thought and practice. The mobilization of the diaspora to justify whatever political or military action Israel might undertake constitutes its crucial element. Innocent though it may appear, the automatic identification of the state of Israel both with Jews and with Judaism suggests that ethnic nationalism can better protect modern humans than modern, pluralist liberal society. It comes as no surprise that an increasing number of Zionists in Europe[28] and North America,[29] despite their former espousal of left-wing values, support right-wing parties that admire Israel as a model of proud and combative ethnic nationalism. At the same time, many young Jews in the United States find pluralist society closer to their Jewish principles than "Jewish ethnocracy": "A Judaism that just preserves the Jews stands for nothing. … Real Jewish issues are not about the Jewish tribe. They speak to real problems, and make our ancient religious mandates seem radically new again—and utterly crucial."[30]

Several signs of the growing awareness of the danger Zionism represents for Jewish continuity can be detected. "The 21st century reality is that Judaism will only survive in America as an attractive ethical and moral force, not as an unyielding foreign policy voice in behalf of Israel."[31] The Tikkun Community, a movement launched by Rabbi Michael Lerner based on the periodical *Tikkun*, has echoed these very concerns and spoken out against the effort to reduce Jewish life in the United States to support for Israel.[32] Rabbi Lerner has on several occasions been attacked and received death threats because of his activities.

Unconditional support for Israel has given rise, on both sides, to a level of verbal violence that contrasts with the manners and customs of liberal democracies. Anti-Zionist activity of whatever kind is denounced as anti-Semitism, a tactic that serves to further consolidate identification of Judaism and Jews with Zionism. For Reform rabbi David Goldberg, of London, the Jews would be committing an "ahistorical error" in confounding the political stances of the opponents of Israel with the theological hatred of the Jews incarnated by classical anti-Semitism:

> We Jews do ourselves a disservice if we cry "anti-Semite" with the same stridency at a liberal commentator who criticizes the Israeli army's disproportionate response to terrorist outrages, and at a National Front lout who asserts that the Protocols of the Elders of Zion is a genuine document.[33]

One veteran of Jewish organizations who has taken a critical distance from his institutional past and from "Jewish community McCarthyism" has stated that for many Jewish organizations, "if you do not support the government of Israel, then your Jewishness, and not your political judgment, will be called into question."[34] An American Jewish author argues about fears that the Zionist establishment might succeed in imposing its will and "excommunicating" any Jew who might not unconditionally support the Zionist state, that:

> if that is so—if, after all these millennia, the Conference of Presidents really gets away with instituting a kind of Jewish excommunication over its rapturous rallying behind Sharon [the then Israeli prime minister]—then Zionism will forever distort, and even threaten to destroy, the creativity, the diversity, the genius of American Jewishness. Zionism, God forbid, will turn out to be the greatest peril Jewish America has ever faced.[35]

Some Jews living in liberal Western societies are deeply concerned lest militant Zionism destroy Jewish moral values and endanger the lives of Jews inside and outside of Israel. Indeed, Jewish tradition contains elements that can, when a minority gains a majority position, be used to foment racism and xenophobia. While preferential attention to the needs of the Jews threatens no one where Jews are in the minority, the same attitude, when applied in a Jewish-majority society, can give rise to multiple injustices. Ethnocentrism can be ethical only when the group in question is threatened, or at least in a minority position. Otherwise it can lead to monstrous outcomes, which the Israeli expert in the history of Nazism Yehuda Bauer describes as "genocidal nationalism."[36]

Indeed, associating the state of Israel with both Jews and Judaism risks weakening confidence in the equality and tolerance demonstrated by those Jews who prefer to live throughout the world. It suggests that ethnic sovereignty can better protect the Jews than liberal and pluralist society. Human rights, which emancipation had extended to the Jews, continue to reassure them. It is significant that European right-wingers, who are opposed to this kind of society, often seek to replace it with ethnic nationalism; as will be discussed in the context of Israel's international relations (see Chapter 9), they find Zionism inspiring since it has functioned as both an internal and colonial variant of ethnic nationalism from its very earliest days.

In the Footsteps of European Nationalisms

The Zionists, as we have seen, were inspired by the rise of organic nationalism in Central and Eastern Europe, where nationalists struggled, at
the turn of the 20th century, to create a state, and thus a legal and political framework for a nation that they considered as already existing. The
exclusive character of German, Polish, or Ukrainian nationalism exerted
a strong influence on Jewish nationalists; those influences were to remain
determining for the Zionist movement and later for Israeli society. The
Zionist activists who emerged in Eastern Europe never knew the tolerant
variety of nationalism that makes a clear distinction between nation, religion, society, and the state; the kind of nationalism we find in countries
like Canada or the United States, which are home to large Jewish communities numbering quite a few critics of Zionism. A striking example of the
way in which Jewish nationalism came to substitute for Judaism was the
call issued by a young Jew to Vladimir Jabotinsky (1880–1940), a Russian
author and Zionist leader: "Our life is dull and our hearts are empty, for
there is no God in our midst; give us a God, sir, worthy of dedication and
sacrifice, and you will see what we can do."[37]

The response came swiftly and took its inspiration from the mass
movements that were then appearing in many European countries: Betar,
a paramilitary youth organization that mobilized tens of thousands of
young Jews. Even though it replaced Judaism, Betar inherited its insistence on wholehearted, unswerving devotion but redirected it to the
Zionist cause. Its members subscribed to a slogan borrowed from a lyric
poem by the Russian-Jewish poet Haim Nahman Bialik (1873–1934):
"There is one sun above, one song in a heart—and no second coming."[38]

To buttress the legitimacy of his approach, Jabotinsky recounted his
conversations with Joseph Trumpeldor (1880–1920), a veteran of the Russian army who fought with the Jewish legion at Gallipoli during the First
World War and in the Russian Revolution of 1917. Trumpeldor, who had
become an icon of Zionist education, confided in him that the Jews must
become a people of iron:

> Iron, from which everything that the national machine requires should be
> made. Does it require a wheel? Here I am. A nail, a screw, a girder? Here I am.
> Police? Doctors? Actors? Water carriers? Here I am. I have no features, no feel-
> ings, no psychology, no name of my own. I am a servant of Zion, prepared for
> everything, bound to nothing, having one imperative: Build![39]

There was a distinct Russian flavor to his rhetoric: iron and steel were the Bolsheviks' metaphors of choice. Stalin (whose *nom de guerre* means 'man of steel') used his private conversations with Lenin to legitimize his own policies of mass mobilization. Other mass movements in Europe adopted similar methods and rhetoric.

The language of redemption is omnipresent in the Zionist movement. Ben-Gurion's Laborites, for long the dominant section, made a particularly coherent use of redemptive imagery. For example, they used the expression *geulat haaretz* (redemption of the land) to signify the purchase of Arab land by Jews, transactions that were often "suspect," adds Shlomo Avineri.[40]

The Passover *Haggadah*, a seminal formative Judaic text about redemption, also became an instrument of secularization, undergoing major changes at the hands of Zionist educators. While references to God disappeared, the *Haggadah* read in certain leftist kibbutzim replaced God with the human effort of the Zionist pioneers.[41] The transformation of the language of redemption and of religious values into secular concepts infused the Zionist pioneers, who saw themselves as the vanguard of the Jewish people, fashioning history with their own hands as they went. They used Judaic terms familiar to the masses of Eastern Europe to facilitate the propagation of their ideology, which, though radical, retained some traditional forms in order to appease widespread apprehension.

The manipulation of religion, writes Israeli historian and political scientist Zeev Sternhell, is not specific to Zionism, but can be found in the many varieties of organic nationalism propagated in Europe from the mid-19th century onward. While keeping intact the social function of religion in order to unify the people, Zionism eliminated its metaphysical content. In the same way religion became a vital element of many varieties of nationalism; for example, neither the Polish variant nor l'Action française (in spite of the atheism of some of its leaders) made any effort to disguise their Catholic traits. Sternhell defines this trend as "religion without God," religion that has preserved only its outward symbols.[42]

Berl Katznelson (1887–1944), the Russian-born leader of the Labor Zionist movement, applied this radical principle by simply rewriting the text of the *yizkor* ("He shall remember") commemorative prayer. The original prayer implores God to preserve the memory of the deceased without mentioning the cause of death; the Zionist version calls upon the Jewish people to remember its heroes "who have given their lives for the dignity of Israel and the Land of Israel."[43] As with other European nationalisms, the memory of fallen heroes—Trumpeldor high among them—became an instrument in the struggle for political independence, transforming as it did the meaning of a religious symbol borrowed from Judaism. In the outburst of messianic enthusiasm that followed the war of 1967, the chief rabbi of the IDF, Shlomo Goren, reinstated the traditional beginning "The Eternal will remember" into Katznelson's text, which remained a part of the official day of commemoration. However in 2012, following a complaint by the mother of a dead soldier all mention of God was removed.[44]

Jewish tradition is rather reserved with respect to the state. While some, like Rabbi Goren, see the state of Israel as part of the messianic redemption of cosmic magnitude, those rabbis who only tolerate the state of Israel frequently warn that the existence of a state is not guaranteed once and for all.[45] However Zionism, like all nationalisms, emphasizes the vital role of the state as a national value, as the center and essence of the Jewish nation. The expectations of the state are clearly quite different.

Unlike the Russian Zionists, who had rejected the Jewish tradition, Herzl's relationship with Judaism was a more pragmatic and functional one. So remote from that tradition as to refuse to have his son circumcised, he nonetheless recognized that it could serve as bait to attract those Jews "still sunk in the old ways," precisely those who, in spite of their mistrust of the new ideology, were deemed most susceptible to Zionist overtures. On the political level, Herzl conceived Judaism as a useful tool for state building, very much along the lines of clericalism in Christian lands.[46]

The nationalist exploitation of Judaism touched off strong reactions:

> But there is worse, a sort of disqualification at once religious and moral, a spiritual corruption at the hands of lies and hypocrisy that borders on blasphemy, in the fact that a people could make use of the Torah to strengthen its national pretensions, while the majority of its members, as well as the social and political regime that it has adopted, have no connection with religious faith, and see in it nothing but legends and superstitions. This is a kind of prostitution of the values of Judaism, which amounts to using these values as a cover for the satisfaction of its patriotic urges and interests. And if there exist Jews willing to join the national-occupationist trend, and go so far as to make a "Greater Israel" … the essential element of their faith, a religious commandment, well then, these people have become the heirs of worshippers of the golden calf who also

proclaimed: "Behold your God, O Israël." The golden calf need not necessarily be made of gold. It may also be called "nation," "land," "state."[47]

The appropriation of Judaic concepts for secular ends nonetheless proved quite effective. The rituals of the Hassidic Jews fascinated Herzl, who analyzed them with a certain cynicism and who hoped one day to recruit these rituals to his cause.[48] Herzl was aware of the opposition his ideas provoked among the German rabbis, Orthodox as well as Reform, who were motivated by a concern to protect all that the Jews had achieved in the greater society around them (*Protestrabbiner*). However, he underestimated the intensity of the hatred and indignation of the Orthodox rabbis to the East, and particularly in Russia, precisely where Zionism was to find its most fervent recruits.

The nationalist conceptualization of the Jews and of their history can be traced both to Zionism and to the racial anti-Semitism from which the Jews suffered in the 20th century. Herzl counted upon the assistance of the anti-Semites to bring the Zionist project to fruition. It must be remembered that both Zionism and anti-Semitism originated in Europe, the home of colonialism and racial discrimination. The dominant current of the Zionist movement continued to take inspiration from European nationalisms by encouraging settler colonialism that excluded and ultimately dispossessed the local population. Zionism succeeded in setting up a state just as the nations of Europe were recoiling from ethnic nationalism in the wake of the atrocities of the Second World War. Moreover, the Zionists intended to establish sovereignty over a territory in which they constituted an immigrant minority made up of disparate ethnic groups. For these reasons, Zionism can best be described as a belated "illegitimate son of ethnic nationalism."[49]

Settler Colonialism

The application of the colonial model to Israeli history no longer raises the slightest eyebrow. It is considered "legitimate and desirable"[50] by mainstream experts such as the Israeli historian Anita Shapira, even though her approach is far from enjoying unanimous support among the Zionist public. The Zionist ideological positions developed by the labor movement denied the existence of a conflict with the local population, which according to that vision was indifferent to Zionist colonization or even benefited from it. But the exclusion of Arab workers from the labor market that began in the early 20th century clearly harmed them. Not only was the labor market segregated, Arabs could not be employed on land sold or rented by the JNF. Acquisition of land by the JNF was irreversible and immutable.

From its very beginnings, the Zionist movement sought to colonize with Europeans a territory in Western Asia inhabited by a variety of ethnic and confessional groups. The first Jewish immigrants, at the end of the 19th century, settled on the land in a random and disparate manner, employing Arab workers on their farms. Unlike them, those who migrated to Palestine in the early 20th century practiced a concentrated form of colonization: they set up exclusively Jewish settlements, which entailed the displacement of local populations. The accent placed on the establishment of ethnically homogenous settlements could not but have created resistance. The two slogans adopted by the Zionist pioneers clearly illustrated their intentions: "conquest through labor" and *hafrada* (separation). In other words, the Zionist movement adopted a policy of separate development that remains in force up to the present, and explains in large measure the perpetuation of the conflict with the Palestinians and the isolation of the state of Israel in the region.

A lasting resolution of the Israel–Palestine conflict would necessarily involve a form of decolonization. Since the Zionist colonists have no country to which they could return (as happened with the French colonists in Algeria), decolonization might follow the South African model. There, the leadership of the African National Congress recognized the legitimacy of the presence of white colonists in their country. What then becomes the issue is the reapportionment of vital resources, beginning with land and water, not to mention the economic disparities that can be observed between the Jordan and the Mediterranean.

Anita Shapira writes, "Zionist psychology was molded by the conflicting parameters of a national liberation and a movement of European colonization in a Middle Eastern country."[51] The resort to force proved indispensable for achieving these two objectives, as Israeli historian Benny Morris explains:

> Zionist ideology and practice were necessarily and elementally expansionist. Realizing Zionism meant organizing and dispatching settlement groups to Palestine. As each settlement took root, it became acutely aware of its isolation and vulnerability, and quite naturally sought the establishment of new Jewish settlements around it. This would make the original settlement more

"secure"—but the new settlements became the "front line" and themselves needed "new" settlements to safeguard them. After the Six Day War, a similar logic would underlie the extension of Israeli settlement into the Golan Heights (to safeguard the Jordan Valley settlements against Syrian depredations from above) and around Jerusalem (to serve as a defensive bulwark for the districts of the exposed northern, eastern and southern flanks of the city).[52]

Israeli foreign policy is built on the same logic. Having established military superiority, first over the Palestinians and then over the Arab countries, for a few years Israel fueled a fear of Iran. Several Israeli commentators have noted that the strengthening of Israel's military capacity—already far and away the most substantial in the region—has not affected its self-image as victim.[53] The shift in the balance of power to Israel's advantage has not led to a change in the awareness of power among the Israelis; the disparity between real power and the sense of powerlessness has only served to sharpen the sentiment of potential victims emanating from Israel. Some critics have likened this attitude to the Biblical curse "you shall flee though none pursues" (Leviticus 26:17).

As a settler colony, Israel possesses several original traits. First, the right to self-determination is utopian in the most literal sense ("utopia" means "in no place"), for it applies to the "Jewish people," a group dispersed to the four corners of the earth, rather than to a population concentrated in a particular territory (the citizens of Israel). Second, the territory claimed is not delimited. Third, transnational organizations (such as the Jewish Agency and the JNF) have been integrated into the state functions of the management of the territory but are not subject to the kind of control normally exercised by institutions of the state. This kind of right to self-determination undermines the status of state and territorial citizenship and obstructs the full and complete inclusion of the Arabs in the political process. At the same time, it reinforces the "Judaization," or more precisely the "Zionization," of the territories by theoretically integrating Zionist Jews residing outside Israel into the eminently political process of immigration and colonization. This form of government was named "ethnocracy" by several Israeli scholars.[54]

The Zionist geographical imperative forms an integral part of the political program and the practical colonization that assumed their respective forms at the turn of the 20th century. The same imperative remains in force today. In fact, space and discourse have become fused in the ongoing process of social construction. Colonization rests upon a settler society, ethnic nationalism, and ethnic capital.

Settler societies like Israel pursue the objective of modifying ethnic structures by applying a coherent strategy of immigration and ethnic settlement. Australia, Canada, New Zealand, and the United States are examples of settler societies that, by their practices, were successful in dispossessing, and in certain cases exterminating, native populations. Settler societies fear being thrust into minority status by native peoples, and encourage selective immigration by offering economic and political advantages to new arrivals. Canada, for example, attracted white immigrants while marginalizing not only its native peoples but also residents of East-Asian origin who were seen as resistant to assimilation. The policy of "White Australia," which was enforced for decades, reinforced the domination of the continent by European immigrants and their descendants. Such are the kind of measures that Israel has been applying ever since its creation, continuing the policies of the Zionist organizations that selected immigrants from the earliest days of the British mandate.

We have already seen that ethnic nationalism is hardly unique to Israel. Estonia, Hungary, and Serbia continue to practice this variety of nationalism, which postulates that the survival of an ethnic group depends on control of a given territory, and devises historical interpretations designed to support that postulate. But Israel is unique in that Zionism defines the group in transnational terms, all the while affirming that it is native to the colonized territory.

Integrated into the Zionist project, capital and labor are mobilized in tandem to create ethnically segregated structures. Segregation extends from relations between Arab and Jewish residents to those among Jews, where the founding sub-group (Eastern European Ashkenazis) assumes the dominant position.

Israeli society is democratic but, faithful to its founding principles, in a selective manner, so it functions as an ethnocracy. The Law of Return allows any Jew to migrate to Israel and to acquire citizenship, while the same citizenship is often inaccessible to those who have been living in the country for generations. The Zionization of the land, that is, its "de-Arabization," much more than simply declaring the state "Jewish," has maintained and reinforced segregation in its various forms, and constitutes one of the pillars of the Israeli Zionist identity.

Zionization of the land took a radical turn after 1948. Until then, the

Zionists had not been able to assert control over more than 7 percent of the land of Mandate Palestine, while 10 percent was under the control of the state authority, in this case the British administration. A year after the unilateral declaration of independence, the state of Israel, in association with the JNF, controlled 93 percent of these lands, an outcome achieved primarily by the expropriation of land belonging to the Palestinian refugees whose return was forbidden by the Israeli authorities. In addition, two-thirds of the lands belonging to the Arab citizens of Israel were also acquired and "Zionized," leaving to their former owners a meager 4 percent despite the fact that they constitute nowadays nearly 20 percent of all Israeli citizens. Zionization has been rendered irreversible as the JNF controls these lands "in the name of the Jewish people," a conceptually vague entity that covers, without their knowledge let alone consent, all those who consider themselves Jews, irrespective of their relation with Zionism and the state of Israel. As a result, Israel's Arab citizens cannot purchase, rent, or even use most of the land in the country of their citizenship.[55]

An estimated 500 Palestinian villages were obliterated after the dispossession of the native population following the creation of the Zionist state. Between 1949 and 1952, the ground on which some of those villages had stood was used to build 240 collective settlements (*kibbutzim* and *moshavim*).[56] These new settlements accentuated the segregation between Jews and Arabs, as well as between European Jews and those of Asian and African origin. Many settlements, in fact gated communities, are authorized to select future residents and thus to ensure the continuity of ethnic, religious, and social segregation.[57]

Jewish critics of the Zionist policy of segregation are numerous. Even the Haredim, who make up one of the most self-segregated groups among Jews, have raised their voices, as humanists and secular pacifists have done, against the oppression of the native population:

> The Zionist movement was not only a heretical departure from Judaism .... It was monstrously blind to the indigenous inhabitants of the Holy Land. In the 1890s, less than 55% of the Holy Land's population was Jewish, yet Theodore Herzl had the nerve to describe his movement as that of "a people without a land for a land without a people." Time and again both Revisionist and Labor Zionists, the former overtly and the latter under the clouds of deceptive rhetoric, have sought the elimination of the Palestinian people from their state. They have dispossessed thousands and refused them the right of return or

minimum compensation .... This aggression has plunged the region into its never-ending spiral of bloodshed.[58]

Unlike many Zionist socialists who refused to recognize Zionism as a colonizing movement, Jabotinsky was proud to proclaim it. In truth, the leaders of the socialist movement shared Jabotinsky's views without ever admitting as much. In a speech to a congress of his political movement in 1922, Ben-Gurion "declared the intentions which," says Sternhell, "he was to hold throughout his life:"

> It is not by looking for a way of ordering our lives through the harmonious principles of a perfect system of socioeconomic production that we can decide on our line of action. The one great concern that should govern our thought and work is the conquest of the land and building it up through extensive immigration. All the rest is mere words and phraseology [*parperaot u-melitzot*] and—let us not delude ourselves—we have to go forward in an awareness of our political situation: that is to say, in an awareness of power relationships, the strength of our people in this country and abroad.[59]

Resorting to his usual disdain of religious Jews, Ben-Gurion stated, "We are not yeshiva students debating the fine points of self-improvement. We are conquerors of the land facing a wall of iron, and we have to break through it."[60] Ben-Gurion's socialism, Sternhell reminds us, was inspired by the German National Socialism of the years immediately following the Great War. The Zionist socialists were quite close to the thought of Spengler, who in turn had paraphrased a remark by Heinrich von Treitschke: "Socialism means power, power, and again power."[61] In 1923, Jabotinsky published in Russian an article that borrowed, without naming Ben-Gurion, the concept of a "wall of iron," and reaffirmed his belief that victory can be won only by force.[62] An admirer of Mussolini, who reciprocated his esteem, Jabotinsky mobilized the Jews for war, revolt, and sacrifice.

Jabotinsky's influence would be long lasting. From the ranks of Betar emerged, in the 1930s, the founding members of the Zionist terrorist organizations Lehi and Irgun, many of whose members were to meet their end at the hands of the British authorities. Menahem Begin (1913–1992), Binyamin Netanyahu, and Ariel Sharon (1928–2014) number among his most illustrious admirers and disciples.

Unlike Jabotinsky, who openly endorsed the colonialist and therefore violent character of Zionism, the majority of the Zionist pioneers,

as already mentioned, refused to acknowledge conflict over the land between the immigrants and the local population. The Zionist left found
it convenient to ignore the national character of the Arab opposition to
its settlement policies. In fact, its attitudes toward the Arabs form the
basis of the systemic violence that haunts the Zionist enterprise down
to the present day. But the defensive ethos made it possible to maintain
a united façade of hope for peace and fraternity, even though behind
this façade loomed shadows of fear and suspicion. The realities of the
1930s and 1940s, the Arab revolt and, at a distance, the Nazi genocide, led to cynicism and pessimism, and introduced a new, offensive
ethos that foreshadowed the inevitability of a frontal conflict with the
Palestinians.

Such an ethos reflected the horror of total destruction, a horror well
founded in the colonial mentality that characterized Herzl's Zionist movement. Even today, despite Israel's uncontested military superiority, this
specter continues to haunt its collective consciousness. The cause can be
found in the words of Lord Balfour who, in 1919, avowed that:

> in Palestine we do not propose even to go through the form of consulting the
> wishes of the present inhabitants of the country. The Four Great Powers are
> committed to Zionism. And Zionism, be it right or wrong, good or bad, is
> rooted in age-long traditions, in present needs, in future hopes, of far pro-
> founder import than the desires and prejudices of the 700,000 Arabs who now
> inhabit that ancient land.[63]

Balfour's recommendations, when applied, could only perpetuate the
struggle over land and water.

Still, the ethical heritage of the diaspora, inspired by the millennia of
pacifist and moralist Jewish tradition, only disappeared slowly under the
impact of Palestinian realities. According to Anita Shapira, "colonization
in Palestine took place in the shadow of an ongoing conflict between a
'Diaspora mentality' (i.e., a deeply-rooted psychology and Jewish socialist
ideology) and the evolving Palestinian realities."[64] It comes as no surprise that the generation following the pioneers in Palestine reflected the
dreams of the founders: the new generation should be pragmatic, muscular, aggressive, and ready to take up arms. Even though the advocates
of the defensive ethos abhorred Jabotinsky and his militarism at least in
word, the realities of the conflict touched off by the Zionist enterprise in
Palestine would lead to the triumph of his doctrine, whose ideas today

may seem timid when placed against the background of contemporary Israeli politics. Moreover, the differences between the Zionist left and right disappeared even though "the myth of 'progressive Zionism' persists among Western liberals."[65]

Today, the term "security" has replaced the concept of self-defense that was widely employed before the creation of the state. Everything regarding security remains today a sacred cow in Israeli society. The term for "security" in Modern Hebrew, *bitahon*, was borrowed from the rabbinical literature, where it means "trust in divine providence." A Judaic concept was thus taken over by the modern language and given a meaning contrary to its original one: rather than put their trust in Providence, the New Hebrews would henceforth rely on the force of arms. As so often happens, language expressed this transformation in the most convincing way.

The Creation of a New Language

Language is a critical ingredient in the creation of European organic nationalisms, of which Zionism is only one. It becomes even more vital when other elements of collective identity begin to fray, leaving a vacuum that must, like all vacuums, be filled. Modern national identity usually rests on a shared language and upon the possession, frequently romanticized, of a given territory. The creation of Modern Hebrew is an exploit unparalleled in history. It came about far from a common territory and instituted a new relationship with the language, which was no longer "the language of holiness" (*leshon ha-kodesh*): that is, one of prayers, the study of the Torah, and scholarly communication.

While some rabbinical authorities had proposed the creation of a modern Hebrew language as early as the mid-19th century, they did so by citing the example of European nationalism rather than Jewish tradition.[66] The rebirth and renewal of Rumanian, Polish, and Lithuanian kindled hopes that a modern language based on biblical or rabbinical Hebrew could be forged. The Zionists were not the first to insist on the use of a national language in their homes: the same policy was adopted by many other nationalists in Central and Eastern Europe whose languages had been ignored by the elites using a universal vernacular, either German or Russian. More than a few national elites within the multi-national empires at the end of the 19th century were obliged to learn the language of the peasantry, the only people who spoke it regularly, and then enrich it for scientific, philosophical, or political use. For Hebrew, the challenge was quite the opposite: it was necessary to adapt the language of the rabbis for use in agriculture and industry. The challenge was all the greater considering that at the end of the 19th century there did not exist either farms or factories where the new language could be used.

Nineteenth-century Central Europe abounded in nodes of encounter and conflict between competing nationalisms. Inspired by Johann Gottfried Herder (1744–1803), the ideologist of the 18th-century German cultural renaissance and a Protestant partisan of the restoration of the Jews in Palestine, many members of the nationalist elites of Central and Eastern Europe made a conscious effort to speak to their children in the national language. Their goal was to produce a literature in that language, thus creating a sense of historical continuity and giving shape to a "national spirit" seen as the indispensable ingredient of a nation-state in the making.[67] The vernacular Hebrew enthusiasts were surrounded with encouraging experiments and examples to be emulated.

The first novel written in Hebrew takes a Bible story as its subject matter but in a format characteristic of European nationalist movements.[68] It was written in the heart of the Russian Empire, in Lithuania, where two nationalisms—Lithuanian and Polish—were in fierce conflict, each of them glorifying its past through the use of diverse literary forms, and naturally each in its own national language. Literary creativity in Hebrew spread rapidly throughout the Austro-Hungarian Empire and elsewhere, but the Russian Empire, with its male Jewish population better educated in biblical Hebrew than in Russian, provided particularly fertile ground for the propagation of Modern Hebrew. Many former students of the famous Lithuanian *yeshivas*, that of Volozhin for instance, abandoned the practice of Judaism and went on to become the pillars of the new Hebrew literature and cultural icons of Zionism. A segment of the Jewish intelligentsia also employed Hebrew in journalism, drawing inspiration from the *Ha-Meassef*, published in 1784 in Königsberg within the framework of the German *Haskala*, the Jewish version of the Enlightenment.[69]

When Zionism was in its infancy, literature and journalism close to the new movement also developed in the imperial *linguae francae*: German and Russian, the very languages that could be understood by the most assimilated of the Jews, who included almost the entire Zionist leadership. A particularly creative literary center emerged in the city of Odessa. Several Jewish authors—including Ilya Ilf, Isaac Babel, and Mikhaïl

Svetlov—chose Russian, and went on to acquire great renown in the Soviet Union.

Vladimir Jabotinsky, who also opted for Russian and became a recognized master of the language, set himself apart from this circle by becoming a Zionist. No lesser a light than Maxim Gorky, the future dean of Soviet literature, regretted that Zionism had torn such a promising writer from the sphere of Russian *belles-lettres*. Best known as the founder of the movement within world Zionism and as the theoretician of its political and military doctrine, Jabotinsky was also the author of several theatrical works and historical novels whose subjects were drawn from a rather literal reading of the Torah.

Perhaps more revealing, this ideologue of Jewish military power is also the author of a romantic literary work based on the story of Samson who, blinded, kills himself and brings his enemies down with him in death (Judges, chapters 13–16). It draws on the same heroic spirit that the founders of Zionism, and later of the state of Israel, sought to inculcate into young people. The rabbinical tradition, however, places a high premium on life and condemns suicide. As a result, the majority of rabbis rejected both such novels and the glorification of suicide as foreign to Judaism. This is why it is at Masada, where Jews surrounded by Roman troops committed collective suicide almost two millennia ago, that future officers of the IDF for decades swore their oath to the state. Many Zionists are proud to have created a new nation by convincing millions of Jews, both in Israel and elsewhere, to abandon their traditions the better to adopt a new identity combined with a national language.

The triumph of Hebrew over Yiddish can thus be interpreted as that of an ideology that refutes the notion of exile and all that could be seen as "exilic"[70] in its pursuit of creating a "New Hebrew Nation." The Zionist leaders perceived Yiddish as a threat, since so many new immigrants spoke it. Legislation was passed by the Knesset to hinder the opening of a Yiddish theatre and the publication of a newspaper in that language. Arab-speaking Jews, Christians, and Muslims were far more numerous in the early 1950s. Arabic, however, was not considered a threat as Zionist ideologues saw the local social milieu as "backward" in comparison with Zionist society and its European roots. These same ideologues, even on the left wing of the Zionist movement, looked upon Palestine as a "culturally virgin soil on which a new national culture could become the definitive, ultimately hegemonic cultural force of a new metropolis."[71]

French philosopher and orientalist Ernest Renan (1823–1892) once noted that "the essence of a nation is that all individuals have many things in common, and also that they have forgotten many things."[72] Indubitably more zealous than their European counterparts, Zionist ideologues spared no effort to banish Jewish continuity from memory. They sought to:

> discard diasporic Jewish culture and to obliterate its very existence from collective memory in order to realize its own ideology and vision. The success of the new creation depended on the suppression of the old one, including its most emblematic element, the Yiddish language.[73]

This vision of the Jewish past also impinged upon the nature of the archeological excavations that the founders of the state encouraged in order to lay the foundations of a new national consciousness: all attention was focused on the vestiges of the biblical period, while official archeologists long ignored Jewish monuments from the post-biblical era, such as Sephoris, when rabbis lived in relative harmony and compromise with the Roman authorities and developed the tradition of non-violence that is characteristic of rabbinical Judaism.[74] The creation of Modern Hebrew, which drew its legitimacy from the concept of renewal of the ancient heritage, was accompanied by the creation of a historical past adapted to the needs of Zionism.

The creators of the new vernacular transformed the language by attributing a modern, secularized meaning to traditional Judaic concepts, a process that had nothing to do with the natural evolution of the language. Eliezer Ben Yehuda (1858–1922), who initiated the Hebrew revival in the land of Israel, received Talmudic education in the Russian Empire. The creation of a national language soon became his obsession. Established in Jerusalem in 1881, his home was the first to employ Modern Hebrew as a vernacular. Rebelling against Judaism, he advocated the secularization of the language, a transformation that tended to alienate the New Hebrews from traditional sources, while simultaneously attracting Jews accustomed to familiar terms. The process of distancing impinged on the very meaning of words, which morphologically retained their original form.

The transformation of the "language of holiness" into a national vernacular remained, for many pious Jews, a brutally offensive act. Haredim recalled that when the Zionists consolidated their control over certain religious schools in the 1920s, they employed the pretext of providing them with teachers with a greater mastery of Hebrew the better to introduce

Zionist ideas. As a result Hebrew came to symbolize Zionism, and many Haredi schools continued to teach in Yiddish (some in English) rather than adopt Hebrew as the language of instruction. Modern Hebrew has been, for some of them, nothing less than "a language created by the Zionists."[75]

Zionist educators encouraged love of the language alongside love of the land, the two most precious elements in the "national treasure house." As in other European nationalist movements, from the beginning of the 20th century hiking in the countryside became an integral part of Zionist education. It was a love that embraced knowledge of nature but at the same time both forgot and rejected recognition in any form of the Arab presence in Palestine. From the first days of colonization, Zionist enthusiasts described in minute detail the flora and fauna, while ignoring the Arab villages and their inhabitants.

The invention of vernacular Hebrew, despite its apparent proximity to biblical sources, had little or no connection with Jewish continuity. Coeval with the efforts of Ben Yehuda, some Palestinian Jews protested about the profanation of the sacred language, while others pointed to a plot to appropriate and deform it. The introduction of secularized Modern Hebrew naturally roused the ire of the rabbinical authorities, who saw in it a particularly pernicious attack on Judaism, affecting as it did the pupils of the yeshivas, who could understand—and thence succumb to—the new literature. One such authority "pointed out many other falsifications of the Holy Tongue committed by the Zionists, and his blood would boil with anger whenever he heard someone speak a word or expression of Modern Hebrew."[76]

A substantial number of Jews, primarily Haredim, but also those coming from other streams of Judaism, refused to speak Hebrew. It happened, however, in the 19th century, that Sephardic notables were obliged to use Hebrew to speak with other Jews, even though Arabic was then a more common means of intra-Jewish communication. But when the Zionists began to exploit Hebrew for their own ends, Palestinian Jews abandoned it with revulsion as a spoken language. "Old Yishuv stalwarts not only desisted from using it but utterly excoriated those that did."[77]

In the United States, the Reform Jewish theologian Marc Ellis rejected Modern Hebrew, as "it is used less as a praise of God's presence," adding, "Is 'our language' spoken with such vehemence—the language of power and might—that it marks a return to the Jewish ghetto mentality, now armed with nuclear missiles, a nuclear ghetto if you will?"[78]

The initial usage of the term "state of Israel" was clearly intended to be ironic, but the Zionists would later employ it in a positive sense. According to Ravitzky, the term originated in an early 20th-century rabbinical diatribe against the secular nature of the Zionist movement and the idea of organizing Jewish life on a national basis, thereby severing it from the Torah and its commandments. So grave did the disaster appear that he invoked a passage from the Book of Esther that relates the threat of the total extermination of the Jews: "For how can I endure to see the evil that shall come unto my people? Or how can I endure to see the destruction of my kindred?" (Esther 8:6). The term "state of Israel" is introduced thus:

> For I know the devastation they are wreaking upon the congregation of Israel. My heart sinks within me, my eyes grow dark and my ears wax heavy at what is being done and said. Their valor in the land is not for the sake of the true faith, nor is it for this that they wave their banners (while we raise the banner of God). What sort of 'nation' can they have if they throw over our holy Torah and its precepts (perish the thought)? How can I bear that something be called 'the State of Israel' without the Torah and the commandments (heaven forbid)?[79]

On the other hand, the expression appealed to Rabbi Abraham Isaac Kook, often referred to as Rav Kook (1865–1935), the Russian rabbinical authority whom the British would appoint as chief rabbi of Palestine, one of the few to declare support for Zionism. He gave it a radically different interpretation from the avowed intentions of Israel's secular founders. He looked forward to "an ideal state, upon whose being sublime ideals would be engraved," a state that would become "the pedestal of God's throne in this world." For him, the state would be the earthly expression of a messianic "kingdom of Israel," a Jacob's ladder uniting earth with heaven.[80] The term underwent a radical transformation in its connotation, but it was a transformation that by no means obliterated the two diametrically opposed meanings. Both would recapture their original power, derived from the Torah, in the language of the religious anti-Zionists (who, like most Haredi Jews, refrain from uttering the words "state of Israel") but also in the language of National Judaism, inspired by Rav Kook's vision of redemption.

Attitudes toward the state were to divide the various factions of Orthodox Jews even more than their attitude to modernity. Though non-religious leaders like Ben-Gurion frequently highlight the association between the state of Israel and redemption,[81] only the followers of National Judaism consider the state to be the realization of the messianic promise. These include the very same settlers who, in their revolt against Judaic pacifism, have committed violence against the Palestinians, and even on occasion against the Israeli security forces.

The new language also serves to underline the Zionists' departure from Jewish tradition:

> Only for them could the Hebrew language become a national language and virtually lose its religious value …. Only for them could the collective Jewish identity be considered in historical terms utterly devoid of a religious burden. Only for them, at this or any stage in the evolution of Jewish national thought, could Eretz Israel be thought of in political terms and viewed through the glass of romantic nationalism, while the Orthodox attitude was set aside.[82]

The secularization of the *leshon ha-kodesh*, the language of prayer and of the Torah, makes itself felt when the Israelis, whose mother tongue is Hebrew, study the classic texts of Judaism. They discover that their language is often not up to the task, that it must enrich itself with other words and concepts, a task that proves quite daunting; that they must relearn a Judaic vocabulary long expunged or transformed on the wave of secular Zionism. The recent publication of a translation of the Torah into Modern Hebrew, undertaken by a Christian publisher,[83] illustrates the distance between the two languages, which is measured not only in thousands of years but in conscious reshaping of the language in the framework of the Zionist project.

While Ben-Gurion proudly declared that "we spoke, once again, the language our forefathers had used in their first contact with Egypt,"[84] the vernacular introduced by the founders of the state appears to have divided rather than united Jews. In their prayers, many Jews avoid Israeli Hebrew, using the traditional pronunciation instead. Even though prayers are recited in Hebrew, a secular Israeli who found himself in a Yemenite, Hassidic, or Lithuanian synagogue would have hard time understanding the words.

The Ashkenazi roots of Modern Hebrew have contributed to the alienation of the Arab Jews who made up important communities extending from Morocco to Yemen. The well-known Israeli author Albert Swissa considered this language "a completely modern invention: a modern, national and alienating language that has little, if anything to do with its

Jewish origins."[85] At the other extreme, Christian admirers of Zionism see in it a biblical connection that reinforces the image of the state of Israel as the culmination of Jewish history, even though in reality the inhabitants of the Holy Land in Jesus's day barely knew Hebrew. In our time, at least for one linguist, Ghil'ad Zuckerman,[86] Modern Hebrew cannot be even considered a Semitic language, but rather an Indo-European one: an idiom created by native speakers of Yiddish, Russian, and Polish who simply grafted Hebrew words onto the syntactical structure of those languages.

He argues, in fact, that the new language should not even be called Hebrew but "Israelian," the vernacular of a country called Israel. Such a conceptualization of Modern Hebrew is essentially post-Zionist, one that breaks the link between the country and its biblical past. But if it were truly "Israelian," the language would belong like the state itself to all who live in Israel, to all confessions and nationalities, rather than to world Jewry, mostly unfamiliar with any kind of Hebrew.

In the minds of the early Zionists, the relationship with the land resembled that between the Russians and Russia: it was romantic and organic. The dozens of Russian songs translated into Hebrew between 1900 and 1930 were intended to instill the love of the motherland (*moledet*) into the new arrivals. The "motherland" was so named because she would always welcome her prodigal sons for whom her love was generous, unconditional, and natural. The mother is the ultimate refuge, and in fact the state of Israel has often been presented as the Jews' ultimate guarantee of security. But such a romantic image is quite foreign to Jewish tradition.[87] Even though the metaphor of the land of Israel as mother can be found in the Talmud, it was never adopted by Jewish tradition and remains firmly anchored in its original context, which makes no reference to settling in the land of Israel.[88]

The adoption of Modern Hebrew provided the means by which the new immigrants could transform themselves and join the "New Hebrews." Uprooted and disoriented, immigrants, facing the need to become someone else in order to be "absorbed," would learn a particularly active form of Jewish self-hatred that has been the hallmark of the Zionist ideology of national revival from its very beginnings. Such a break was not an easy matter for the converts to the new vernacular, particularly for those whose mother tongue was Yiddish; one of them later remarked with a degree of nostalgia that "in Yiddish they loved us as we were."[89]

The New Hebrew Man Arises

A choice falls upon you, who have been raised and educated in the Land of Israel. A choice of two paths stands before us: either a complete transvaluation of values in every aspect of our lives—and national rebirth, or continued traversal of the tried and beaten path; your time has now come to make this choice, and may you choose the path of life![90]

These were the terms used by the director of the Tel Aviv Hebrew Gymnasium (*Gimnazia Ivrit*) in 1915 as he addressed the school's first graduating class.

The Zionists were not the first Jews to take up residence in Palestine. The Old Yishuv, the term used to designate the Jewish settlements in the Holy Land prior to the Zionist colonization, existed in Jerusalem and in several other Palestinian towns before the arrival of the first Zionist settlers. The Old Yishuv had long survived on charitable contributions from the diaspora. In the mid-19th century several philanthropists made it possible for pious Jews crowded in the Old City to move to a new healthier neighborhood known as Mea Shearim. (The term means "one hundred measures," a reference to Isaac's harvest: "sowed in that land and reaped a hundredfold the same year and the Lord blessed him" [Genesis 26:12]. Mea Shearim, known today for its large Haredi population, is often mistranslated as "one hundred gates.")

Although the Arabs long remained receptive to Zionist economic overtures, the Jews who then resided in Palestine reacted with fear and horror to the arrival of secular Jews from Russia. The proverbial "Jewish solidarity" that so many anti-Semites deplore was nowhere visible. On the contrary, aware of the particular responsibility that Jewish tradition imposes upon the Jewish inhabitants of Eretz Israel, which "vomits" the impious, they accused the new settlers in dramatic terms: "They do not walk in the path of Torah and fear of God … and their purpose is not to bring the redemption close but to delay it, God forbid."[91] But the new settlers gave not the slightest indication of repentance, and worse yet, attracted the youth of the Old Yishuv to the Zionist project. Thus began the conflict between traditional Judaism and Zionism in the Holy Land, a conflict that is far from being resolved more than a century later.[92]

When the first "proto-Zionist" Jewish settlements of Hibbat Tzion were established in Palestine in the early 1880s, largely in reaction to the pogroms in Russia, numerous rabbis lent their support to the settlers. However enthusiasm quickly turned to disappointment, with rabbis issuing public warnings against the dangers of the new settlements.

In 1882 Rishon Letsion, a settlement on the coastal plain, was founded. It would rapidly set itself apart from traditional Jewish communities. This colony was led by followers of the Haskala and reported to Jaffa, the center of secular colonization, in contrast to Jerusalem and Safed, which were known as centers by pious Jews. In other settlements, such as Petah Tiqwa, the difference was less pronounced: the settlers received aid from the *haluka* (the system for the distribution of charity funds among pious Jews), and traditional Jewish education was dispensed alongside the Zionist secular schools that would eventually prevail.

The Old Yishuv continued to oppose the Zionist settlers, who quickly learned to profit from the presence of religious Jews in the land of Israel. In 1911 a Zionist emissary, himself a recent immigrant from the Russian Empire, travelled to Yemen disguised as a representative of the traditional communities of Jerusalem.[93] The strategy paid off as hundreds of Yemeni Jews left their homes to become manual workers in the Ashkenazi settlements in Palestine. The distancing of the Yemeni Jews from the Torah and their economic exploitation by the Zionists would remain a source of bitter condemnation by varied strata of Israeli society for several decades. The secularization of Jews arriving from Muslim countries where the effect of the Haskala was minimal has divided Israeli society up to the present day.

Jewish tradition teaches that the Jews must take into account the impression they may make on others, even those who have persecuted them in the past. For example Moses, in his discussion with God (Exodus 32:12), is concerned about the impression Divine action might have on the Egyptians, even though they had exploited his people during two centuries of enslavement. But the Zionist education system from its inception has promoted the use of force, self-affirmation, and combativeness. The Zionists looked upon the requirement to behave as moral exemplars with scorn and ridicule, caring little for the impression they, and later their state, make upon the world, and above all upon its immediate neighbors. Ben-Gurion formulated the proposition thus: "What matters is what the Jews do, not what the *goyim* think."[94]

This deep-seated disdain led the Zionist movement, and later the state of Israel, to undertake exceptional foreign public relations efforts (*hasbara*). Today, these efforts include the mobilization of Israeli tourists and supporters in various countries for *hasbara*-related tasks. The

Internet has become an important platform for promoting Israel, and Israel's supporters, coordinated from a government ministry in Jerusalem, have been particularly active in responding to critics of, and proactively promoting, the Zionist state. Still, Israel's image remains (as it has been in recent years) strongly negative among the populations of the Western countries,[95] even though Western elites lend it increasingly unconditional support.

The Zionist reeducation program is part and parcel of a lengthy series of pedagogical experiments carried out throughout the 20th century, which aimed to tear the children from the influence of their parents and shape them according to the dominant model. Nationalist varieties of socialism tended to use psychological and cultural models the better to control society, precisely the objective of Ben-Gurion and his associates.[96] In the USSR, thousands of orphans and children of "enemies of the people" were sent to reeducation camps spread across the entire country in order to make them part of the new Soviet people.[97] In Israel, kibbutz members, a majority of whom were Ashkenazi, decided for themselves to have their children educated by the collective. In contrast, non-Ashkenazi parents, most of who had come from Muslim countries where they had preserved their Jewish traditions, were often forced to leave their children in the charge of the state. These policies contributed not only to their secularization, but also to the delinquency that flourished in conditions of poverty and the disintegration of the traditional family.[98] The zeal with which the young were torn from their families and from tradition is one of the principal issues in the religious critique of Zionism.

The institution known as Aliyat Hanoar—youth *aliya*—was an instrument of choice in the campaign that was to affect immigrants from almost all countries. Adolescents, removed from their families and inspired by the grandeur of the Zionist vision, were assimilated into the dominant culture and became a vector for the integration of their families into Israeli society. It should come as no surprise that Aliyat Hanoar has been the target of virulent attacks by religious Jews lashing out at the secularization campaign and denouncing the breakdown of the family underlying it. The struggle against Judaism has certainly lost most of its vigor as practicing populations from the lands of Islam are now long established in Israel. Today, Aliyat Hanoar receives principally young people from the ex-USSR whose degree of allegiance to Judaism is on average even lower than in Israel.[99]

The new Israeli identity's opposition to Jewish tradition is well documented and helps explain the presence of the widespread hostility to Judaism frequently encountered in Israel. It has no parallel in the diaspora, where such violent rejection of Judaism is nowadays unknown. The press regularly reports manifestations of this hostility, particularly toward Haredi Jews.

"Nowhere else are Haredi Jews as feared and hated as in Israel," writes Israeli historian Noah Efron. "Israel is a bastion of a classic sort of anti-Semitism, aimed not against all Jews but against the ultra-Orthodox, the overly Jewy Jews."[100] This should come as no surprise, for the image of the "New Hebrew Individual," a reflection of European anti-Semitism, rejects the image of the traditional Jew, who is depicted as a degraded, degenerate being. In fact, argues Efron, Zionism's promoters have simply refined the hateful image of the traditional Jew as painted by Voltaire and Fichte:

> One need not search hard to find denigrating images of the Altjude [traditional Jew] in Zionist rhetoric and pamphletry. Herzl had already noted in 1894 that Jews had "taken on a number of antisocial characteristics" in the ghettos of Europe, and that Jewish character was "damaged." [The poet David] Frishman [1859–1922, of Russian origin] opined that "[traditional] Jewish life is a dog's life that evokes disgust." [Another Russian poet,] Joseph Haim Brenner [1881–1921], likened Jews to "filthy dogs, inhuman, wounded dogs." [Yehuda Leib] Gordon [1831–1892, an active opponent of Judaism, also of Russian origin] wrote that European Jews were parasites. [Micha Joseph] Berdyczewski [1865–1921, a poet and philosopher born in the Russian Empire] christened traditional Jews "spiritual slaves, men whose natural forces had dried up and whose relation to the world was no longer normal," and elsewhere, "a non-people, a non-nation—non-men, indeed."[101]

Haim Hazaz (1898–1973), a Kiev-born author and Zionist ideologue, expressed similar views through one of his protagonists:

> Zionism and Judaism are not the same thing, but two very distinct things. In fact, there can be no doubt that they are two self-contradictory things. When one can no longer be a Jew, one becomes a Zionist. Zionism has emerged from the ruins of Judaism, as the people faced exhaustion …. One thing is certain, Zionism is not a continuation—nor is it the remedy for a sickness. It uproots and destroys. On the contrary, it misguides the people, defies it, goes against its will and its spirit, empties and uproots and abandons it for another path,

toward a distant but specific goal, it, with a handful of men in the vanguard [who seek to become] the seed of another nation! Attention: this nation is neither new nor renewed, but only different. He who believes otherwise is either mistaken or lying.[102]

André Malraux (1901–1976), unlike the Christian Zionists who see the modern-day state of Israel as a continuation of biblical history, demonstrates greater perspicacity; in his view, the Israeli is not a continuation of the Jew but a mutation.[103]

In this context, the role played by eugenics and social Darwinism in the Zionist venture appears quite natural. Paternalism had characterized the Zionist movement from the earliest days, well before Russian Jews were able to seize control of it.[104] It was proposed that marriage be viewed "not as a personal act … but rather as an important public act upon which depends the future of the race."[105] The entire Zionist initiative thus became "a eugenics revolution" that sought, according to Arthur Ruppin (1876–1943), an influential Zionist leader often called the "father of Jewish settlement," "the purification of the race."[106] Ruppin maintained his ties with the German theoreticians of racial science even after the National Socialist regime took power.[107] Later still, in the wake of the Nazi genocide, the Zionist movement often tended to "blame the victims for the violence they suffered," or worse, to accept "the Nazi vision that saw the Jews as less-than-human."[108]

This vision is reflected in the deep fear the secular majority feels of the Haredim. Efron writes:

> Several friends and colleagues have independently told me about nightmares in which they are captured and held by Haredim and, in some instances, tortured. [The secular] feel squeezed between two burgeoning enemies—the Palestinians on the one hand and the Haredim, on the other.[109]

No one is truly safe: "no matter how rationally children are raised, they may be ultimately lured into the Haredi camp."[110] It comes as no surprise that many secular Israelis feel a visceral hatred of the Haredim. During the 1991 Gulf War, when dozens of Iraqi missiles rained down on Israel and a chemical attack seemed imminent, most Israelis experienced a new sense of solidarity with one another. Efron reports a remark that he overheard during the war from a group of Tel-Aviv University students in the humanities, who affirmed that "the best thing for the country would be if there were a chemical attack in Bnei Brak [a bastion of Haredi Judaism] now, before they get new masks [adapted for bearded men]. That would get rid of all of them at once."[111]

The antagonism between secular Zionism and Haredi Judaism is unique to Israeli society. Assimilated Jews in Canada, France, and Russia are conscious of their distance from their "Jewish roots" and—should they feel the need—can seek them out in Judaism. They can join a synagogue, become members of a beginners' Torah study group or participate in Yom Kippur services—all gestures that can bring them closer to a Jewish way of life. To take such a step in Israel is far more difficult, as it would mean betraying your secular identity and "going over to the enemy." This degree of polarization is without parallel anywhere else in the world, even though Israeli media contain information about Judaism that reaches the secular majority.

The elevation of the secular identity to the status of an ideal has not eliminated the sacred; it has transferred it instead from Judaism to symbols of nationalism that are rendered sacrosanct in turn. Jewish nationalism is not the only domain to have absorbed the Jewish idealism that had been previously focused on the Torah: science, literature, and the struggle for justice and peace can also become "sacred." This is how a secular Israeli describes the peculiar relationship with poetry maintained by the sister of Israel's national hero, Moshe Dayan (1915–1981):

> But my mother's love for poetry was not just a passing fancy; it was a way of life. If you ask me, the sickness of my mother and of many of her generation, of reciters and declaimers was this: they did not only love poems; they believed them .... My poor mother took poems as an option, as a way of life. She quoted endlessly and believed in rhymes and in her notebook the way a religious person believes in mitzvahs and bible stories .... The poet Natan Alterman [1910–1970, a leading poet and pillar of the Israeli cultural establishment] was to my mother as the author Leo Tolstoy was to my grandmother Dvora. When we were children, my mother used to cut out his weekly column from the Friday edition of the newspaper *Davar*.[112]

The rendering sacrosanct of culture, and more specifically of "high culture," came to characterize the secularized Jews in Russia, Germany, France, and other Western countries. It contributed to the shaping of the Israeli secular identity that replaced, often without a trace, traditional Jewish identity. Once, at a marriage celebrated in a secular moshav near

Netanya, I struck up a conversation with the couple that shared my table. They were leftists, disgusted by the warlike nature of Israeli society; they had attempted to settle in Europe, only to return to Israel. "People like you have no problem adapting," they told me in terms bordering on reproach. "You can settle in any country you like, find a synagogue, a Jewish school and a kosher bakery, and there you are. All set! But we no longer have any of that. We are tied to the land and the language; we're culturally trapped here. We're the hostages of our grandparents who wanted to create a new species, the New Hebrew Individual, and deprived us of everything Jewish."

Their analysis was as laconic as it was insightful. After all, "Zionism had claimed: 'no more tradition's chains shall bind us,' [quoted from the Internationale] and consigned to oblivion all that had been so unfortunate as to precede it."[113] Some Israelis, born free of tradition's chains, are conscious of their alienation from Judaism, which they attribute, with some bitterness, to the atheistic Zionism of the founding fathers; at the same time, they are reluctant to return to the tradition of their ancestors. There are also quite a few attempts to create alternative spaces for the study of Judaism. In recent years, the city hall of Tel Aviv, the quintessential secular city, has become a space for all-night study of Judaic sources on the night of the holiday of Shavuot, a secular take on a venerable Jewish tradition.[114]

The encounter at the *moshav* reminded me of a critical remark made a century before by Rabbi Haim Soloveitchik (1853–1918), a renowned Talmudic scholar: "The Zionists do not drive away Jews from the Torah in order to get a state. They need a state in order to drive Jews away from the Torah."[115] The secularists who founded the state and established its contemporary structures were well aware of this fact. As recently as the early 21st century, they continue to oppose the movements of religious, non-Zionist youth by denying them the budgetary allocations earmarked for youth movements. The reason? The non-Zionists do not conform to the model of a youth movement that must, above all, be devoted to the state rather than to the Torah.[116]

Leibowitz, in his critique of Zionism, notes that without the markers of Judaism, the existence of such Jews—now a majority of the Jewish people—represents a break with the preceding millennia. These Jews, he argues, are seeking a national identity that exists only in and for itself, for they no longer have any concrete, empirically observable ties with Judaism. For Leibowitz:

The danger is that [national identity] be transformed into statism and will to power, into a national identity in the Mussolinian sense .... Nonetheless, a portion—a minority, but a significant one—of the human group heretofore considered as the Jewish people insists on keeping alive its historical religious heritage by rejecting both this national identity and its symbols. Suddenly, it becomes clear that the notion of "Jewish national identity" today possesses two meanings, and, moreover, two contradictory meanings.[117]

Atheist Israelis generally do not feel that their relationship with Judaism is deficient, an image that mirrors their social milieu: they live in Israel, speak Hebrew, and serve in the IDF. They see themselves as much better Jews, or rather Israelis, than those people with the long beards whom they occasionally pass in the streets.

The New Hebrew would thus be the antithesis of everything the Torah seeks to inculcate in a Jew. "The only thing required of a Jew is national feeling. Whoever pays a shekel [symbolic contribution to the Zionist movement] and sings the Ha-tikva [national anthem] is thereby dispensed from all the commandments of the Torah."[118] Still, Rav Kook hoped that the return to the land of Israel would bring the new secular Hebrew back to tradition. Contrary to the prevailing view, he had little appreciation for the ideology of the founders of Zionism, recognizing that "the destruction of faith and religion proceed in step with the spread of Zionism."[119]

Kook's hope was that the Holy Land would exert a mystical influence on these intrepid pioneers. Today, almost a century later, this hope seems not to have materialized. Nothing indicates that the land has had any spiritual impact on the majority of Israelis. Neither the language, nor the land of Israel appear to have led to commitment to Judaism, and several observers argue that only in Israel, among secular Jews, can "de-Judaization" be so fully accomplished. The president of Hebrew University and Reform rabbi Judah Magnes (1877–1948) noted bitterly after several decades spent in Palestine: "It is now harder and harder to be a Jew and be faithful to the spirit of Israel among those new-fashioned Hebrews."[120] In the view of Rabbi Adin Steinsaltz, Israel Prize winner, thinker, and distinguished translator of the Talmud, the Israeli nation lacks a specific Jewish character. Judged by its outlook and lifestyles, he argues, it has become less Jewish than any other non-Jewish nation: "Will we be able to preserve ourselves and to survive in that quality of Israeli non-Jewishness?"[121]

The value of the national preservation of the Jew who no longer has any connection with Judaism lies at the heart of the debate over the new Israeli identity as a substitute for Judaism. Jay A. Gonen, author of a psycho-history of Zionism, asserts, as have others, that abandoning the relation-ship with God eliminates the sole distinct trait that the Jews possessed.[122] The new Jewish identity must therefore find a new common denominator: the interminable concern for the security of the state of Israel would be called upon to fill this role, in Israel as well as in the diaspora.

We have seen that the shift in identity was to give rise to condemnation in a variety of Jewish contexts. At the beginning of the 20th century, Rabbi Shalom Dov Baer Schneerson (1860–1920), the fifth Lubavitch rebbe, whose influence extended well beyond the Hassidic community, accused the Zionists of promoting a Jewish identity devoid of any allegiance to the Torah. With perspicacity he pointed to the root of this transforma-tion in the nationalist interpretation of the Torah and its precepts and the abandonment of tradition that Zionism had fomented.[123] Even though in recent decades it has toned down its public criticism of Zionism and become committed to a hawkish line on Israel's security, the Lubavitch movement, certainly the most Russian of the Hassidic movements, used to take a firm and intransigent position against the "Zionist temptation," which originally attracted Russian Jews above all others.

The Russian Dimension

In the 19th century, Russian Jewry was concentrated in the Pale of Set-tlement, caught in the vice-grip of a bureaucracy as corrupt as it was arbitrary. The great majority experienced frustration at the limitations and persecutions to which they were subjected. Throughout the cen-tury the imperial government introduced legislation that purported to favor the integration of the Jews, but restrictions remained in place. Educational levels as well as Russification increased rapidly: by 1880, the number of Jewish students in Russian universities had surpassed the number of young people studying in the yeshivas of the Empire.[124] With Tsar Alexander II's death by terrorist bomb in the center of St. Petersburg in 1881, the relatively liberal period came to an abrupt end and a wave of pogroms swept over Russia, the first for more than two centuries.

Because of the geographic concentration imposed by the tsarist regime and thereby its remoteness from the centers of Russian culture, a culture which wielded an undeniable attraction, the secularization of the Jews of

Russia did not bring about massive assimilation. While leaving the Torah behind, these secular Jews developed "a proto-nationalist character and a national sensibility."[125] Indeed, they possessed at least two of the fundamental attributes of a "normal" nation: a common territory (the Pale of Settlement) and a common language (Yiddish). Several national movements (Polish, Finnish, Lithuanian) came into being at the same time that the wave of secularization was sweeping over the Jews of Russia at the turn of the 20th century. Zionism was but one among many of these radical movements; it would become dominant only in the context of the murderous anti-Semitism that rose throughout Europe before and during the Second World War. But this version of Zionism, unlike its visionary original, was a reaction to ambient hostility. Prophetically, well before then, the *Jewish Chronicle* of London, which gave a favorable but prudent welcome to settlement projects in Palestine, wrote, "It is oppression, and not prosperity, which will lead us back to our proper place in the Holy Land."[126]

Even though fewer than 1 percent of Russian Jewish emigrants at the turn of the 19th century made their way to Palestine (55,000 versus 2,127,000 who migrated to North America from 1881–1914[127]), Russian nationals formed the hard core of Zionist activists. The version of Zionism that emerged from Eastern European Jewish culture was to exert a powerful influence on the entire Zionist movement: despite a conscious effort to erase the past, the Zionist elites reproduced in Palestine the cultural models they had brought with them from Eastern Europe.

Russian Zionism witnessed its most rapid growth among the supporters of the Haskalah, those Jews who had been educated in the *yeshiva* system before acquiring a European culture of sorts, more often than not self-taught. Some of these Haskalah supporters mastered Hebrew, while abandoning the despised Yiddish, which had been the mother tongue of the great majority. Unlike aficionados of Hebrew in Western Europe, they wrestled with social issues, denounced economic injustice, and fiercely criticized the Jewish communities of the day.

Another unmistakable sign of the difference between the supporters of the Russian Haskalah and their Western counterparts was their alienation from the Russian Empire, which the majority perceived in rather critical terms. Zionism, like other transformative movements, provided them with a positive voice and paved the way toward a radical idealism that would mark the growing Zionist enterprise throughout its first decades.

Furthermore, the pogroms of the last 20 years of the 19th century also pushed them toward secular nationalism.

Reactions among Russian Jews to the pogroms were quite diverse. More traditional Jews, motivated by concern for the future of their families, sought escape via emigration to the United States. The most Russified Jews, bearers of modern European values, were not satisfied with individual escape, however massive, and sought, following Herzl or Marx, a collective solution to "the Jewish problem."

The shock, anger, and frustration caused by the pogroms among many Russian Jews were channeled toward the clandestine, radical parties that stood for political violence.[128] Jews flocked to the Russian oppositionist movements, but also created several that were specifically Jewish, such as the socialist Bund, anti-pogrom self-defense groups, and a variety of Zionist parties. The atmosphere of nihilism and contempt for human life that weighed upon oppositionist circles in Russia as the 19th century drew to a close would engender a form of political terrorism whose shadow continues to haunt the world.[129]

While the world's other Jewish communities remained faithful to the tradition of non-violence and envisaged no armed action against the populations among whom they lived, in Russia this tradition was to be increasingly called into question, and a substantial number of Jews were won over to the idea of political violence. Many Jews turned to this operating method in a variety of political organizations, all of which were illegal in Russia. The choice of radicalization and violence was a logical one in a social context that excluded Jews, and prior to the 1905 revolution, forbade all forms of political activity. Russian autocracy drove many Jews into extremism, or at least those who, unlike their forebears, were not inclined to interpret suffering as a stimulus to moral self-improvement.

The pogroms only increased the insecurity of the Jewish populations of the Russian Empire. The fear of violent death became particularly acute during the riots of 1881, and a generation later, in 1903, during the Kishinev massacres. In more general terms, at issue was fear of the non-Jew, of the neighbor who might at any moment kill, rape, and plunder. Unlike Jewish reactions during the pogroms of the 17th century, which were far more violent, the violence encountered as the "century of progress" drew to a close lost all religious significance for an increasing number of secularizing Jews. These Jews who had broken with the Torah reacted in a radically new way. Rather than calling into question their own behavior, while adjuring violence, and intensifying their penitence as required by Jewish tradition, they emphasized their pride and called for resistance. Self-defense units were set up in some parts of the Pale of Settlement, most of them by the activists of the Bund workers' movement.

Feelings of shame, indignation, and a burning desire to be respected combined to drive many Jews toward Zionism. "Opposition to exile … for me was transformed," admitted a Zionist of Russian origin, "into hatred! I hate it like a shameful infirmity to get rid of which one is ready to sacrifice one's life."[130] The motive of pride now made its appearance with a renewed meaning. While Judaism, as do all religions, considers it a vice, pride became the motivation for many secularized Jews. Heroic romanticism, foreign to Jewish tradition, now took up residence in these emergent Jewish circles. Herzl—who in his youth admired Bismarck and dreamed of becoming a German aristocrat—fought in a duel and considered it a true manifestation of manhood.[131] The Jewish protagonist of one of his plays is mortally wounded in a duel "in the name of Jewish honor," exclaiming before his death: "I want a way out, out of the ghetto!"[132] Such were the traits that the Zionists sought in their quest for respect, drawing on the European criteria for success: a national homeland, an army, and national sovereignty. What inspired the extraordinary activism of the Zionist movement in Russia was not so much the suffering of the victims of the pogroms as a humiliation similar to that of the rejected suitor, the humiliation felt by those whose hopes of integration into Russian society had been shaken by the pogroms.

Russian Jewish intellectuals, even those like Ahad Ha-Am, who had earlier decried the cruelty with which the Zionists treated the native population of Palestine, now called upon the Jews to defend themselves against violence in Russia. Ahad Ha-Am drew a clear distinction between Jew hatred, widespread in Eastern Europe, and the animosity that the Zionists provoked by their actions among the Palestinian Arabs. But it was Haim Nahman Bialik, a Russian author who later became a cultural icon in Israel, who stoked the fires of revenge and violence. In a poem written following the Kishinev pogrom of 1903, he castigated the survivors, heaping shame on their heads, and calling upon them to revolt not only against their tormentors, but also against Judaism. By blaming the victim, Bialik lashed out at the men who hid out in stinking holes while their non-Jewish neighbors raped their wives and daughters.

The anger that had swept over many Jews caused Bialik, a former *yeshiva* student, to turn the old Jewish value system on its head. He mocked the tradition that attributed all adversity to short-comings in the behavior of the Jews: "let fists fly like stones against the heavens and against the heavenly throne."[133] Bialik broke violently with Judaism and issued a ringing challenge: defend yourselves or perish!

Brenner, another poet and like Bialik the son of a pious Russian Jewish family, rebelled as well against Jewish tradition, meeting a violent death during the Jaffa riots of 1920. He radically transformed the best-known verse of the Jewish prayer book, "Hear, O Israel, God is your Lord, God is one!" one of the first verses taught to children and the last to be spoken by a Jew before his death. Brenner's revised version proclaimed: "Hear, O Israel! Not an eye for an eye. Two eyes for one eye, all their teeth for every humiliation!" In using the Biblical verse "an eye for an eye," he gave it a literal interpretation in total contradiction to Jewish tradition, for in the rabbinical legal system, this principle is interpreted solely as the obligation to pay a corresponding monetary compensation.

Borrowings from European nationalism in the conceptualization of Zionism by Jews of Russian origin in Palestine were all the more determinant because, to begin with, the future Zionist elites had little intellectual training in either Talmudic or European culture.[134] By way of example, the thought of Aaron David Gordon (1856–1922), developed in the course of his activities as the administrator of a landed estate in Russia, played an important role in the shaping of Zionist ideology.

Large numbers of rabbinical thinkers protested against the Zionist vision of the Jew, which laid emphasis on the national dimension of Jewish identity, historically subordinate to the religious one. To this vision they counterposed the Jewish concept of the nation, based on allegiance to the Torah rather than on belonging to an ethnic group or a territory. It was a concept close to that of religion in the West but not entirely, for it also contained an objective aspect: someone born of a Jewish mother remains a Jew even if their allegiance to the Torah leaves much to be de-sired. These rabbis realized that in the Zionist version of Jewish identity "a total inversion of traditional values has occurred: that which had before been a simple means to an end now became the objective, and what had been an objective now became a means to an end."[135] It was an inversion that would become natural for the majority of Jews in the USSR. Though foreign to Judaism, they possessed a "Jewish nationality" made official by Stalin, which remains the main pillar of identity in Israel. It was easy for them to adopt Zionist ideas and to integrate more rapidly into the country's political life than most other immigrants.

The ideological shift among large numbers of Jews that occurred as the 19th century was ending produced a similar shift in the meaning of Jewish history in the eyes of young people thirsting for Jewish activism. The atheist version of Jewish history stripped it of the privileged relationship between God and the Jews, and transformed them into victims of a historical injustice. It was a historical vision that tended to stimulate a powerful drive to act. Many of the founders of Jewish armed groups, in both Russia and Palestine, also recognized that the use of force was a way of tearing the Jews from Jewish tradition.

Vladimir Jabotinsky was adamant in affirming national pride. As an organizer of the Jewish Legion during the First World War, he glorified the use of force as the most convincing way of bringing about this affirmation. According to his biographer, "The Jewish Legion had become a cherished legend and an inspiring precedent."[136] Militarism was a feature of many 20th-century nationalist ideologies; Zionism was no exception.

Another figure that embodied the romantic heroism in the Zionist curriculum was Joseph Trumpeldor, a veteran of the Russo-Japanese war of 1904–05. While a prisoner of war in Japan, he organized a Zionist cell later recognized by the World Zionist Organization. Killed in a skirmish with the local Arab population, he allegedly managed to utter the last words, "How good it is to die for the fatherland." The phrase, a variant of the Latin *dulce et decorum est pro patria mori*, was to become, alongside the officers' oath at Masada, one of the symbols of the new determination to take up arms.

In its Zionist version, the teleology of return reduced Jewish history to a continuum of suffering that could only lead to Jewish self-emancipation and to the enfranchisement of the Jews as a modern people on its own land. An expression frequently heard in Israel is *ein berera* ("we have no choice"), which dismisses any but the Zionist option available to the Jews of the world. *Ein berera* also means that there exists no other choice but the use of force, a belief that Israel's increasingly overwhelming military actions have come to embody.

The widespread legitimacy of the use of force set the Jews of Russia apart from those of other countries, where armed resistance against non-Jews was neither necessary, nor even conceivable. Traces of Russian cultural influence are likewise visible in more recent history:

Israeli military heroes Moshe Dayan, Ezer Weizmann, Itzhak Rabin, Rehavam Zeevi, Raphael Eitan, and Ariel Sharon are all descendants of Russian Jews, whose propensity for the use of force goes hand in hand with their estrangement from Jewish tradition. Only by rejecting Judaism and its humility could the Russian Jews acquire a newfound confidence in their own strength and in their capacity to reconquer and defend Israel.

The Russian dimension of Zionism cannot be overestimated. One telling indicator is the composition of the Knesset 12 years after the founding of the state. Despite the almost total prohibition of emigration from the Soviet Union for more than four decades, over 70 percent of the members of this political elite were Russian-born, while 13 percent were born in Palestine/Israel of Russian parents. The American Zionist elites, whose support was crucial for Zionism's success, were also composed primarily of Jews of Russian origin.[137] The replacement of the Jewish elites of German origin with those originating in Russia also contributed to the shift, between the two world wars, of Jewish public opinion in the United States in favor of Zionism. The essentially Russian character of Zionism stands revealed in its concepts, its methods, and in the support it received from American Jews.

It was in the Netherlands that Russian Jewish students initiated the journalist and barrister Jacob de Haan (1881–1924) into Zionist ideology. He subsequently strengthened his commitment following a two-year sojourn in Russia. Zionist ideas and activities, even in Morocco, were introduced almost exclusively by Russian Jews.[138] It comes as no surprise that an American historian has described Israel as "a European fragment of the Russian revolutionary movement."[139]

According to public opinion polls, the image of the state of Israel was more favorable in Russia than in other industrialized nations in Europe.[140] This is partly because the Russian press uses freelancers among Russian expatriates in Israel who usually reflect the positions of the Israeli nationalist right wing. Interestingly, a Russian weekly argued that the cruelty shown to the Chechens and the Palestinians accounts for the mutual sympathy that can be observed between Russia and Israel at the beginning of the 21st century. "It is not Dostoevsky's Russia that has opened her eyes, and come to adore Israel," but rather the Russian militarists who had suddenly discovered affinities with Sharon.[141] Naturally, it is not only in Russia that Israel enjoys sincere admiration for its use of force: right-wing parties in European countries or in former European colonies also take their inspiration from Israel.

Russian Jews make up the most reliable electoral base for the Israeli right wing. "It is quite natural for the Russians to gravitate to right-wing parties; they form a political camp that has long drawn sustenance from the ideological heritage of the great leaders of Zionism, Jabotinsky and Begin, both born in the Russian Empire," notes a Russian journalist with overt sympathies for the Israeli right.[142] The right-wing party Israel Beitenu ("Israel our home"), most of whose members and supporters are recent Russian-speaking immigrants, casts the Russian dimension of the Zionist project in sharp relief. Soviet-born Avigdor Liberman, former Israeli deputy prime minister and foreign minister, is often described in the Israeli press as a fascist. Many extra-parliamentary activists of Soviet origin farther to the right than Israel Beitenu have built up solid ties with right-wing extremist groups, in Russia above all.[143]

The majority of immigrants from the former USSR, at least one third of whom cannot be considered as Jews according to rabbinical law, have contributed handsomely to this shift to the right. Their paradoxical situation has not eluded several keen-eyed observers among these new Israelis. To paraphrase the Russian poet Nikolay Nekrasov (1821-1878), "You may not be a poet, but you must be a citizen," to a formula more pertinent in Israel, "You may not be a Jew, but you must be a Zionist." Immigrants from the former USSR, for whom it is only natural to see themselves as belonging to the Jewish nationality, dovetail with the image of the secular Zionist, who is at once the pillar and the *raison d'être* of the state of Israel. Created in large measure by Jews who originated in Russia, the state of Israel continues to awaken among their former compatriots around the world a singularly positive response. Early in 2012, the World Forum of Russian-speaking Jews was established, with local sections in several countries, including Israel, Russia, the United States, and Canada.[144] It coordinates Zionist activities in the former Soviet republics and plays a key role in the Israeli government's efforts to improve the image of the Zionist state in world public opinion. These efforts often cite the Nazi genocide as the ultimate justification of the Zionist project.

Chapter Five

The Nazi Genocide, Its Memory, and Its Lessons

The industrialized massacre of millions of Jews during the Second World War has, as an event, remained central to the Zionist discourse. Certain Zionists, such as Jabotinsky, foresaw the murderous tragedy and began to call for massive migration to Palestine in the early 1930s. It is hardly surprising that for the great majority of Zionists, the Nazi genocide stands as ultimate proof of the dangers that threaten Jews around the world. It would also irrefutably legitimize the creation of the state of Israel. After the Second World War, the Zionist movement presented its political project as a rescue operation for the survivors of the tragedy, and obtained United Nations approval for the creation of a separate state a mere two years after the last crematory fires had been extinguished. Prevention of another genocide became the justification for the military hegemony that the new state quickly achieved and has constantly reinforced ever since. But as we will soon see, many Jews drew from the tragedy entirely different conclusions.

Throughout the Second World War, the Zionist movement maintained an ambiguous position. Zionist activities in the Western countries, especially between the two wars, laid emphasis on Palestine's role as a place of exile for the persecuted Jews. They knew that their plan to create a Jewish state did not enjoy unanimous support among Jews in the United States and in other countries where Zionist fund-raising campaigns were held. At the same time, internal discussions clearly indicated that Zionism was above all an ideological movement of self-determination rather than a pragmatic plan for the rescue of the Jews in distress, a kind of "Red Cross for Jews."[1] Russian-born Haim Weizmann is claimed to have said, "Nothing can be more superficial and nothing can be more wrong than that the sufferings of Russian Jewry ever were the cause of Zionism. The fundamental cause of Zionism has been, and is, the ineradicable national striving … to have … a national centre."[2]

In the face of restrictions on immigration to Palestine, the Zionist organizations undercut efforts to welcome Jews anywhere else, drawing sharp criticism from Reform and Haredi rabbis and, much later, from a significant number of Israeli intellectuals. All the critical voices concurred in accusing the Zionist leadership of being much more concerned about the future state than about the fate of Europe's Jews. The upshot was that several planned attempts to save the Jews, in Hungary and elsewhere, appear to have encountered resistance from the Zionist leadership. Even before the war, the Zionists attempted to block diplomatic efforts, particularly at the Évian Conference in 1938, to find a place of exile for Jewish refugees.[3] In response to an appeal to come to the aid of the Jews of Europe, Itzhak Gruenbaum, prominent Zionist leader and future Israeli minister of the interior, replied, "One cow in Palestine is more important than all the Jews of Poland."[4] Another, Sol Meyer, a wartime Zionist functionary, refused to save thousands of lives by paying the Nazis, arguing, "If we do not have sufficient victims, we shall have no right to demand an independent state …. It is insolent [and] shameless to ask monies for the enemy to succor our blood, for only by blood shall we obtain the land."[5] One of the first to articulate this vision was William Hechler, a Christian Zionist, one of Herzl's prophetic inspirations, who in 1931 told a Jewish Zionist, "a part of European Jewry will be immolated for the resurrection of your Biblical homeland."[6] On the other hand, the Nazi genocide deprived the future Zionist state of much of its population base by exterminating millions of Ashkenazi Jews.[7]

In 1938, following the Kristallnacht, which set off a wave of physical violence against Germany's Jews, Ben-Gurion said:

> If I knew that all Jewish children could be saved by having them relocated to England, but only half by transferring them to Palestine, I would chose the second option, because what is at stake would not only have been the fate of those children, but also the historical destiny of the Jewish people.[8]

In early 1943 Hypolinary (Apolinari) Hartglass, the former head of Poland's Zionist Federation and future director general of the Ministry of the Interior in Israel, declared that people should save "only children (the best prospective material for the *Yishuv* [Zionist settlement]) and members of the Zionist youth movements, as well as some adult Zionist activists."[9] The pioneer youth needed to be rescued first, particularly those who had received training and were intellectually capable of carrying out the Zionist program.[10]

Consistent with his vision, Ben-Gurion:

was opposed ... to the creation of a strong, competent official agency with the necessary resources to undertake rescue operations, as well as to the use, for such operations, of funds raised by Zionist organizations. Nor did he call upon the American Jews to raise significant funds to be used for this purpose.[11]

The Zionist position with regard to the massacres reflected the conviction that "Zionism was an operation whose aim was to save the nation and not an operation to rescue the Jews as individuals."[12]

Reform rabbis reproached the Zionists for the same crime that their Haredi counterparts had earlier accused them of: to have sabotaged all initiatives to rescue the Jews of Europe, including a decision by President Roosevelt to seek out, in the earliest days of the war, countries willing to grant them asylum.[13]

Morris Ernst (1888–1976), an American Jewish human rights activist with close ties to Roosevelt who reported the president's remarks, set out to test the veracity of what he had heard, and informed his Zionist friends of the White House initiative:

> I assure you that I was thrown out of parlors of friends of mine. And they said very frankly, and they were right from their point of view, "Morris," they would say, "this is treason—you're undermining the Zionist movement." I'd say, "Yes, maybe I am. But I am much more interested in a haven for a half a million or a million people—oppressed throughout the world."[14]

The above quote points at a policy of saving primarily those who, from a political and economic point of view, could make an active contribution to the Zionist enterprise. According to Weizmann, "The old ones will pass. They will bear their fate or they will not. They are dust, economic and moral dust in a cruel world .... Only the branch of the young shall survive .... They have to accept it."[15]

It was an attitude that did not go unnoticed in the Western press. Shortly after the war, Leonard Sussman, a Jewish-American human rights advocate, wrote, "Who can tell how many thousands of Jewish lives might have been saved from Hitler's claws if these anti-Jewish pressures exerted by Jews had not been effected?"[16]

Historians concur in their assessment that Ben-Gurion and his inner circle hindered attempts to save the European Jewish communities from extermination.[17] The Zionist leadership, they argue, did its utmost to subordinate rescue efforts to their primary objective, which was the establishment of a Jewish state and the creation of a New Hebrew Man (women were expected to be just as muscular and intrepid as men). In so doing, it treated human beings as "human material," reducing the survival and the death of millions to a matter of political expediency.[18]

These observations, made by Israeli historians in the late 20th century, confirm the statements that rabbis in black frock coats had been making for decades, except that Jewish consensus had not taken the latter seriously. Such accusations were no less ignored when voiced in Reform circles, albeit fully integrated into American society.

On his return from a visit to the Jewish communities of Europe prior to the Second World War, American Reform rabbi Morris Lazaron (1888–1979) protested against the tendency to concentrate on financing projects in Palestine to the detriment of the rescue of the Jews threatened by the Nazis in Europe. He also protested against the Zionist claim that Palestine represented the only place of safety for the Jews, and lashed out at Zionist propaganda that the world would sooner or later reject the Jews because they were Jews. In his view, there was no good reason to undermine the confidence of American Jews by inviting them to forfeit their trust in emancipation because of German politics.[19] For many Jews, the principle of equality remained a vital one, despite Nazi persecutions—and also because of them.

An Israeli scholarly work found that:

> The Jewish communities scattered across Central and Eastern Europe were important to the founders chiefly as a source of pioneers. They were considered to have no value in themselves. Even at the height of the Second World War, there was no change in the order of priorities: it was not the rescue of Jews as such that topped Berl Katznelson's order of priorities but the organization of the Zionist movement in Europe …. Thus every event in the nation's life was evaluated according to a single criterion: the degree to which it contributed to Zionism.[20]

Ideology may thus provide the ultimate explanation for the indifference of which both historians and rabbis accuse the Zionists. The Nazi genocide simply served to reinforce the political determination of the Zionist leaders to obtain a Jewish state: in fact, it provided them with an argument of rare power.

To a certain extent, there existed a conceptual, if not political, affinity between the Zionist movement and National Socialism: both considered the Jews as a foreign people who could never be assimilated and had no place in Europe. Rabbi Joachim Prinz, a Zionist activist in Germany, greeted the ascent to power by the Nazis and celebrated "the end of liberalism" in his book *Wir Juden* (*We Jews*), published in Berlin in 1934.[21] From the safety of Britain, he later confirmed that the Nazis treated the Zionists like favorites, in stark contrast to the treatment meted out to other Jews.[22] Following migration to the United States he continued both his rabbinical vocation and his involvement in the Zionist movement, going on to become president of several Jewish organizations in the 1960s.

To ensure the cooperation of the Nazi authorities, Zionists in Germany proudly displayed their devotion to their own form of nationalism. In this vein Kurt Tuchler, a member of the German Zionist Federation, invited Baron Leopold Edler von Mildenstein, a high-ranking SS officer, to write a pro-Zionist article for the Nazi press. The baron, "an ardent Zionist"[23] who had attended Zionist congresses and would later recruit Adolf Eichmann to the Sicherheitsdienst (SD, the Nazi security service) Jewish Department, agreed on condition that he first visit the Zionist colonies in Palestine. The two men, accompanied by their spouses, set out a few months after Hitler had seized power:

> What had brought them together on this journey to Palestine was their common desire, motivated by radically different objectives, to make Germany "free of Jews," or as the Nazis put it, *Judenrein*. Where the National Socialists had not yet worked out a solution to "the Jewish question," the Zionists, with their ambition to establish a Jewish homeland and their sponsorship of Jewish emigration to Palestine, had an answer.[24]

The baron kept his word; following his visit, in the fall of 1934, a series of articles appeared in the daily *Angriff* (*Assault*), founded by Joseph Goebbels in 1927 (and discontinued in May 1945, literally under fire from Soviet tanks in the streets of Berlin), which played a key role in the rise to power of the National Socialists.[25] After the war Tuchler, who settled in Palestine in the late 1930s, and von Mildenstein resumed their friendship and spent summer vacations in the Alps. The Zionists also concluded an agreement with Hitler for the transport of tens of thousands of German Jews with their capital to Palestine, in violation of the economic boycott of Nazi Germany.[26]

While during the war, the Zionist leadership was in no hurry to recognize the extent of the Nazi massacres, the lesson they drew from them was prompt and simple: it was imperative to acquire a state at any price, to make it strong and to populate it with Jews against any form of Arab resistance. The Israeli Declaration of Independence is explicit: "The catastrophe which recently befell the Jewish people—the massacre of millions of Jews in Europe—was another clear demonstration of the urgency of solving the problem of its homelessness by re-establishing in Eretz-Israel the Jewish state." In the words of the Israeli historian Moshe Zimmerman:

> The Shoah is a frequently used instrument. Cynically, one is tempted to add that the Nazi genocide is one of those objects that so readily lend themselves to the manipulation of the public, the Jewish people in particular, both in Israel and abroad. In Israeli politics, the lesson is conveniently drawn from the Shoah that an unarmed Jew is worth no more than a dead Jew.[27]

However, another lesson that could be drawn from the tragedy that befell the Jews of Europe would be to encourage distrust of powerful states that scorn individual morality, practice racial discrimination and commit crimes against humanity. Today, the entire world recognizes the role of the Nazi massacres in the creation of the state of Israel. In the wake of the Second World War, Israel's founders convinced the majority of the United Nations that the only possible reparation, and at the same time the only solution to the "Jewish problem," consisted of establishing a state for Jews. In their view, the presence of Jews in the diaspora was a danger; only an independent state could protect them. The Zionists established a direct connection between what was a case of extreme violence and the state of Israel, which is presented as rebirth after extermination. The way the victims are commemorated reflects the conclusions that people wish to draw.

The official commemoration established by the Israeli government was initially entitled *Yom ha-shoah ve-ha-gevurah* (Day of the Shoah and Heroism), as if the "honorable" death of some could offset the "shameful" death of others.[28] (*Yom ha-shoah*, Day of the Shoah, is the term in current use.) The better to underline the connection between two major events in Jewish history, it is held a few days before *Yom ha-atsmaut* (Independence Day). The choice of the date can be explained by the desire of the leadership of the newly declared state to temper remembrance of "passive suffering," which the Zionists have always looked down upon, by introducing the theme of resistance: the Warsaw Ghetto revolt of 1943. Independence Day follows immediately the official Day of Remembrance for soldiers and security agents fallen in the service of their country. The term used in Hebrew, *Yom ha-zikaron*, is another secular reinterpretation of a biblical term, which Jewish tradition understands very differently, as remembering your sins for purposes of self-improvement on the occasion of the Jewish New Year.

During the early post-war years, the Israeli press presented almost exclusively articles devoted to the memories of resistance fighters, while those that dealt with "simple survivors," accused by Zionist public opinion of having gone "like sheep to slaughter," were often published at their author's expense or by associations of survivors.[29] During the first Zionist commemorations of the Warsaw Ghetto uprising, not a word was spoken of the 6 million victims of the Nazi genocide.[30] Some historians described the commemorations organized by survivors outside the official Zionist framework as a "semi-clandestine act."[31] In any event, the Israeli press lent far greater weight to the accounts of Zionist resistance fighters than to those of other members of the resistance, the Bund for example, creating the impression that Zionists held a monopoly of anti-Nazi resistance.[32] It was not until the trial of Adolf Eichmann in 1961 that survivors' accounts, including their explanation of the absence of resistance on their part, emerged into Israeli public awareness.[33]

Yom ha-shoah begins with a military ceremony the night before at Yad va-shem, the memorial to the Nazi genocide in Jerusalem; then a siren sounds at 10:00 am, inviting the Israeli population to observe two minutes of silence; throughout the day special programs are broadcast on radio and television, and public lectures are held. The principal message of the commemoration could not be clearer: there can never be another Shoah because our state will protect us. The Zionists frequently claim that if the state of Israel had existed before the Second World War, the Nazi extermination would never have taken place.

According to a manual issued to the educational officers of the IDF, Yom ha-shoah should encourage young recruits to develop a sense of belonging to the people and of loyalty to the state:

> The Zionist solution establishing the state of Israel was intended to provide an answer to the problem of the existence of the Jewish people, in view of the fact that all other solutions had failed. The Holocaust proved, in all its horror, that in the 20th century, the survival of the Jews is not assured as long as they are not masters of their fate and as long as they do not have the power to defend their survival.[34]

The official text adds, "The position taken by the Jews during the Shoah reflects the moral and spiritual power that continues to provide the principles of our position in the ongoing conflict." In other words, the activities of the IDF are presented as the logical continuation of the resistance to the Nazis. As early as 1947 the memory of the genocide was used to mobilize Zionist combatants in Palestine for the conquest of the country and the ethnic cleansing that accompanied it: "we have avenged our bitter and lonely death with our fists, our heavy, burning fists."[35] They were fighting in Palestine the battles they wished they had fought in Europe.

The enlistment of memory to transmit a message of combat readiness has been a constant. In the course of an air show in Poland, over the protestations of the Auschwitz museum, three Israeli fighters bearing the star of David and piloted by descendants of survivors of the Nazi massacres overflew the former Nazi extermination camp while 200 Israeli soldiers observed the flyover from the Birkenau death camp adjacent to Auschwitz. The remarks of one of the Israeli pilots stressed confidence in the armed forces: "This is a triumph for us. Sixty years ago, we had nothing. No country, no army, nothing. We now come here with our own planes to honor those who can no longer be with us."[36]

Israeli soldiers and officers are often taken to the places where the Nazi genocide took place. But these visits do little more than reinforce what state schools have already accomplished: the Nazi genocide accounts for more than 15 percent of the contemporary Jewish history program. More than half of all students and teachers consider the Shoah the most important event of the 20th century. Even among students of Arab, Turkish, and Iranian origin—whose elders had never experienced the Nazi regime—83 percent considered themselves as "Shoah survivors." The same percentage of young Israelis fear the destruction of the state of Israel, while a third believe that another Shoah is possible.[37]

It is highly symbolic that the first Israeli astronaut Ilan Ramon, a descendant of Second World War survivors, carried with him aboard the US space shuttle a memento of that era: a lunar landscape drawn by an adolescent in the Theresienstadt concentration camp.[38] The message was meant as one of rebirth, of pride in belonging to Israel as against the indignity of dying in Europe.

The official commemorations of the Shoah offer numerous occasions for transmitting the same message. The chief of the Israeli General Staff

proclaimed, at the foot of the monument to the resistance fighters of the
Warsaw Ghetto, "If you wish to know the source from which the Israeli
army draws its power and strength, go to the holy martyrs of the Holocaust and the heroes of the revolt. ... The Holocaust ... is the root and
legitimization of our enterprise."[39] However, linking the history of the
Warsaw Ghetto revolt to the Zionist cause is not always as easy at it might
appear. The daughter of a Jewish fighter in the Warsaw uprising raised
painful questions:

> As long as hundreds of Palestinians are not being lined up and shot, but are
> killed by Israelis only one a day, are we Jews free from worrying about mo-
> rality, justice? Has Nazism become the sole norm by which Jews will judge evil,
> so that anything that is not its exact duplicate is considered by us as morally
> acceptable? Is that what the Holocaust has done to Jewish moral sensibility?[40]

Marek Edelman (1919–2009), a veteran of the Warsaw Ghetto uprising,
identifies with the Palestinian resistance and finds in it many similari-
ties with his own struggle against the Nazis. "Nothing infuriates Zionists
more than the arguments of anti-Zionist Jews, who have such a courageous and principled history."[41] It is hardly surprising that his memoirs,
published in Poland in 1945, were only published in Israel a half-century
later.

The same was true of Hannah Arendt's book *Eichmann in Jerusalem*,
published in Hebrew 37 years after it first appeared in English. The book
undermines one of the founding myths of Zionism, the belief that anti-
Semitism must be seen as an eternal, constant, and mystical force. Arendt
did not find Eichmann "guilty of crimes against the Jewish people," the
verdict of the court. She saw, instead, a case of the "banality of evil," a
largely unconscious development of normal human behavior under the
impact of an implacable bureaucratic system. Arendt's conclusion carries
instead a universal meaning, which should stand as a warning to any state
that adopts ethnic discrimination as state policy. This was one of the motives heard at a conference on her intellectual and moral heritage finally
held at the end of the 20th century, and which yielded a book entitled
Arendt in Jerusalem.[42]

Zionist educators must continually draw attention to the profound insecurity of Jewish life outside of Israel, for a fortuitous event, even of the
dimensions of the Nazi massacres, cannot provide Zionism with lasting
legitimacy. It was in this light that Reuven Hammer, Israeli minister of

education, himself a member and leader of National Judaism, maintained, "The Holocaust is not a national insanity that happened once and passed, but an ideology that has not passed from the world and even today the world may condone crimes against us."[43] It is hardly surprising that only 4 percent of Israeli students draw universal rather than specific conclusions from the Nazi genocide (the necessity to fight against discrimination, racism, and so on).[44]

The state is also seen as protection against any future threat to the Jews, a belief that explains how support for Israel in the diaspora is often seen as an insurance policy. But among Orthodox rabbis, even those who share to a certain extent the philosophy of National Judaism, doubts persist. For example, Rabbi Moshe Sober (1955–2006), educated in the spirit of National Judaism, remained skeptical about Israel's capacity to come to the aid of American Jews in any meaningful way if ever the American government were to persecute them. He found the idea ridiculous, and citing the Talmud, concluded, "Your guarantor needs a guarantor! It is like taking out a life-insurance policy with a company that is guaranteed to go bankrupt on your death."[45]

From a traditionally religious point of view based on the premise of the existence of divine justice,[46] the tragedy of the Shoah calls out for the closest scrutiny of personal behavior, and for individual and collective atonement. It is not an occasion for accusing executioners, and even less an attempt to explain their behavior by political, ideological, or social factors. The executioner— whether Pharaoh, Amalek, or Hitler—in this perspective is an agent of divine punishment, an admittedly cruel means of bringing the Jews to repentance.[47]

Following this same logic, only divine providence—and not historical accident—can explain the catastrophes that have afflicted the Jews, affirmed Rabbi Elhanan Wasserman (1875–1941), disciple of Hafetz Haim and an eminent authority on Lithuanian Judaism. Born in Lithuania, then a part of the Russian Empire, he trained under renowned rabbinical masters, culminating in the Talmudic Academy of Brisk (Brest-Litovsk). He served as director of several *yeshivas*, the best known of which was the Novardok *yeshiva* in Baranovichi, currently in Belarus. While on a fund-raising mission to the United States on behalf of his *yeshiva*, he learned of the Nazi attack on Poland. Well aware of the Nazi threat to the Jews, he refused to abandon his students and returned to Europe. He was arrested in 1941 and put to death by Lithuanian collaborators. His last words have been preserved:

In Heaven it appears that they deem us to be righteous because our bodies have been chosen to atone for the Jewish people. Therefore, we must repent now, immediately. There is not much time. We must keep in mind that we will be better offerings if we repent. In this way we will save the lives of our brethren so that Jewish life may continue.[48]

Well known for profound insights, Wasserman was the author of several collections of Talmudic innovations, as well as of a book on the events of his lifetime. His brief work *Ikveta de-Meshiha* (*The Epoch of the Messiah*) remains to this day one of the basic sources of the orthodox Jewish critique of Zionism.[49] He composed it toward the end of his life, fully conscious of the danger that National Socialism represented for the Jews, but he saw in it no innovation, no departure from the divine order. Similarly, his contemporary in Germany, Rabbi Simon Schwab, interpreted the beginning of the Nazi persecutions as a call to repentance: "God is calling them now and they make no reply."[50] Only a handful of individuals returned to religion.

The Nazi persecutions brought about little or no return to Judaic practice. The exclusion of the Jews from all aspects of social and cultural life in Germany indeed caused an effervescence of Jewish community existence, but rarely if ever a rediscovery of Judaic practice. Rabbi Schwab lamented in Germany in 1934:

They have set up athletic associations and even an honest-to-goodness "cultural league," so that, God forbid, we should not "get back into the ghetto again." ... True, we are depressed, but we are not contrite. We are downcast but not humbled, least of all in our relationship with God. ... If this is so, is it still the people of God?[51]

Only a few months after Hitler was appointed chancellor, Rabbi Schwab predicted that the Jews would be "decimated" in "measure for measure" divine retribution. The rabbi maintained those passages in the English-language version of his book, published in the United States several decades after the Nazi genocide.

Wasserman viewed the Nazi persecutions, of which he would himself be a victim, as a direct consequence of Zionism. Of all the many and varied "isms" of which Wasserman was a contemporary, he attacked Jewish nationalism with particular virulence, describing it as movement that had led to war between the Jews and the Heavenly Kingdom. In his view, the goal of Jewish nationalism was to extirpate God from the hearts of the children of Israel. As long as the Zionist leaders did not turn back from their chosen course of action, as long as they refused to repent their sins, there could be no salvation. Lashing out at the socialism promoted by Zionists in Palestine, Wasserman saw divine justice in the notion that the union of nationalism and socialism, the two idols worshipped by the East European Zionists, had ostensibly engendered the very National Socialism that was unleashing—measure for measure—all its wrath on the Jews of Europe.

> Nowadays, the Jews have chosen two "idols" to which they offer up their sacrifices. They are Socialism and Nationalism. … These two forms of idol worship have poisoned the minds and the hearts of Hebrew Youth. Each one has its tribe of false prophets in the shape of writers and speakers who do their work to perfection. A miracle has happened: in Heaven these two idolatries have been merged into one—National Socialism. There has been formed from them a fearful rod of wrath which hits at the Jews in all corners of the globe. The abominations to which we have bowed down strike back at us.[52]

He remained convinced that the genocide, the extent of which he had intuited, could be nothing but punishment for the abandonment of the Torah that the Zionists had for so long encouraged and practiced. It followed that as long as the Zionist enterprise lasted, the Jewish people would continue to pay in human life for the transgressions inherent in Zionism. The violence from which the Israeli population has suffered for more than a century would in this view be ongoing punishment for the violation of the Talmudic oaths prohibiting violent conquest of the Holy Land.

An even more categorical condemnation comes from anti-Zionist militants in Jerusalem: "If it were not for Zionist sinning, the tragedy of Europe would never have come about." They took strong exception to the widespread idea that if the state of Israel had existed in the 1930s, it would have been able to absorb the Jews of Europe. "This is outright heresy. I repeat that the Holocaust came as a retribution for Zionist sinning."[53]

This categorical statement was the work of Rabbi Amram Blau (1894–1974). Born in Jerusalem into the Haredi community, he early on became an anti-Zionist activist, initially joining the ranks of Agudat Israel (also known as Aguda), a movement founded in Europe in 1912 to combat Zionism. He went on to become the editor of *Kol Yisroel*. Distressed by the later collaboration of Agudat Israel with the Zionist enterprise, in 1937 he founded the Neturei Karta movement. Rabbi Blau was on intimate terms with many leading personalities, particularly Rabbi Avraham Yeshayahu Karelitz (1878–1953), better known as Hazon Ish, a prominent mid-20th century Haredi leader. Often imprisoned for his acts of protest against certain policies of the Zionist state, such as conscription of women, Rabbi Blau became the symbol of militant Haredi resistance. His position remained firm throughout his life: justice must be restored; political control of the Holy Land must be handed to the Palestinians. Jewish life would be better protected under Arab control than in the Zionist state. For Blau, Zionist aggression was the sole cause of Palestinian hostility. "If you'd just been expelled from your home by someone who acted like the owner who took everything you owned, would you react any differently?" Condemning the Zionists for their routine cruelty, he was unable to see in what way a Palestinian government would be any worse than other non-Jewish regimes, "in Switzerland or America, for instance."

In 1965 Rabbi Blau remarried. His wife, Ruth Ben-David (1920–2000), née Madeleine Ferraille, was born into a Catholic family. A member of the Resistance during the Nazi occupation, she gained experience in clandestine action. In 1951 she converted to Judaism and later joined the Haredi community in Aix-les-Bains, France. An inveterate activist, she became a militant anti-Zionist, and participated in many anti-Zionist operations in and outside of Israel before marrying Rabbi Blau.[54]

Another Haredi leader, Rabbi Joseph Zvi Duschinsky (1868–1948), who at the time represented the traditional Ashkenazi community in Palestine, also declared before the United Nations in 1947 that Zionism was responsible for the violence and friction with the Arabs, forcing the British government to limit Jewish immigration to Palestine in the early 1930s. Zionism stood accused, in his eyes, of making it impossible to save millions of Jews from death: "the colossal massacre of millions of our brethren at the hands of Nazism during the second World War might have been averted to a very substantial degree for many of them might have been able to live peacefully in the Holy Land."[55] The rabbi concluded that if the traditional leaders devoid of even the slightest national ambition had continued to run the Jewish communities in Palestine, the long history of neighborly coexistence with the Arabs would have made it possible to open the doors to the threatened Jews of Europe.

This was an opinion expressed well before the massacres of the Jews in Nazi-occupied Europe. In 1937, following the recommendations of the Peel

Commission for the partition of Palestine, Rabbi Judah Magnes, president of Hebrew University, objected to the idea of partition in a letter to the *New York Times*:

> We have failed. We have not known how to make peace. … With Arab consent we could settle many hundreds of thousands of persecuted Jews in various Arab lands. That is worth a real price. Without Arab consent even our 400,000 in Palestine remain in jeopardy, despite the momentary protection of British bayonets.[56]

The leaders of the Jewish organizations of the day failed to respond to his appeal, which was rapidly forgotten.

Zionist educators proved far more successful in convincing the Israelis, as well as the young Jews of the diaspora, that the state of Israel constituted reparation for the millions of deaths in Europe, and made use of a wide variety of strategies to achieve their aims. By far the most impressive has been the March of the Living, organized in 1988, which brought Jewish teenagers from various countries first to the extermination camps in Poland, most often to Auschwitz, and then to Israel to celebrate Independence Day. The message conveyed is a forceful one: after death, life; after the dark barracks of Auschwitz, the sun-drenched streets of the towns and cities of Israel decorated with the blue and white flag in honor of Independence Day. Israeli youth joined this annual march thanks to the ideologists of the kibbutz movement, concerned about the identity crisis among young secular Israelis. All the while many kibbutzim opposed the construction of synagogues on their premises, even for the customers of the kibbutz-run hotels.[57]

The state of Israel has used the memory of the Nazi genocide in a wide variety of ways. For example, only the need to discredit the Palestinian leadership can explain why the *Encyclopedia of the Shoah,* published in Israel, lends more attention to Amin el-Husseini (1893–1974), a minor Nazi collaborator, than to Himmler, Goebbels, and Goering.[58] In 2015 the Israeli prime minister went as far as to accuse el-Husseini of convincing Hitler to exterminate the Jews.[59] Not for the first time the history of that tragedy had been manipulated for political ends. In addition to providing Israel with a highly persuasive *raison d'être*, the memory of the genocide has proved a powerful means of leveraging aid. As an Israeli parliamentarian commented:

> Even the best friends of the Jewish people refrained from offering signifi-

cant saving help of any kind to European Jewry and turned their back on the chimneys of the death camps. ... Therefore all the free world, especially these days, is required to show its repentance ... by providing diplomatic-defensive economic aid to Israel.[60]

This quotation, taken not from a polemical work but from a political analysis by religious Zionists, indicates that the ideological and political use of the Shoah has become a matter of habit and routine, and that it includes manipulation of collective guilt feelings.

Remorse over the genocide has brought substantial reparations from Germany and later from other countries into the coffers of the state of Israel and many of its citizens. For decades, Israeli diplomacy has invoked the Nazi genocide to mute criticism of, and to generate sympathy for, the state, which it presents as the collective heir of the 6 million victims, and which is still threatened by enemy encirclement. However, this function has apparently begun to lose its effectiveness. The generation that experienced the war is no longer in power in Europe; some are beginning to assert that Israel has overused this powerful argument. The Israeli novelist Amos Oz has spoken out against this manifestation of the Israelis' proverbial *chutzpah*:

> Our sufferings have granted us immunity papers, as it were, a moral *carte blanche*. After what all those dirty goyim [non-Jews] have done to us, none of them is entitled to preach morality to us. We, on the other hand, have *carte blanche*, because we were victims and have suffered so much. Once a victim, always a victim, and victimhood entitles its owners to a moral exemption.[61]

Then there are those Israeli political commentators who fear that to use the memory of the genocide in this way will awaken antagonism even among Israel's allies, and thus become a self-fulfilling prophecy:

> the centrality of the holocaust myth, and the core values of Jewish history and Jewish peoplehood is relevant to understanding why Israelis apparently prepared to behave in a manner that not only many of its friends but even some of its citizens consider irrational.[62]

By way of example, political analysts Charles S. Liebman and Eliezer Don Yehiya cite a letter from then prime minister Menahem Begin to U.S. President Ronald Reagan during the Israeli invasion of Lebanon in

1982. Begin reassured the American president that he felt like someone who had led "a courageous army to Berlin to eliminate Hitler in a bunker."[63]

For some Zionists, the president of Iran, the Palestinians, and even the Muslims have become the "new Nazis." Having lost sight of the decisive role of the Soviet army in the defeat of Nazism, many Americans see the United States as a force for good, which in winning the Second World War liberated the Jews from the Nazi threat. "What has bound America and Israel together is their shared constant need for another Hitler to destroy."[64] This is a convincing case of the durability of the phenomenon remarked by the historian Enzo Traverso with respect to the 1947–49 war: "Their action was physically taking place in Palestine but their mindset and their moral universe remained in Europe."[65]

Reference to the genocide pervades Israeli political life as well. We need only recall that on the eve of the assassination of prime minister Itzhak Rabin (1922–1995) by a follower of National Judaism, thousands of leaflets depicting him in an SS uniform had been distributed. Subsequently, the unilateral evacuation of the Zionist settlements in Gaza, decreed by prime minister Ariel Sharon in 2005, touched off an eruption of comparisons with the Nazi genocide. Opponents of the evacuation used terms like "deportation" and "*judenrein*" ("cleansed of Jews"), distributing posters that likened Sharon to Hitler. On the other side of the ideological divide, the philosopher Yeshayahu Leibowitz described the settler-vigilante partisans of National Judaism as "Judeo-Nazis."

Among pious Jews, views of the massacre of the Jews in Nazi Europe were articulated differently. It is generally accepted that the destruction of the Temple of Jerusalem stands as the prototype to which Jewish tradition refers each time calamity has struck the Jews down through the centuries. According to tradition, nothing can elude Divine Will except for the fear of God, which remains firmly lodged in the heart of every human being. Free will can be seen as the gift that if misused will provoke God's wrath. A crucial distinction is often drawn between a tragedy inflicted by God (for example, the destruction of Sodom and Gomorrah) and a tragedy that occurs because of the removal of Divine Providence. From this perspective, God punishes only the guilty; however, when God withdraws ("hides his face") and when punishment comes from humans, the innocent will suffer as well. The Talmud warns, "Once permission has been granted to the Destroyer, he does not distinguish between righteous and wicked."[66]

It also articulates the idea of communal responsibility, underlining that God may punish a Jew for the transgressions of another.[67]

Both the Zionists and their detractors agree that the hostility encountered by the Jews over the centuries stands outside the bounds of normality: it is a form of hostility unlike any other. But while the Zionists generally explain this hostility by the political and military weakness of the Jews, pious Jews tend to see it as a punishment for the sins committed by the Jews themselves:

> Whenever in the course of history the Jew loses consciousness of his heritage and mission in life, it becomes necessary that his enemies rouse him and restore him to the possession of his faculties. The magnitude of his enemies and the severity of the methods they employ in awakening the Jew depend entirely on the intensity of the latter's lethargy.[68]

An analogy may be found in the case of a man who is asleep in a burning house:

> If he sleeps lightly, a gentle nudge may suffice to make him aware of the danger; however, if he has sunk into an extremely sound and deep slumber it may be necessary to strike him hard in order to save his life. Similarly when the Jewish people are on the whole conscious of their Jewishness, anti-Semitism expresses itself as minor annoyances which suffice to prevent Jews from forgetting their destiny. However, when Jews completely ignore the covenant which God made with their ancestors and desire to live like other peoples of the earth, then the hordes of beastly anti-Semites swoop down upon them with terrific force and fury, as is the case in our own day.[69]

Rabbi Wasserman's point is that the slightest distancing from the Torah entails a corresponding punishment designed to return to the path those Jews who have strayed: "The reason for our present plight, unparalleled in Jewish history, must be attributed to the abandonment of the study of Torah."[70] The Judaic literature that presents this vision of the Nazi persecutions is abundant, based on classical sources, and begins well before the Nazi genocide. The betrayal of exile by the Zionists is seen as having brought about the catastrophe, and as Zionist transgression is collective, the punishment will also be collective.

Ruth Blau, Rabbi Blau's widow, adds a historical footnote to the relationship between Zionism and the Nazi massacres. Recalling the message that Theodore Herzl and Max Nordau were actively propagating in the early 20th century among European leaders—"the Jews constitute a foreign and destructive element for the countries they inhabit"—she quotes a minister of Emperor Franz-Joseph's government: "If the malicious propaganda that would cast the Jews as a danger to the world and as revolutionaries continues, instead of establishing a Jewish State the Zionists will bring about the destruction of the Jews of Europe." She concluded, "Hitler, less than fifty years later, unfortunately would make the Austrian minister's fear a reality."[71]

Wasserman for his part believed that ignorance of the Torah and the extinction of faith among many Jews had made them "the most unfortunate of men. They do not know the reason for their suffering; they have no one to turn to in time of trouble. Who can imagine the extent of their despair and disillusionment?"[72] He asserted that the loss of the traditional framework for the interpretation of adversities has left the Jews powerless, driving them to violence against others and against themselves. Clearly, the majority of Jews no longer recognize the traditional exegetical schema that makes it possible to seek existential meaning in the apparently senseless massacres perpetrated by the Nazis and their collaborators.

There can be little doubt that after the Nazi genocide, the use of force became an article of faith for a large number of Jews. To cast doubt upon the legitimacy and efficacy of force is, in Zionist circles, tantamount to treason. When the secular Jewish sensibility encounters that of the traditionalists, who see the hand of God in all that happens to them, including the massacre of millions of Jews, the encounter is bound to create a certain resistance or even anger among secular Jews.

A touching collection of Hassidic stories told by survivors provides many examples of the unshakable faith in God and in His providence. One short story deals with Jewish women being led to slaughter by the SS in a ghetto. These same women requested and obtained permission to immerse themselves before death in the *mikve*, the bath used for ritual purification. The German commanding officer asked one of them for the reasons for this strange request from this "filthy race, the source of all disease and vermin in Europe." She answered, "God has brought our pure souls into this world in the pure homes of our parents, and we wish to return to the purity of our Father in Heaven."[73]

It was this same trust in God that gave a Hassidic rabbi the courage to request that the commander of the Bergen-Belsen camp provide him with flour and an oven to prepare *matzoh* for Passover. And as he recited and discussed the *Haggadah* at the Passover meal, he assured the Hassidim that their predicament was "the beginning of our Redemption." As they returned to their barracks, the Hassidim were "sure that the sounds of the Messiah's footsteps were echoing in the sounds of their own steps on the blood soaked earth of Bergen-Belsen."[74]

It is noteworthy that the author, in her preface, feels obliged to reassure the reader that "this collection of Hassidic tales is not ... a negation of the value of armed resistance and the physical struggle for one's life or death with honor."[75] However, none of the stories in the collection mention armed resistance; they bear witness only to an interpretation by the genocide victims rarely heard in commemorative ceremonies, one that affirms Jewish tradition and draws from it spiritual meaning.

It is hardly surprising that those Jews who cannot identify with Zionism commemorate and interpret the Nazi genocide so differently from the Zionists. Despite the wide variety of reactions, a common thread runs through the belief shared by all traditionalists: the genocide, brought upon us by our sins, calls us to repent. As we have seen, some religious thinkers hold Zionism responsible for the genocide, identifying as decisive factors the challenge to the nations it represented and the rejection of the Torah that they accuse it of having promoted and encouraged. In their view, the Torah contains warnings about both the Holocaust and the creation of the state of Israel.

Rabbi Moshe Dov Beck, a consistent opponent of Zionism, welcomed me to his modest home in Monsey, New York State, wearing a striped caftan identical to those worn in Meah Shearim. He began speaking in Yiddish, but in order for me to understand him he agreed to make an exception to his habit of not speaking Hebrew "for profane purposes" and addressed me in *loshen ha-kodesh*, the rabbinical version of Hebrew spoken with an Ashkenazi accent. He explained that the Nazis had certainly caused the gravest suffering but that God had never abandoned us, nor did He even hide his face. He deplored the Zionist insistence on seeing in the Nazi genocide only the physical weakness of the Jews, their lack of an army and a state:

> Like a dog that bites the stick that strikes it, the Zionists are incapable of seeing the hand of God behind the Shoah. And, it goes without saying, that they have drawn from it false and dangerous lessons.[76]

In Haredi circles, there is a sense of categorical rejection of the heroic romanticism observed in the official commemoration of the Nazi genocide. Dying with weapons in hand certainly represents an act of heroism in European culture, and this conception of revolt has penetrated the collective conscience of the Israelis as an act of courage and an example to be emulated. But the Haredim have an entirely different vision of revolt: "To die a hero's death just for the sake of dying a hero's death is not compatible with the Jewish faith .... Let them not long for false heroism, which has no basis in Judaism."[77] They thus condemn the leaders of the Warsaw Ghetto revolt:

> It is as clear as day that people who believe in the Lord and live according to His will do not do anything to hasten their deaths by even one moment and certainly not something that will hasten the deaths of tens of thousands of their brethren.[78]

Provoking the annihilation of the Warsaw Ghetto by an uprising that had no chance of success against the Nazi war machine constitutes an act of heroism for some, and a crime for others. For this question, as for so many other questions arising from the confrontation between Zionism and Jewish tradition, there seems to be no intermediate or compromise position. Of course, there exists a gamut of other views held by Jews on this tragedy: Bundists, communists, followers of National Judaism and of Reform and Conservative movements, to name just a few, interpret the Nazi genocide in different ways. Quite a few find it inexplicable and prefer to remain silent.

Chapter Six

The Making and
Maintaining of the Zionist State

Political and Military Aspects

In the conflict with the Ottoman Empire during the First World War, the United Kingdom sought out local allies and encouraged Arab nationalists striving to free themselves from Ottoman control. At the same time, in November 1917, as British troops fought to conquer Palestine, the Cabinet approved a brief declaration:

> His Majesty's government view with favour the establishment in Palestine of a national home for the Jewish people, and will use their best endeavours to facilitate the achievement of this object, it being clearly understood that nothing shall be done which may prejudice the civil and religious rights of existing non-Jewish communities in Palestine, or the rights and political status enjoyed by Jews in any other country.[1]

Thus read the Balfour Declaration, named for the foreign minister of the day, Arthur Balfour. Its principal objective was to consolidate U.S. support for the war rather than to gain the sympathy of the Zionist settlers in Palestine, who were too few to wield any influence. The Zionist leaders behind the initiative, Haim Weizmann and Nahum Sokolow (1860–1936), both Russian Jews, encouraged Balfour, who was known for his anti-Semitic views, to believe in the political influence of "world Jewry," in the United States and Russia above all.[2] What they did not tell him was that such influence was largely their own invention, and that moreover the Zionist movement was far from being popular among the Jews.

The Cabinet then appointed a Zionist Jew, Herbert Samuel (1870–1963), a veteran civil servant and expert in colonial affairs, as the first British high commissioner for Palestine. In the course of his mandate, from 1920 to 1925, Samuel put in place the infrastructure that would soon facilitate Zionist settlement. He also successfully tempered criticisms of the U.K.

commitment to Zionism expressed in Parliament in the early 1920s. While British promises to the Arabs to set up independent states were short lived, the commitment to Zionism proved more long lasting, thanks in no small measure to the tireless efforts of the Zionist representatives in London.

The Zionist leadership outside Palestine, which took tangible form in the establishment in 1922 of the Jewish Agency for Palestine, concentrated its efforts in the corridors of power in London. Events in Russia from 1917 on, however, had much greater impact on the situation in Palestine. Even though the new Soviet authorities proscribed Zionism, as they did all political movements independent of the Bolsheviks, "the first homeland of the working class" exerted a powerful attraction among Zionists already established in Palestine. A certain number of left-wing Zionists faced a serious dilemma: should they struggle for socialism in Palestine or participate in building socialism in the Soviet Union? More than a few elected to return to their homeland, and joined the ranks of Jewish communists in the USSR. Their common political—not to mention cultural—affinity made it easy to forge links between the Zionist left in Palestine and the Soviet Union.

But British support remained essential, particularly in dealing with unrest among the local population in Palestine. Violent incidents broke out frequently during the 1920s and 1930s. Certainly the best known was the Hebron pogrom of 1929. Arab resistance remained focused above all on the British authorities, whose responsibility in the intensification of Zionist settlement activity was clear-cut. Zionist paramilitary units joined with the British in reprisal operations, preparing the ground for collaboration that allowed the Zionist militias to benefit from the experience of the British colonial administration.

Meanwhile, Jewish immigration to Palestine continued throughout the British Mandate. More than 40,000 Jews arrived between 1919 and 1923 alone from the former Russian Empire, which lay devastated by the First World War and the civil war that followed it. These migrants came from the same ideological and cultural environment as the Zionist pioneers; many of them rapidly integrated into the socialist-inspired agricultural structures set up by the settlers. The intensification of anti-Semitism in Europe and the restrictions on immigration introduced by the United States in 1924 brought more than 80,000 Polish and Hungarian Jews to the Holy Land in the next five years. These immigrants were primarily city dwellers from the lower middle classes. The ideals of socialism and Zionism mattered little to them, as they congregated in the greater Tel

Aviv area.[3] A significant portion of these immigrants, around 75 percent, moved on as soon as they could find a country prepared to accept them.[4]

The period between 1930 and 1939 was marked by the rise of National Socialism in Germany and of fascist movements elsewhere in Europe. While fascism was a minor irritation for Italian Jews, many of whom had joined Mussolini's movement before 1938, most European fascist groups were openly anti-Semitic. Some of these groups, particularly in Poland and Germany, collaborated with the Zionists not only in providing them with military and agricultural training, but also in encouraging the Jews to leave their homelands. For example, the SS policy in the mid-1930s was "based ... on the promotion of Jewish emigration to Palestine ... [and] was remarkably like the Zionist programme."[5] The Zionist project dovetailed with the anti-Semites' desire to rid Europe of Jews. In 1937 Adolf Eichmann, one of the top Nazis in charge of the "Jewish question," traveled to Palestine to meet with Labor Zionist officials.[6] Attachment to the people and to the land was common to Zionism and quite a few other forms of European nationalism between the two world wars.

It was during this period that 250,000 Jews arrived in Palestine from Germany, Austria, and the Eastern European countries. Among them were lawyers, scientists, engineers, industrialists, artists, and architects, who were to lay the foundations of the future state in industry, higher education, and research, and who contributed substantially to the cultural advancement of the Zionist enterprise. Over and above the immigration authorized by the British authorities, several Zionist organizations encouraged illegal immigration, which saw more than 100,000 European Jews seek refuge in Palestine between 1933 and 1948.[7]

Arab resistance to Zionist settlement grew stronger toward the end of the 1930s. The UK authorities moved to limit Jewish immigration to Palestine, and even to restrict purchase of land by Jews. Several commissions of inquiry were set up to deal with the future of Palestine. Division of the country into two states emerged as an increasingly thinkable perspective. In 1942 the Zionist leadership, meeting in the United States, adopted as a matter of policy the creation of a Zionist state.

From 1943 onward, violence intensified in Palestine. Zionist militias attacked the British authorities. Shock units (*Palmakh*) affiliated with the labor movement carried out operations against British installations while extreme right-wing nationalist militias perpetrated much deadlier attacks, the most spectacular of all being the 1946 bombing of the King

David Hotel, which housed the offices of the Mandate Administration in Jerusalem.

The Second World War, which was to kill millions of European Jews, touched off a groundswell of sympathy for the Jewish victims of Nazism, and by extension for the Zionist project. Addressing the United Nations, the Soviet foreign minister Andrei Gromyko (1909–1989) expressed the then common sentiment:

> The fact that no Western European state has been able to ensure the defense of the elementary rights of the Jewish people, and to safeguard it against the violence of the fascist executioners, explains the aspirations of the Jews to establish their own state. It would be unjust not to take this into consideration and to deny the right of the Jewish people to realize this aspiration.[8]

The General Assembly of the United Nations adopted on November 29, 1947 a resolution recommending the partition of Palestine into two states, one Jewish, the other Arab. The Soviet Union and the United States voted for the resolution, which passed thanks to the support of several Latin American countries, as well as Liberia and Haiti, which caved in to American pressure.

The aim of Resolution 181 was the creation of two states: a Jewish entity of 14,000 km^2, composed of 558,000 Jews and 405,000 Arabs and consisting of three distinct components: the coastal plain, the lands along the Syrian border, and the Negev Desert; and an Arab state of 11,500 km^2 populated by 804,000 Arabs and 10,000 Jews and consisting of four parts: a zone surrounding the city of Gaza, the mountains of Judea and Samaria, most of the Galilee region in the north, and the city of Jaffa. The resolution also created a zone under international administration covering the Holy Places, Jerusalem and Bethlehem, inhabited by 106,000 Arabs and 100,000 Jews. Despite the avowed intention to create two states of similar dimensions, the partition actualy decided by the United Nations heavily favored the Zionists. Even though they possessed 7 percent of the territory they were allocated 60 percent, including 80 percent of Palestine's grain-growing areas, and most of the coastal areas.

The Zionist leadership accepted the resolution. But, adopted against the will of the majority of the population of British Palestine and of all the neighboring countries, the UN decision reflected the vestiges of the colonial mentality: a decision of an international body took no account of the realities on the ground and in the region. Thus it only fanned the flames of the conflict. In the months that followed the UN resolution, the numerically superior and better-armed Zionist forces attacked and drove hundreds of thousands of Palestinians from their homes and land. The cities of Jaffa, Tiberias, Safed, and Haifa fell to the Zionist units as the majority of their inhabitants fled the combat zone or were deliberately expelled.[9] Even before the end of the British Mandate, the Palestinian forces had been defeated.

On May 15, 1948, the same day that the British forces left Palestine, David Ben-Gurion, in the name of the Zionist executive, proclaimed the creation of the state of Israel. The neighboring Arab countries attacked the fledgling state but, divided and poorly prepared, they failed in their attempt to smother the "Zionist entity." At the same time, the IDF, the newly formed Israeli army made up of several pre-existing Zionist militias, seized the opportunity to expand Israel's territorial holdings. Summary expulsions took place in the Arab towns of Lod and Ramleh. The war ultimately helped Israel increase its portion of Palestinian territory by 40 percent above the UN partition plan.[10]

The events surrounding the unilateral declaration of independence by the Zionists in Palestine continue to fuel debate among historians, politicians, and even simple citizens, in Israel and elsewhere. Even the text of the Declaration of Independence drew sharp criticism. One of those critics, Yeshayahu Leibowitz, notes:

> Contrary to what is said in our Declaration of Independence, "The Land of Israel was the birthplace of the Jewish people," ninety or one hundred generations have maintained, rooted in their consciousness, the memory of the fact that a people—that preexisted—had once invaded the land of Canaan and made of it the land of Israel. ... In its historical conscience, the people existed outside any connection with a given territory. It remembered—and it well remembered—that it was a stranger in the land of Egypt. ... It later became independent, not in a state, but in the desert, something with no defined frontiers. ... The historical image is clear: it is the people that created the state and not the state—nor the land—that created the people.[11]

Several myths fabricated during the first decades of the Zionist state have since been fundamentally revised.[12] The first concerns the number of belligerents. It has now been established that the Zionist military and paramilitary forces were more numerous and better equipped than the Palestinian militias: a fact that undercuts the image of victims that many Israelis have about themselves, and above all about their place in history.

A second myth concerns the intentions of the Arab armies in 1948, particularly their most significant component, Transjordan's Arab Legion. Israel alleged—and continues to this day to insist—that their aim was the destruction of the newborn state and that consequently all the operations of the Israeli forces were purely defensive. However, Israel's New Historians—for example, Avi Shlaim at Oxford[13]—have shone new light on the agreement between the Zionist leadership and Transjordan to divide between them the territories designated by the United Nations as the future Arab state in Palestine. While the Zionist forces carried out frequent attacks on the Arab Legion on lands allocated to the Arab state, the Legion itself launched only two offensive operations, one in Jerusalem, the other at Gush Etzion, against the Zionist militias.

Yet another myth concerns the Palestinian refugees. More than 800,000 non-Jews left Palestine in 1947–49, dispersed among the neighboring Arab countries. In violation of numerous UN resolutions, the Israeli government forbade the refugees to return to their homes and confiscated their properties. Several thousand non-Jews who remained within the new country likewise looked on as their villages and dwellings were destroyed or confiscated without compensation. More than 500 villages were leveled. In the early 1950s the Knesset adopted legislation authorizing the expropriation of land belonging to Palestinians. To avoid legal action under international law, these properties were transferred to the control of a third party, the JNF, whose mandate was to act for the benefit of the Jewish people, as defined by Zionist institutions. This institution has played a crucial role in the development of the Zionist state. In response to an anti-discrimination action brought against the JNF in 2004, the organization confirmed that "the loyalty of the JNF is given to the Jewish people and only to them is the JNF obligated. The JNF, as the owner of the JNF land, does not have a duty to practice equality towards all citizens of the state."[14]

To explain the exodus, the Israeli version of events points to the calls by Arab leaders to the local population in an effort to protect them from the hostilities. But according to at least one of the New Historians, Benny Morris, this account more closely resembles Israeli propaganda. Only six villages were evacuated on the initiative of the local Arab authorities. What actually happened could best be described as ethnic cleansing operations. Most of the inhabitants of the abandoned towns and villages fled before the assaults of the Zionist forces or were expelled outright from their land. Morris regrets that these operations were less thorough than in the Americas and that the "Palestinian problem" continues to haunt Israel: "If he [Ben-Gurion] had carried out a full expulsion—rather than a partial one—he would have stabilized the State of Israel for generations."[15]

Furthermore, a number of well-to-do Arab families seeking to avoid the armed conflict also departed precipitously. By May 15, 1948 the leadership of that part of Palestine allotted to the Arabs had almost entirely abandoned their country.

Since the proclamation of the state, Israeli policy has remained constant. It reflects the imperative to perpetuate a state established against the will of the native Arab population and situated predominantly on lands that had once belonged to that population. Despite numerous calls from the United Nations to allow those displaced by the hostilities of 1947–48 to return, Israel repulsed all those who attempted to return to their ancestral homes, and killed thousands of others in the first years of independence.[16] Since then Israeli forces have intervened with impunity in neighboring countries. Armed Palestinian resistance has drawn an increasingly disproportionate response, with the result that the spiral of violence set in motion has continued for more than six decades. Ben-Gurion's choice to base Israel's regional policy on priorities of the military and the security services has given them influence and prestige that have enabled former military and security officials to hold key positions in Israeli governments.

Diplomacy now serves primarily the interests of the military. All of this tends to support Ben-Gurion's conviction that military victory rather than diplomacy made possible the creation and the perpetuation of the Zionist state. What could be described as "warrior pragmatism" has grown stronger over the years, a trend born out by the fact that Israel, the sole country whose establishment was decreed by the United Nations, has chosen systematically to ignore the international organization's many resolutions censuring its treatment of the Palestinians. Israel's behavior, the incarnation of the principle "might makes right," has undermined the very bases of international public law conceived to reduce conflict and promote peace.

Israel looms first and foremost as a military power, while its occasional faint-hearted attempts to compromise with the Palestinians can be seen as striking exceptions. The "peace process" that has been under way since the early 1990s has allowed Israel to consolidate and extend its control over the Palestinian territories occupied in 1967.[17] Because of Israel's treatment of the Palestinians, the peace agreements signed with Egypt and Jordan have remained unpopular among the general public in those countries. The temptation to hang onto the Palestinian territories seems too strong, and the Arab League's peace proposals formulated at the beginning of the 21st century have remained on the table without Israel even having deigned to respond.[18]

Israel's military superiority and Western support, which have grown steadily since 1948, combined to reassure the country's leadership that it would not benefit from seeking peace. Despite its apparent diplomatic flexibility, it remained faithful to the policies set out by the state's founders: to occupy the maximum amount of land with the minimum of Arabs. The unilateral evacuation of the Gaza Strip settlements in 2005 was more a reflection of military tactical considerations, as was demonstrated during the Israeli attack on the area in the winter of 2008–09 and later in 2014, than of any desire to conclude an agreement or to coexist with the Arab population. The spirit of unilateralism, combined with overwhelming economic, technological, and military advantage, has transformed Israel into an overtly Western enclave increasingly foreign to the Middle East. Whatever may befall the Palestinians, Israeli society and its leaders have displayed a firm resolve to consolidate their power and to dominate the region.

Arabs and Non-Arabs

Paradoxically, the countries that attacked Israel in 1948 were those that contributed, a few years later, to reinforcing it. Massive immigration of Jews from Muslim-majority countries began with the declaration of independence. In the following three years, 93,000 persons arrived in Israel from Egypt and Morocco, 180,000 from Iraq, Turkey, and Iran, and 48,000 from Yemen and Aden.[19] According to Ben-Gurion, in August 1939 the number of registered Zionists in these countries accounted for 0.38 percent of the total of Jewish immigrants, compared with 40.9 percent from Eastern Europe.[20] The figures illustrate yet again the Eastern European character of Zionism, which has been an obstacle to the integration of Arab Jews, and *a fortiori* Muslims and Christians, in Israel.

As did most of the newly arrived immigrants, the Arab Jews (or Arabs of Judaic faith) underwent a kind of cultural sterilization, the fate reserved for the "generation of the desert," a biblical reference to the Hebrews that wandered for 40 years in the wilderness and finally perished there in order that the next generation, purified of every trace of the past, could enter into and conquer the Promised Land. In order to become a part of the new society, they would have to leave behind them their age-old modes of behavior, their ancient values, tastes, and melodies, and adopt the manners and customs of the New Hebrew individual.

Meanwhile, a smaller number of Arab Jews were encouraged to continue their Arab culture and thus become useful to Israeli intelligence. Some of them, such as Egyptian-born Eli Cohen (1924–1965)—viewed as a hero in Israel—became extremely effective spies, working in the Arab countries under the supervision of higher-ranking officers of predominantly Eastern European origin. But at no time was the Arab culture and sensibility of these Jews, regarded as a military advantage, ever considered a means of building bridges with the neighboring Arab societies.

While Arabic and Farsi-speaking immigrants found themselves obliged to discard almost every distinguishing feature of their culture, others, from Eastern Europe, integrated thanks to the culture of their countries of origin. After all, theirs largely inspired the new Zionist/Israeli culture, which sees itself as resolutely European. So it was that dozens of songs, nursery rhymes, and children's stories were translated from Russian into Hebrew during the early years of Zionist settlement.[21] Today, Israeli society has become considerably more diverse, leaving behind heavy-handed policies for shaping the new Zionist culture.

On the other hand, Arab Jews face a quadruple handicap. First, they are the bearers not only of the culture of their countries of origin, but of the culture—and the language—of the Arab enemy, which surrounds and threatens Zionist society. Second, because Arab culture was seen as non-European and thus inferior, the New Hebrew Man looked down upon it: a Eurocentric attitude that remains strong and appears to be growing stronger. Third, the Arab Jews were often pauperized before leaving their countries of origin, which reinforced their feelings of inferiority. Fourth, even though the landscape of Palestine reminded them of their geographical heritage, the structures of the new society, modeled as they were on the experience and interpretation of Eastern European realities, were clearly foreign to those who grew up in Muslim-majority countries. For these populations the concept of the atheistic Jew, which played (and continued to play, though to a lesser degree) a leadership role in Israel, was totally foreign to their experience. True enough, after the first electoral defeat of the Labor Party in 1977, the culture of Arab Jews in Israel has undergone a rehabilitation of sorts, accompanied by a return to Judaism expressed politically by the Shas Party.

Arab Jews, for the first time in their history, had to choose between Jewish nationalism and Arab nationalism. First the Zionists, and then the Arab nationalists, postulated that it was impossible to be both Jew and Arab. However, contrary to what the Zionist paradigm asserts, the affinity between an Arab Jew and an Arab Muslim was often stronger and more natural than between a Yemenite Jew and a Russian one, particularly if the latter no longer practiced Judaism. The founding—and the policies—of the state of Israel destabilized the Jewish communities in the Arab world and, with a few exceptions, ultimately uprooted them.

The Arab Jews had to choose between two identities. In the majority of cases the choice was made for them rather than by them. In some countries they were marginalized by the Muslim majority in its indignation over the partition of Palestine and the dislocation of the Palestinians; in others, Zionist agents fomented instability, spread rumors of impending anti-Jewish violence, and reportedly on occasion embarked on false-flag actions in order to cause the largest possible number of Moroccan and Iraqi Jews to leave for Israel.[22] The departure for Israel almost never reflected an ideological commitment to Zionism, and even less to the state constructed by and for Eastern Europeans. Throughout the history of the Zionist enterprise, ideologically motivated *aliya* have never accounted for more than 2 percent of the population.[23]

There exists a symmetry between the Zionist vision of the land of Israel, supposedly neglected by the Arabs and made to bear fruit by virtue of the work of European Zionists, and of the Arab Jews, who were likewise seen as empty, passive vessels that the life-giving spirit of Zionism should reshape and transform.[24]

It was hardly surprising that the principal function allotted to the Arab Jews was to increase the Jewish demographic composition of the newly formed state. Frequently assigned to former Arab villages on the periphery, they were faced with incursions by Palestinians trying to return to their homes and lands. Thus they became the instruments of Palestinian dispossession while at the same time suffering from inferior status within Israeli society. Ella Shohat, an expert in Arab Jewish studies, pointed to a "structural analogy" between the function attributed to the Jews of the Arab countries in the colonization of Palestine, and the role played by the African-Americans in the dispossession of the native populations throughout the territory of the United States.[25] Moreover, the socio-economic gap between Jews of Arab and of European origin has not appreciably narrowed, and according to some studies, may have widened for the second generation born in Israel.[26]

Israeli and other specialists agree that:

> Zionism was founded in Europe by utopian visionaries seeking new lands to cultivate, following the example of the Boers in South Africa, and the Pied-noirs in Algeria. Militarily well outfitted ... the military and paramilitary units that repelled the Arab armies ... had been given or had undertaken the mission of "cleansing" the conquered regions of their Palestinian inhabitants. ... The Arab houses and villages thus emptied of their population were handed on a priority basis to Jewish immigrants from the Arab countries, and for whom the messianic dream of "return to Zion" would quickly evaporate in the face of systematic exploitation.[27]

According to these observers, entire populations—particularly those originating in Muslim countries—underwent a "deculturation" whose main element was their frequently forced detachment from Jewish tradition.[28] Ruth Blau used similar terms to describe the situation of the North African Jews in Israel:

> They grow up resembling Palestinian children, nourished on the bitterness of their parents. Without the Torah, which was the source of their grandparents' dignity, they became revolutionaries. Their parents fell silent in resignation. They understood that they had been brought there to serve as unpaid soldiers. To risk their lives. To defend a state governed by Ashkenazim for Ashkenazim. From the Zionists they learned revolt. Taught to hate, they came to loathe their Ashkenazi masters.[29]

For Rabbi Blau, Zionism brought about much greater injury to the Jews than to the Arabs. The Arabs may have lost their land and their homes, but by accepting Zionism the Jews lost their historic identity. His wife, who had visited the Jews of Morocco before their departure for Israel in the 1950s and 1960s, raised the same question several decades later:

> Their faces shone with goodness, simplicity and great purity. These Jews, whose relations with their Arab neighbors were excellent, led modest but happy lives around their rabbi. ... Often, since then, I have thought back to the Jews in that

village lost in the Atlas. Where are they now? Have Israeli agents forced them to leave? Are they in Eretz Israel? Do they still resemble Jews?[30]

The excessive zeal of the triumphalist Zionist of the first decades of Israel continues to be the target of criticism, particularly by religious Jews. In the early years of the state several hundred children of Yemeni immigrants were taken from their parents in order to make them into true Israelis, on the secular model of the New Hebrew individual. Government authorities apparently assured the immigrant parents that their children were dead. Only years later, when some of these same parents received conscription notices from the army, were their suspicions aroused.[31] The kidnapping of the Yemeni babies during the early years of the Zionist state could be seen not only as a simple act of profit-seeking through their sale to Ashkenazi Jews, but also as part of a much larger modernization scheme. Physicians, nurses, and social workers contributed, each in their own way, to guarantee a European-style future to Jews who would otherwise have remained "prisoners of their Arab past."

The Yemeni immigrants, renowned for their devotion to the Torah and for their Torah knowledge, were subjected on their arrival in Israel at the end of the 1940s to a secularist re-education campaign, often in isolated camps. The measure was intended primarily for the young people who, without necessarily being kidnapped, were subjected to a campaign designed to estrange them from tradition. Physical coercion was brought to bear, particularly when secularist camp commanders sought to restrict access by religious young Jews who were attempting to bring relief to their interned brethren. The Knesset was the scene of the following description, by an Israeli legislator:

> I cannot employ other terms to describe the situation prevailing in these camps but spiritual constraint and inquisition against the Jewish faith. I see nothing else in what is being done in these camps than a cultural and religious murder of the tribes of Israel.[32]

Indeed, their Zionist educators obliged the young Yemenite Jews to harvest oranges on the Sabbath, to go about with their heads uncovered, to cut off the curls that they had always worn in their homeland. For many Yemenites, the contrast with their country of origin could not have been more acute:

The Arabs whom we lived among did not bother us, not even in the slightest of our religious observances. Quite the opposite: the government recognized our religion, our rights and our faith. If an official or a member of the police force happened to be among us on the Sabbath, he would not dare smoke, nor profane the Sabbath in any way whatsoever. But here they commit outrages; they force us to profane the Sabbath; they mock us, deride our traditional faith, our prayers and the religious observance of our Holy Torah.[33]

The fate of the Jews living in the Arab countries had, at the same time, become a major subject of controversy: the Zionists encouraged the spread of accounts of atrocities that were said to have been committed against Jews, while their opponents held that it was the fault of Zionism that relations with the Muslims had so deteriorated. From the Zionist point of view, Jews residing in the Arab countries had no other choice than to flee for their lives by migrating panic-stricken to Israel. They were to be seen as refugees, exactly like the Palestinians in 1947–49; what had happened was an exchange of populations, a kind of rough justice after the fact. A thoroughgoing revision of the history of the Jews in Muslim countries has been underway since the end of the 20th century, in an effort to integrate that history into the essentially Ashkenazi narrative of endless suffering, thus reinforcing the Zionist perspective. At the same time, there exist ample testimonials to the existence of good-neighborly relations between Jews and Muslims in those countries, including the Holy Land.

Chapter Seven

Jewish Opposition to Zionism

Zionism was, at its inception, a marginal movement. Opposition to the Zionist idea was articulated on the spiritual and religious as well as the social and political levels. Most practicing Jews, both Orthodox and Reform, rejected Zionism, referring to it as a project and an ideology that conflicted with the values of Judaism. Jews who joined various socialist and revolutionary movements saw Zionism as an attack on equality and as an attempt to distract Jewish masses from pursuing social change. Finally, those who, thanks to the Emancipation, had integrated into the broader society and become dedicated liberals were convinced that Zionism was, no less seriously than anti-Semitism, a threat to their future. Jewish nationalism was thus rejected because it was seen to imperil not only Judaism but also the social status and political values of the emancipated Jews.

Religious and Spiritual Opposition

The outlook of the Zionists, and their ideas, were to a great extent foreign to Judaism. Opposition to Zionism is far from circumstantial, it is fundamental:

> It was the Zionist threat that offered the gravest danger, for it sought to rob the traditional community of its very birthright, both in the diaspora and in Eretz Israel, the object of its messianic hopes. Zionism challenged all the aspects of traditional Judaism: in its proposal of a modern, national Jewish identity; in the subordination of traditional society to new life-styles; and in its attitude to the religious concepts of diaspora and redemption. The Zionist threat reached every Jewish community. It was unrelenting and comprehensive, and therefore it met with uncompromising opposition.[1]

While the respected Israeli intellectual Boaz Evron argues that "Zionism is indeed the negation of Judaism,"[2] the words that, for decades, have been inscribed on the walls of the Haredi quarter of Meah Shearim in Jerusalem echo this basic position: "Judaism and Zionism are diametrically opposed to each other." Such declarations, published regularly in the Haredi press and occasionally in mainstream media,[3] reiterate the claim that the state of Israel not only does not represent the Jews, it is hostile to their interests.

Zionists themselves have looked with disdain upon all forms of Judaism: "Ben-Gurion saw Judaism as the historical misfortune of the Jewish people and an obstacle to its transformation into a normal nation."[4] Furthermore, in attempting to gain the sympathies of the governing elites of Russia, the United Kingdom and elsewhere, Zionists presented their movement as an antidote to the radicalization of the Jewish masses. Zionism denounced the emancipation of the Jews and the liberal values that nurtured it as a shortsighted and dangerous illusion.

While political opposition to Zionism has a modest presence in the historiography of the movement, religious opposition is for the most part lacking. Even though Jewish religious opposition to Zionism—a variant of the more general phenomenon of religious opposition to nationalism[5]—is well known, it is rarely broached in the histories of Zionism. Zionism thus signifies a rupture not only in Jewish history but also in historiography that appears to follow the ideological imperatives of the moment.

Aside from a handful of monographs and collections of essays devoted specifically to the history of relations between Zionism and Judaism,[6] the great majority of the history books written in Israel and elsewhere hardly mention rabbinical resistance. Even the "New Historians" who pay serious, and even sympathetic, attention to Arab opposition to the Zionist enterprise tend to ignore the Jewish opposition and the Zionist establishment's reactions to it. Polemical and adversarial literature that reflects the religious anti-Zionist viewpoints is quite abundant,[7] but little used in the historiography of Zionism and of the state of Israel.

In the European Jewish world of the late 19th century, the Zionist movement, even though its Protestant origins were then little known, appeared as an incongruous and threatening paradox. One the one hand, it claimed to be a modernizing movement that had risen up against Jewish tradition; on the other, it idealized the Biblical past, utilized traditional symbols, and aspired—it claimed—to realize the millennial dream of the Jews. In his intellectual history of Zionism, Avineri observes that:

> Jews did not relate to the vision of the Return in a more active way than most Christians viewed the Second Coming. As a symbol of belief, integration, and group identity it was a powerful component of the value system; but as an activating element of historical praxis and changing reality through history, it was wholly quietistic.[8]

Sincere secular commentator that he is, Avineri acknowledges that it would be, to use his own words, "banal, conformist and apologetic" to link Zionism to the traditional religious longing for the land of Israel. It would be better to speak of a transformation of Jewish consciousness than of the triumphal conclusion of centuries of yearning for the Holy Land. The ensuing transformation of messianic aspirations took place under the influence of several factors, one of which, as we have seen, is located outside of strictly Jewish experience, and is of Protestant origin.

The messianic nature of the return to Zion raised suspicions that any Zionist or "proto-Zionist" initiative might in fact be false messianism. Zionism offers, above all, a new definition of what it meant to "be Jewish." According to the Israeli historian Yosef Salmon:

> Put briefly, the general Haredi conception of Zionism was of a secularizing force in Jewish society, following in the footsteps of its predecessor, the Haskalah movement. Since its major programs were associated with the Holy Land—the object of traditional messianic hopes—it was infinitely more dangerous than any other secularizing force in Judaism and, accordingly, it had to be attacked.[9]

Seen in this light, the opposition between the Zionists and their adversaries was so fundamental that it antedated the First Zionist Congress, held in Basel in 1897. Three years before then, Rabbi Alexander Moshe Lapidos (1816–1906), a leading Russian rabbinical authority, expressed his disappointment with Hibbat Tzion's first attempts to establish colonies in Palestine in the early 1880s:

> We thought that this sacred sapling would be a sapling true to the Lord and to His people, and that it would restore our souls .... But O weariness! While still in its infancy it sent forth weeds and its evil odor is wafted afar. ... We withdraw our support and shall stand aside and oppose them to the best of our ability, for we muster our forces in the name of the Lord.[10]

Moreover, Rabbi Samson Raphael Hirsch (1808–1888), a pillar of enlightened Orthodoxy in Europe, refused from the very beginning to support the Zionist movement.

Given that Zionism is a European-inspired movement, imitation of the "nations" became a recurring theme in Judaic critique of Zionism:

It manifestly is absurd to believe that we have been waiting for 2,000 years in so much anguish, with such high hopes and with so many heart-felt prayers merely in order to finish up by playing the same role in the world as an Albania or a Honduras. Is it not the height of futility, to believe that all the streams of blood and tears, to which we ourselves can bear witness in our own time apart from the testimony of our ancestors, should have been fated to the acquisition of this kind of nationhood which the Rumanians [sic] or Czechs, for instance, have achieved to a *greater extent* of success without all these preparations?[11]

As early as the First Zionist Congress in 1897, the influential Viennese rabbi and historian Moritz Güdemann (1835–1918) rejected any attempt to separate the Jewish nation from its monotheistic faith.[12] In his view, the Torah should be free of territorial, political, or national considerations. Jewish nationalism would, in spiritual terms, be a step backward with regard to the sublime vision of the messianic realm that the Jews had developed in the diaspora. To return to a pagan concept of Jewish nationality would be a self-destructive form of collective assimilation for the Jews.

As we have seen, to a great extent Zionism became a "Russian affair," and as such, it was altogether natural that resistance to it would come from Russian rabbis. In the Romanov Empire, opposition to Zionism turned fierce. Several rabbis set up a "black bureau" (*lishka ha-shehora*) to propagate anti-Zionist ideas. These rabbis, including Haim Soloveitchik, a leading innovator in Talmudic scholarship, were quick to grasp that Zionism, which offers a national identity devoid of any normative content, could be a balm to the conscience of those who wish to abandon the practice of Judaism.

The alliance of anti-Zionist forces produced, in 1900, a book entitled *Or la-yesharim* (*Light for the Righteous*), an anthology of rabbinical critique bringing together Hassidics as well as their opponents, the so-called Lithuanian Orthodox rabbis. It underscored the threat of Zionism for the survival of the Jewish people, and rapidly became a leading reference for critics of Zionism.[13] Two other major books presenting a cross-section of anti-Zionist religious opinions, *Orah le-Tzion* (*Light unto Zion*) and *Daat Ha-rabbanim* (*The Judgment of the Rabbis*), were published in 1902.[14] Among Russian rabbis, the reaction was categorical:

We are dumbfounded to learn that men who do not accept the yoke of the Kingdom of Heaven, who have never followed the path of our Holy Torah, who neither know nor truly love their brothers, boast that they are able to bring salvation to the House of Israel.[15]

Russia aside, the Zionists encountered the most stubborn resistance among the Hassidim of eastern Hungary and western Galicia. There, any expression of sympathy for Zionism is forbidden. The Hungarian Jews, particularly those from Satmar, achieved major stature among the bastions of anti-Zionism. The few Satmar Hassidim who survived the Second World War settled in Williamsburg and in Brooklyn, where they founded the Yetev Lev[16] congregation in 1948, with a scant dozen members. (Several years later, the congregation counted more than 1,000 families.[17]) Satmar groups soon sprang into existence in Jerusalem and Bnei-Brak in Israel, in Antwerp, London, and Montreal, as well as in several Latin American cities. Now global in scope, the group has established links with other organizations, including the Neturei Karta, which is made up principally of the descendants of the Jerusalemites of the 19th and the early 20th centuries, who looked to the Satmar Rebbe as a spiritual leader. It was he who ruled that Zionism is a heresy, a denial of fundamental messianic belief, and a violation of the promise made to God never to take possession of the Holy Land by human effort.

The Haredim have largely remained faithful to the Jewish tradition, viewing exile and redemption as two qualitatively distinct conditions, and holding that the passage from one to another can only be abrupt and discrete, a quantum leap of sorts. Exile is by no means a simple matter of a postal address or of political sovereignty; it is a theological and cultural concept that implies the condition of the entire world. Redemption signifies a radical change that brings harmony to all humanity and extends far beyond the strictly Jewish realm. Exile is seen as a divine decree visited upon the Jews as punishment for their transgressions against the Torah. The Hassidim, more inclined to mysticism, see themselves as invested with the mission of "liberating" tiny sparks of the divine light inherent in all creation that are as scattered throughout the world, as are the Jews themselves. These sparks (or *netsutsot*) are believed to contribute to the establishment of the Divine dwelling on earth, which according to Kabbalah is the ultimate purpose of creation.

While most of the opponents of Zionism were Ashkenazi Jews, the Sephardim likewise formulated strong criticisms of Zionism. The Salonica-born Sephardic luminary, Hakham Jacob Meir (1856–1939), leader of the

Sephardic communities in Palestine, publicly attacked Zionism in 1928, at the ceremony in honor of Sir Herbert Plumer (1857–1932), the British high commissioner who succeeded Herbert Samuel in 1925. When the master of ceremonies presented Hakham Meir along with dignitaries associated with the Zionist apparatus, the rabbi protested vigorously and declared that he neither recognized nor belonged to that group. Moreover, he announced that all pious Jews must separate themselves from it. Along with Sonnenfeld, he drafted a letter to Plumer in which he condemned the Zionists and called upon the British authorities to free the traditional Jews from Zionist control.[18] The League of Nations later authorized the Haredim to remain outside of the increasingly influential Zionist establishment.

Their self-isolation ("right of exclusion" in the language of the day) came to a formal end with the declaration of the state of Israel in 1948, even though the anti-Zionists attempted to obtain at least equivalent status from the United Nations, successor to the League of Nations. While pro-Zionist organizations have been involved in long-term political activity, including some unrelated to Jewish issues, the anti-Zionist Haredim have only been able to make pinpoint breakthroughs whose impact is nonetheless felt.

With the establishment of the state of Israel, opposition to Zionist ideology, which was relatively easy to sustain, turned into opposition to the state, which was present in many spheres of everyday activity. Most Haredi residents of Palestine have become Israeli citizens, but their collaboration with the state does not make acceptance of it either desirable or legitimate. In fact, a majority of Haredi Jews and their rabbis have accepted the state of Israel as a *fait accompli*, and then only as a Jewish community in need of the social and other services normally offered by a state. They reject Zionist thought, whether secular or religious, do not observe Independence Day or any other official holiday, and like the majority of Haredim, avoid contact with the secular majority. Their sons do not serve in the Israeli army and their daughters perform the obligatory alternative service not at all; many do not come to a standstill when, every year, sirens summon the population to observe a minute of silence, in commemoration of the soldiers who died for the state of Israel and of the victims of Nazi genocide.

Refusal to ascribe any Jewish value to the state of Israel has made it possible for some Haredim to deal with it as they would have with any other state. Thus certain Haredi leaders justified their participation in

Israeli governments by arguing that Jews, who continue to be in exile, have always sent representatives to deal with political leaders in order to protect the interests of the community. Likewise, the Haredim reasoned, they could dispatch delegates to the Israeli government in order to defend the interests of pious Jews on a wide range of issues. The positions taken by Rabbi Eliezer Menahem Schach (1898–2001), a respected Haredi leader, to a great extent determined Haredi attitudes toward the Zionist state. He did not approve the colonization of the Palestinian territories occupied in 1967, terming it a flagrant provocation "against the nations." While a firm opponent of all forms of Zionism, he remained open to pragmatic and limited collaboration with successive Israeli governments. Rabbi Schach's positions were a mix of ideological intransigence and circumspect pragmatism. On the ideological level, he stood for uncompromising opposition to the state of Israel, which he termed "a revolt against the kingdom of God."[19] While taking care not to lend legitimacy to the official institutions of the state, on the practical level he focused on an overarching goal: to safeguard the Jews through the survival of the Orthodox minority.

As a result of Rabbi Schach's pragmatism, the Orthodox parties increased their participation in political affairs during the years that he was their leader. His was an approach that could be traced to Hazon Ish, who granted permission for Jews to participate in the Israeli political system while denying its legitimacy: "If a highwayman falls upon me in a forest and threatens me with arms, and I begin a discussion with him, so that he spares my life, does that mean that I recognize his legitimacy? No; for me, he remains a highwayman."[20]

Several groups, hailing from varying geographic, ideological, and cultural origins, both in and outside of Israel, share the pragmatic approach. The most recent Israeli Haredi group to take institutional form is the Shas political movement. Its rapid rise owes much to the influence of Rabbi Schach who, alongside Rabbi Ovadia Yossef (1920–2013), the former Sephardic chief rabbi of Israel and an uncontested authority on Jewish law, provided the link between Haredi anti-Zionism and the frustrations felt by many Arab Jews in Israel.

The Jews who emigrated from Arab countries encountered stronger cultural pressures in Israel than did the European Ashkenazi Jews. The New Yishuv (Zionist settlements) and the state of Israel, as we have seen, largely reflected the realities faced by Jews in the Russian Empire. Most Jews who lived in the lands of Islam found the resulting culture alien to them. Their quality of life had often been much better than that of Jews in Christian Europe.[21] Their relations with their Muslim neighbors were more harmonious, more cordial; they spoke the local languages (Arabic, Farsi, Pashto) with greater fluency; and their history was far less marked by violence and persecution than that of their European co-religionists.

Shas is both a movement that seeks to promote Sephardic pride and a political party that boasts a network of educational institutions and social services.[22] Originally non-Zionist, its leaders can occasionally be heard to utter sharp criticisms of Zionism, all the while continuing to sit in the Knesset, where the party could boast more elected members than any other religious party by the turn of the 21st century.[23] The party relies principally on the ethnic vote of former citizens of Morocco and other Arab countries, who have embraced Zionist values as a path to modernity. The tension between the non-Zionist, even anti-Zionist positions of the Shas leaders, and the nationalist convictions of the electorate were finally resolved with the party's integration into the World Zionist Organization in 2010. The decision was dictated principally by donors in France and Latin America, upon whom Shas depends as a movement. But Shas, despite its official membership in the Zionist movement, continues to criticize the Eastern European secularist structures of the state.

At its inception, Shas was strongly influenced by the so-called Lithuanian Judaic outlook, which had opposed Zionism ever since the end of the 18th century. Lithuania, until the Second World War, had been home to several illustrious Talmudic academies, which stood as bastions against the Haskalah and against secularization throughout Eastern Europe. After the Nazi genocide, and in commemoration of the victims, the Lithuanian *yeshivas* and intellectual tradition spread to Israel and to several countries of the diaspora, with two centers situated in Bnei-Brak and Lakewood, New Jersey.[24] Rabbis who survived imbued their students with the central value of Talmudic studies, which continues to be handed down from generation to generation. The movement has also attracted thousands of recruits among young people from secularized families or, as in the case of the Shas electorate, of African or Asian origin. Certain orthodox groups of German and Alsatian origin grafted themselves onto the main branch of the Lithuanian tradition, historically opposed to Zionism.

A third group consists of the various Hassidic movements that emerged from the rabbinical dynasties of what are today Russia, Ukraine, Poland, Hungary, Slovakia, and Romania. Hassidism, an 18th-century mystical renewal movement, gave rise to a variety of trends structured around influential and often charismatic *rebbes*—heads of rabbinical dynasties. Though engaged primarily in the study of the Talmud, the Hassidim also devote particular attention to the sources of Jewish mysticism, as well as sayings of earlier *rebbes*. The most significant Hassidic movements in terms of their critiques of Zionism at different periods of the 20th century are those of Belz, Lubavitch, Munkacz, Satmar, and Vizhnitz. Most anti-Zionist activists emerged from these two groupings of East-European origin, the Lithuanian and the Hassidic.

Today all these groups have grown closer to Zionist positions, though to varying degrees. Shas has formally joined the Zionist movement; Aguda did not do so, but often adopts pro-Zionist policies (for example, against the return of the territories occupied in June 1967[25]), while the members of certain Hassidic communities have begun to serve in the armed forces. The adoption in 2014 of a law obliging Haredim to serve provoked mass protests, and its enforcement has been postponed for several years.

Elections to the Knesset provide an opportunity to protest about the very existence of the state of Israel.[26] Major Sephardic authorities have also taken Israeli elections as a symbolic *casus belli*. Yakov Mutsafi (1900–1983), a rabbi of Iraqi origin, joined the opposition to participation in Israeli elections, not only deeming them "impure," but consistent with his refusal to recognize the state of Israel, not accepting social welfare payments from Israel's National Security Institute.[27]

Principled opposition to Zionism was also the hallmark of Rabbi Israel Abuhatsera, better known as Baba Salé (1890–1983), revered by many Sephardim and quite a few Ashkenazim. It is said that when he completed reading *Vayoel Moshe*, a scholarly anti-Zionist work written by the Satmar Rebbe Yoel Teitelbaum (1887–1979), he called the author "a pillar of fire[28] whose radiance should lead us all to the arrival of the Messiah."[29]

This shows that while most of the opponents of Zionism were Ashkenazi Jews, the Sephardim also formulated a strong critique of Zionism. The Hakham Salomon Eliezer Alfandari, the "Holy Grandfather" of Istanbul (c. 1826–1930), was the living embodiment of the Sephardic opposition. He forbade all contact with Zionists and inspired other Jewish scholars to attack them publicly. Haim Shaul Dawik (1861–1932), a Sephardic kabbalist of Jerusalem, considered observant Zionists to be hypocrites capable of leading more Jews into error than could the secular Zionists, which brings to mind Hafetz Haim, who compared them to armed bandits (secular Zionists were, for him, unarmed bandits).[30] This school of thought clearly rejects Zionism for intrinsic reasons totally unrelated to the status of religion in the Zionist enterprise.

The Palestine partition plan drawn up by the Peel Commission touched off a negative reaction in Morocco, where Jewish and Muslim notables addressed a letter to the Foreign Office in London, in which they warned the British authorities "of disastrous consequences that would result in undesirable troubles between Arab and Jewish elements." The letter concluded with a call for "an independent Palestinian state to be governed by democratic parliamentary institutions, the only regime that can ensure both groups in Palestine equal rights in the country so dear to them".[31]

Independence Day is, for the adversaries of Zionism, an occasion to display their true colors with regard to the state of Israel. The most radical wear mourning sackcloth, burn Israeli flags, and raise the flag of Palestine. According to *Vayoel Moshe*, to celebrate Independence Day:

> [is] worse than to accept idolatry; it is not only that they accept, but that they celebrate and rejoice in the terrible insurrection against God and His Holy Torah. There are many sinners, and even miscreants, whose hearts are troubled because they do not serve God, but they are incapable of resisting the temptation of the false ideologies that have confounded them. But those who rejoice in their sin are guilty of something graver still: blasphemy.[32]

Most Haredim deliberately turn their backs on everything relating to the national holiday. Even more explicitly, one of the leading contemporary rabbinical authorities, Rabbi Moshe Feinstein (1895–1986), forbade decorating synagogues with the Israeli flag. The state of Israel, he argued, represents no Judaic value and cannot be associated with a Jewish house of worship.[33] Hazon Ish took an even more intransigent position, forbidding entry into a synagogue decorated with an Israeli flag even if there is no other synagogue in the vicinity.

In contrast with the messianic Zionism that has become dominant in National Judaic circles both in and outside of Israel, the precursors of that religious movement warned against precisely such an eventuality. Though it may seem surprising today, Rabbi Isaac Jacob Reines (1839–1915), founder of Mizrahi, which became National Judaism, inveighed against confusing settlement with messianic expectations.

In fact, one of the rare ideas shared by the earliest Zionist ideologues and the rabbinical majority was the negation of any messianic significance of Zionism. These atheist socialists naturally sought to distance themselves from Judaism and its yearning for the Messiah, of which they spoke with irony and condescension. "Israel has no Messiah, so set to work!" thundered the poet Brenner in 1910.[34]

Leading rabbinical authorities condemned the attempt to reconcile Zionism with Jewish tradition undertaken within the framework of National Judaism. Indeed, though the Mizrahi precursors of National Judaism were then rather moderate, their followers now see their movement as part of a "profound revolution within Judaism," more radical than the one that had driven the rise of Reform Judaism at the beginning of the 19th century.[35]

From within National Judaism, whose entire *raison d'être*, as its name indicates, is a commitment to Zionism, we also hear criticism of the state of Israel. In fact, within the heart of National Judaism, whose followers constitute the spearhead of the settlers' movement, there is no longer unanimous support for the state of Israel. After the withdrawal of the Zionist settlements in the Gaza Strip in 2005, deep disenchantment pervaded this normally active and vigorous camp.

"The Jewish character of the state," a concept central to National Judaism and undoubtedly one of the main roots of the conflict in the Holy Land, remains nebulous. For some, it signifies a judicial system based on the *Halakhah* (Jewish law), for others the occupation by the Jews of all the territories mentioned in the Hebrew Bible as comprising the "Promised Land."

But it is principally in the demographic sense that the expression is increasingly being understood. The state's Arab citizens are presented as a threat, even as a "demographic bomb,"[36] which makes it more appropriate to redefine Israel as a non-Arab rather than a Jewish state.[37] The establishment of this state against the will of the nations bordering it, as well as against that of the Palestinian majority of the day, has combined to condemn Israeli society to chronic violence. It also produced a visceral rejection of Arabs, which is felt in many ways, from the increasingly popular demand to deny them citizenship to the appeals signed by hundreds of rabbis calling upon people not to rent apartments to Arabs.[38] Invocations of the "Jewish character of the state" appear increasingly to be a justification for the wholesale expulsion of Arabs.

For many observant Jews, the state of Israel has nothing to do with redemption. For them, the land of Israel has no absolute value detached from the Torah. For the fifth Lubavitch Rebbe, Shalom Dov Baer Schneerson (1860–1920), to seek freedom from the yoke of exile is as pernicious as to seek freedom from the yoke of the Torah. In order to escape their fate as Jews, the Zionists must abandon the Torah and the faith of Israel:

> In order to infuse our brethren with the idea of being a "nation" and an independent polity ... the Zionists must give nationalism precedence over the Torah because it is known that those who cling to the Torah and the commandments are not likely to change and accept another identity, especially such as is implied in leaving exile by force and redeeming themselves by their own power.... Hence, in order to implement their idea, the Zionists must distort the essence [of Jewishness] in order to get [the Jews] to assume a different identity.[39]

It comes as no surprise that anti-Zionist discourse often resembles that favored by those who prefer a more "oriental" society, which in the context of the Eastern Mediterranean would be more authentic. From its earliest days in the Holy Land, Aguda set itself above ethnic barriers and defended all the Haredim, Ashkenazi as well as Sephardi, who were looked down upon by the primarily atheist Zionists from Russia. Both the so-called Oriental Jews (that is, those originating from outside Europe) and the Arabs frequently considered the Ashkenazi elites as their common foe. For example, Rabbi Blau established close relations with the Black Panthers, a protest movement that spread to Jews of North African origin in the 1970s.

Religious critics also pointed out that the threat posed by Zionism was particularly grave in that it closed off the path of repentance. Those who embraced Zionism saw themselves as "good Jews," deplored the fifth Lubavitch Rebbe at the beginning of the 20th century. He noted that Zionism had not brought a single Jew back to Judaism, but had, on the contrary, taken many more far from the truth. Zionism, its promoters argued, should be seen as a successor to Judaism, which would in turn be reduced to the role of a respected but outmoded predecessor. The analogy with Christianity, which claimed to replace Judaism, seems clear; Schneerson was to repeat it more than once.[40]

Schneerson acknowledged the powerful attraction Zionism wielded over the Jews. It spoke a modern language, invoked Jewish symbols to achieve emotional impact, and lent meaning to the life of a Jew whose attachment to the Torah was either weak or nonexistent. But, he warned, appearances were deceptive. He compared Zionists to swine, which have cleft hooves—the signs of a kosher animal—and when they lie down and stretch out their legs, appear to be kosher. But, he cautioned, the Torah forbids swine: "he is unclean to you" [Leviticus, 11:7].[41]

Aside from the basic texts—the works of Rabbis Wasserman and Teitelbaum—a series of stories transmitted by word of mouth have inspired Haredi rejection of the state of Israel. One of these stories relates that when the venerated Hazon Ish received prime minister Ben-Gurion, who was at the time attempting to neutralize Haredi opposition to the newly founded state, the rabbi neither shook his hand nor looked him in the eye. It was apparent that he was acting out of respect for the Talmudic prescription that forbids looking upon the face of an evil-doer.[42]

The European origins of Zionism do not alone explain the rabbinical rejection of Zionism. Its connection with the ambient Western culture is not the only reason for the intensity of criticism. Hassidic rabbis, many of whom remain aloof from Western culture, share the anti-Zionist opinions of the disciples of the German rabbi S. R. Hirsch, who accept and even admire European culture, as well as some Reform rabbis both in Europe and the United States. In comparison with Zionism's followers, the number of its opponents remains quite modest, at most several hundred thousand.[43] But, Ravitzky and other Israeli experts argue, their influence can be felt in much larger numbers of Haredi Jews.

Reform Jews, based on their own interpretation of the Torah, have also been critical of Zionism. Like the majority of streams of Judaism at the beginning of the 20th century, the Reform movement stood in firm opposition to the new ideology. The reforms advocated by the new movement, which originated in northern Germany at the beginning of the 19th century, included a weakening of the ethnic dimension of Judaism. Its followers became "Germans of the Mosaic persuasion" and abandoned all reference to the return to Zion shortly before the Reform movement branched out into the United States in the mid-19th century. Today, the majority of American Jews are members of Reform synagogues. At the inauguration of the first Reform synagogue in the United States, in 1841, these words were heard: "This house of worship is our Temple, this city our Jerusalem, this country our Palestine."[44]

Prior to the rise of political Zionism in Europe, the program of Reform Judaism adopted in Pittsburgh, Pennsylvania, in 1885, rejected all forms of Jewish nationalism and anticipated, to a certain extent, the rapid growth of political Zionism in Europe.[45] Reform Jews were thus prepared to refute Herzl's Zionist theory, which postulated the absolute existence of anti-Semitism, which would in turn justify a state for the Jews. They "detested both the premise and the conclusion of Zionism, i.e., that anti-Semitism was an absolute condition in all nation-states wherein Jews constituted a minority, and that a separate nation-state was a necessity."[46] Mocking "Zionomania," they considered it every Jew's duty to join in against Zionism. "A sober student of Jewish history and a genuine lover of his co-religionists sees that the Zionist agitation contradicts everything that is typical of Jews and Judaism," Rabbi Louis Grossman (1863–1926), professor of Hebrew Union College, the Reform movement's rabbinical academy in Cincinnati, Ohio noted in 1899. The president of the college, Rabbi Kaufmann Kohler (1843–1926), added in 1916, "Ignorance and irreligion are at the bottom of the whole movement of political Zionism"[47]

In 1919, a petition was presented to President Woodrow Wilson entitled "A statement to the Peace Conference." It reflected the then dominant Reform position on Zionism and Palestine. Signed by prominent Jewish Americans, including a former U.S. ambassador to the Ottoman Empire, Henry Morgenthau (1856–1946), and the publisher of the *New York Times*, Adolph Ochs (1858–1935), the petition criticized Zionist efforts to segregate Jews "as a political unit… in Palestine or elsewhere," and underlined the principle of equal rights for all citizens of any state "irrespective of creed or ethnic descent." It also noted that "most inhabitants of Palestine were then non-Jews, suggesting that conflict between Jews and non-Jews could erupt if a Jewish state were created."[48] The same year, Morris Jastrow (1861–1921) of the University of Pennsylvania, one of the signatories of the petition, published a book subtitled *The Fallacies and Dangers of Political Zionism*.[49]

Reform Judaism's anti-Zionism reached its high point during the Second World War when, in 1944, one of its most outspoken members described the idea of a Jewish state as a "Hitlerian concept."[50] The subsequent decline of this kind of anti-Zionism can most easily be explained by the feelings touched off by the catastrophe of European Jewry and the humanitarian arguments voiced by the Zionist movement at the time. Despite their decline, certain groups within the Reform movement continued to oppose the existence of the state of Israel for reasons similar to those put forward by the activists of Neturei Karta. In a speech before an Arab audience in Jerusalem before the Six Day War, Rabbi Elmer Berger (1908–1996), Reform anti-Zionism's best-known representative, asserted that the Zionist threat weighed heaviest against the Jews who "may be [its] last and most tragic victims."[51] The prophetic tone could well have belonged to the anti-Zionist rhetoric of the Hassidic movement, which stands remote indeed from Reform Judaism. The apparent coincidence suggests that rejection of Zionism may well be based on a Jewish religious sensibility shared by a great many, despite the persistent ideological divisions within Judaism.

Reform rabbis focused on the priority of religious identity, and deplored its transformation into a national, and even a racial, concept. In rejecting the new nationalism, in the mid-1940s they proposed the creation of a democratic structure in Palestine in which "neither religious faith nor ethnic derivation would be a deterrent to full participation in the national polity."[52] The Zionist leadership opposed the Reform model, for it threatened the primacy of a Jewish national identity. This fundamental rejection of liberal values introduced a discordant note into the state of Israel's relations with the majority of Jews who made their lives in the world's liberal democracies.

In the 1930s, the Reform movement softened its opposition to the transformation of traditional Jewish identity into a national identity, and adopted an even more conciliatory approach after the Six Day War. Principled anti-Zionism in the ranks of Reform Judaism has survived mainly within the American Council for Judaism, but the synthesis of Reform Judaism and Zionism remains a challenging concept. "Reform Judaism is spiritual, Zionism is political. The outlook of Reform Judaism is the world. The outlook of Zionism is a corner of western Asia," declared Rabbi David Philipson in 1942.[53] Some even asserted that by accepting Zionism the Reform movement had rejected its very philosophical basis. For Reform Judaism, in other words, Zionism is as much of a departure from tradition as it is for Orthodox Judaism.

In today's diaspora, Zionist organizations, far and away stronger than the handful of opposition groups, often bring moral, economic, and even physical pressure to bear against their critics. Threats of reprisal are commonplace for those who refuse to display solidarity with Israel. Arguments that call into question either Zionism or the state of Israel touch off hostile reactions. Indeed, it appears impossible to set up a loyal opposition to Zionism, since the attitude is that "You are either with us or against us." In this connection, the historian and former Israeli ambassador to France, Élie Barnavi, concluded that "deprived of its religious dimension, the dream of a 'Third Kingdom of Israel' could only lead to totalitarianism."[54]

Although the media based in Zionist-controlled Jewish communities have stifled anti-Zionist speech, the Western media have begun to discover Jewish religious anti-Zionism.[55] In their efforts to reach a wider public, critics of Zionism such as Neturei Karta have learned to use modern media, and despite their limited resources have organized protest campaigns, including televised opportunities to denounce the very existence of Israel.

The discourse of the religious critics of Zionism is also present on the Internet. Aside from several highly specialized sites,[56] echoes can be found on the sites of several international left-wing movements and on Arab and Christian sites. In this sense, the religious adversaries of Zionism are visible, even though Zionist circles treat them with contempt, presenting them as "enemy collaborators." In attempting to demonstrate that their anti-Zionism is "not stabbing Jews in the back," they broadcast their views to the widest possible audience, which often finds it paradoxical that a group that seeks to maintain its distinctiveness is opposed to political independence in any form.[57]

The theological arguments put forth by the detractors of Zionism have hardly changed since their initial polemics at the end of the 19th century. Even though Jewish life has since undergone radical transformations and major tragedies, the anti-Zionists have integrated those events into the traditional schema of interpretation, barely modifying the way they express their views. Admittedly they have sharply criticized different aspects of Zionism and of the state of Israel: for some, it stands for the new Jewish identity liberated from the "yoke of heaven," while for others, it represents the militarism inherent in the Zionist enterprise. For still others, Israel stands as an obstacle to the advent of the Messiah.

The apocalyptic prophecies invoked by Zionism's early detractors appear today far better grounded in fact in a nuclearized Israel.[58] Israel's assertive policies and their defense in the name of all Jews by the Zionist organizations in various countries may thus be seen as an extraordinary source of danger. But insecurity experienced by diaspora Jews can only strengthen their Zionist convictions. It is a win–win game for Zionism.

Political and social opposition

Repeatedly, dating from its inception, Zionism has been accused of fomenting anti-Semitism. Racial anti-Semitism took form in Europe only a few years after the emergence of the secular Jewish identity which was indispensable for the emergence of Zionism. Even though it often proved a source of embarrassment, the Zionists frequently received support from anti-Semitic politicians in a number of countries. Herzl's contacts with the tsarist authorities as well as those cultivated by Vladimir Jabotinsky with the Polish anti-Semites underscore the conceptual compatibility of Zionism and anti-Semitism. The anti-Semites wished to be rid of the Jews; the Zionists sought to gather the Jews in the Holy Land. A recent study of the history of Palestine under the British Mandate has pointed up the assistance provided to Zionism by anti-Semites in the Colonial Office in both London and Jerusalem, and the efforts of the Zionist leadership to cultivate the myth of a world Jewish plot.[59]

The connection between Zionism and anti-Semitism is not simply circumstantial, but deeply rooted in the concept of the Jew as belonging to a distinct and separate nation. Lord Balfour, author of the Declaration that bears his name, was opposed to Jewish immigration to the United Kingdom.[60] Today, several European right-wing parties with broad anti-Semitic antecedents are among the most ardent defenders of the state of Israel and of Zionism.[61] For more than a century, this coalition of interests has caused unease among many Jews.

Thus, the reaction of the emancipated Jews of Central and Western Europe to the Zionists was predictable: the latter were seen as the allies of the anti-Semites. Not only rabbis but also German, French, Austrian, and British Jewish notables were all but unanimous in their rejection of Zionism.

From the beginning the Zionist enterprise was rejected by those Jews who saw it as a threat to the process of integration into their countries of residence, as well as a reactionary project that would distract them from the struggle against discrimination and anti-Semitism. In reaction to the Balfour Declaration, Edwin Montagu, a well-known British statesman and a Jew, publicly accused his own government of anti-Semitism.[62] Across the Atlantic, Reform synagogues denounced the British initiative;

the predominately Jewish hatters' and garment workers' unions affiliated with the American Federation of Labor (AFL) refused to endorse the Zionist project.[63] At the same time, the American Protestant establishment enthusiastically endorsed the Balfour Declaration.

In France, the rabbinical establishment was unanimous: Zionism was "mean and reactionary." The Dreyfus trial did nothing to change that opinion. The Jews' identification with France and its republican values held uncontested primacy, which in no way undermined their solidarity with Jews of the Arab countries or of Russia. On the other hand, "the Jews of France always took pains to distinguish between their antipathy for nationalist ideology and their attachment to the Holy Land."[64] In the Netherlands, any Jew joining the Zionist organization risked excommunication.

Opposition to any form of cooperation with the Zionists was particularly consistent in Germany at the start of the 20th century. It should be remembered that the German Jews protested so strongly against the holding of the first Zionist congress in their country that the event was finally transferred to Switzerland.[65] German Jews considered as anti-Semitism any suggestion that they were not a part of the German nation. Since then, the Zionists have successfully inverted the definition of anti-Semitism:

> Another historical irony: there were times in Europe when anyone who argued that all Jews belong to a nation of alien origin would have been classified at once as an anti-Semite. Nowadays, anyone who dares to suggest that the people known in the world as Jews (as distinct from today's Jewish Israelis) have never been, and are still not, a people or a nation is immediately denounced as a Jew-hater.[66]

When the Zionists arrived in Palestine, they discovered a land where for centuries, Jews, Muslims, and Christians had been living side by side. That reality, with its old-stock residents, Jews and Arabs alike, did not correspond to the image borrowed from the Protestants, [67] of a "land without a people" promoted by the Zionists who claimed to represent a "people without a land." But for the Zionist ideologues, the land was empty: the picturesque traditional communities they encountered there were, for them, nothing more than a part of the landscape. Not only did the Zionists ignore the Arabs; they hardly noticed the traditional Jews, whose Sephardic majority were integrated into the Arabic-speaking local economy.

By the early 1920s it had become urgent to find a credible advocate to defend old-stock Palestinian Jews from the Zionists. Jacob de Haan,[68] the best-known political figure in the Haredi camp, fulfilled the need brilliantly. De Haan was the son of a practicing Dutch Jewish family; his father taught Judaism and officiated in the local Zaandam synagogue. Jacob studied law and became involved in human rights issues when, on the eve of the First World War, he visited political prisons in Russia and intervened on behalf of a small number of Jewish socialists (activities that might well have warranted his being considered a precursor of Amnesty International). After the war his Jewish identity asserted itself; he embraced Zionism and took up residence in Jerusalem in 1919. But his acceptance of Zionist principles would be short lived, as we shall see. For it was in Palestine that he intensified his religious practice and soon joined the Haredi circle of Rabbi Sonnenfeld. De Haan, poet, journalist, and barrister, was able to establish contact with influential circles in Europe, acting as "foreign minister" of Aguda. He successfully set up effective communication between the Haredim and two different worlds: those of the British authorities and of the Arab notables.

The November 1917 Balfour Declaration reinforced and formalized London's support for the Zionists, whose pretension to speak for all the Jews was now recognized by the United Kingdom. The anti-Zionists likewise turned to the British authorities and to international bodies, particularly the League of Nations, in an attempt to gain recognition as an independent community. The Haredim wished to be a part of any eventual political arrangement with the British. Their initiatives threatened to delegitimize the pretensions of the Zionists, who took very seriously the danger represented by de Haan: in London, he threatened to adversely affect their plans to position themselves as the exclusive representatives of the Jews in Palestine in the eyes of British decision-makers.

De Haan enjoyed influential contacts in the West and was ready to mobilize them to combat the Zionists and their designs on the traditional Jewish communities in Palestine. He had also to convince his interlocutors in London that the pious Jews represented no danger whatsoever for the local Arab population, with whose leaders he was in regular contact. He pointed to the utter lack of nationalist ambition among the traditionalist Jews, a crucial point that placed their position in a favorable light as tensions were growing in Palestine. But it was a point that often eluded observers of the day, who appeared to confuse the Zionists with their most tenacious detractors, primarily because the two groups both called themselves Jews. The traditionalist rabbis imputed to the Westerners, and particularly to the British authorities, the error of failing to distinguish between the Orthodox Jews who for generations had been living in the Holy Land, and the Zionist settlers.

"The Zionist analysis of the Arabs is an aberration for an Orthodox Jew who, like my husband, was born in the Old City of Jerusalem at the beginning of the century," wrote Ruth Blau. "As Rav Amram, the head of Neturei Karta, used to say, the Arabs have been transformed into a kind of universal enemy of the Jewish people. Nothing could be more false. The Jews and the Arabs lived side by side until the British, then the Zionists, decided that it was in their interest to sow discord."[69]

The rabbis of the Old Yishuv, who sought to ensure the security of the individuals who made it up, established connections with Arab leaders such as King Hussein of the Hijaz. Rabbi Sonnenfeld, who was then the leader of Aguda alongside Jacob de Haan, handed the king a petition intended to confirm the pacific intentions of the Orthodox Jews and to request that they be represented in any discussion of the future of Palestine:

> We assure His Majesty that the Jewish population relates to their neighbors with brotherly harmony wherever they exist, and also in the Holy Land we will adhere to that tradition and in the future will cooperate with all the inhabitants in the building and prospering of the land for a blessing and peace with all ethnic groups.[70]

Their meeting strengthened the ties of cooperation that de Haan had earlier established with Emir Abdullah, Hussein's son. The emir signed a document welcoming Jewish immigrants to Palestine, providing they not evince any exclusivist political ambitions, such as setting up a Jewish state. Abdullah's letter was read out to the Congress of Aguda Israel held in Vienna in 1923. A document of capital significance, the letter accepted the idea of mass Jewish immigration and the peaceful settlement of Jews in the land of Israel. But it excluded the concept of Jewish nationalism, which was foreign to both traditional Jews and the Arabs themselves. According to anti-Zionist sources,[71] the document vanished in the burglary of de Haan's house following his assassination by the Zionists one year later. With it vanished the possibility of peace expressed in terms of individual and equal rights. The nationalist objective of the

Zionists was to prevent that agreement from becoming a reality. But the fact that such a document existed reminds us that peace between Jews and Arabs had been—and remains—possible.

The radical policies of the Zionist immigrants from Russia opposed to the old-stock Jews of Jerusalem brought those plans to a screeching halt. The Jewish Agency, the executive arm of the Zionist movement, gained official status. Histadrut, the trade union federation founded by settlers from Eastern Europe, became the focus of the labor movement in Palestine, providing employment via its network of enterprises and social services that included a system of clinics, cultural clubs, and the like.[72] Since the earliest decades of Zionism, the leaders of the Old Yishuv had considered the Jewish settlers to be a more immediate danger than the native Arab population.[73] The Palestinian rabbis left not the slightest doubt about the origins of the violence that wracked the Holy Land: the Zionists and later the state of Israel were needlessly provoking the nations.

The memory of cordial relations between Jews and Arabs continues to motivate anti-Zionists, who differ from the strong-arm approach that they attribute to the Zionist concept of the state. From this perspective, the mighty Zionist arsenal has been counter-productive. Instead of bringing the advent of salvation, it has perpetuated violence, argue the anti-Zionists who see the state of Israel as the gravest danger now threatening the Jews. A three-volume work by a former BBC journalist intimately familiar with the conflict and its protagonists has recently echoed this view.[74]

As Rabbi Wasserman has noted, "At a time when the peoples talk increasingly about us, great is the danger which threatens."[75] In the context of the ceaseless media coverage of the conflict in the Holy Land, it is easy to understand why a number of anti-Zionist sources insist that all aggressive behavior must be avoided, for it can only be counter-productive.[76]

Convinced of Judaism's universal character, many of the anti-Zionist critics who address non-Jews wish to show the world that not all Jews are Zionists, and that they do not all identify with the state of Israel or with its actions in the name of the Jews. The following advertisement, published in the *New York Times* in 2001, a few days after the electoral victory of the nationalist right wing in Israel, provides an example of the kind of messages addressed to the general public:

In the aftermath of the elections in the state of Israel it has become a commonplace that religious Jews and their parties support a candidate who was in favor of slowing down or stopping the peace process. The impression has been created that ultra-Orthodox Jewry, in accordance with traditional Torah belief, are the staunchest supporters of maintaining Israel sovereignty over "territories" and the Temple Mount in Jerusalem.

In fact, nothing could be further from the truth.

The goal of Torah Jewry is to live in quiet piety and dwell peacefully with all nations and peoples. Those following this Divine agenda are not linked to any wars that are falsely depicted as Jewish wars but are, in reality, Zionist wars.[77]

The advertisement brought a new aspect of Zionism to a broader readership. The administrators of anti-Zionist websites have likewise noted that public interest, reflected in the number of hits registered, has been on the upswing for several years.[78] Their interest is stimulated by the persistent political opposition to Zionism driven by many Jewish thinkers and movements for more than a century.

Even though Jewish opposition to Zionism often assumes a political or social form, it reflects the prophetic tradition that informs it. There can be little doubt that the most explicit expression of this can be found in the work of the contemporary American Jewish theologian Marc Ellis, who not only calls Zionism into question, but also advocates that the fate of the Palestinians be given pride of place in the register of Jewish concerns.[79] In truth, Jews have been sharply critical of Zionist aggression against the local population of Palestine for over a century, at least since an article by Ahad Ha-Am published in St Petersburg after a visit to the Holy Land in 1891 that deplored the "reprehensible behavior" of the settlers, who were provoking anger and hatred.[80] A settler confirmed Ha-Am's observation in 1905, pointing, during a Zionist congress, to the "flagrant mistakes" committed by his comrades against the Arabs. "When we enter into our land we must forget any idea of conquest or deportation."[81]

Sigmund Freud, in 1929, attributed Arab violence to the "unrealistic fanaticism of our people," and refused to sign a public letter casting exclusive blame on the local Palestinian Arabs.[82] These warnings and criticisms, and many more, had little impact on Zionist policy, but proved that the prophetic tradition was still alive, even among those who were apparently far removed from ancestral Jewish practices.

The moral critique that flows from the prophetic tradition, mingled with the universalism of the Enlightenment, gave rise to a solid commitment to the solidarity and equality of all human beings.[83] The socialist convictions of many leading anti-Zionists strengthened the universalist vision that runs counter to any form of restrictive nationalism. Prophetic tradition sensitized and raised awareness, as it brought up burning questions without however offering political solutions. Some Jewish dissidents may deplore certain Israeli actions, all the while affirming Israel's legitimacy based on Jewish national liberation and historical justice. Others deny it that legitimacy and consider it to be "conceived in sin." They do not accept the myth of the self-evident innocence of the state of Israel. The first group, whose position is perhaps best articulated by the American intellectual Peter Beinart,[84] seeks to produce a "Zionism with a human face." It includes movements such as J-Street and Tikkun in the United States, and J-Call in Europe. The second group includes anti-Zionist Haredim, the International Jewish Anti-Zionist Network (IJAN), parts of the Jewish Voice for Peace, Independent Jewish Voices in North America, and the Union juive française pour la paix (UJFP, French Jewish Union for Peace)

More than a few advocates of the prophetic tradition, including Ellis, have paid a high price for their dissidence. But, some argue, "the world has paid an even higher price for ignoring their warnings."[85] Those who warned against the creation of a Zionist state saw their words treated with disdain, or at best with condescension. However, these same Jewish authors have proven to be prophetic in identifying early on the trends that have now appeared in Israeli society and in Jewish communities around the world. They had, in particular, foreseen the upsurge of chauvinism and xenophobia, the creeping militarization of society, and the growing popularity of fascist ideas. This is why their writings today warrant the most serious attention, rather than the "condescension of history."

The Jewish American historian Tony Judt (1948–2010) characterized the Zionist state as an anachronism, and immediately drew fire from supporters of Israel even though there was nothing either new or seditious about the idea. Meanwhile, another historian and long-time Zionist, Walter Laqueur, caused nary a ripple when he wrote, some 30 years earlier, that "the Zionists are guilty of having behaved like other peoples—only with some delay due to historical circumstances."[86] The Polish-born intellectual Isaac Deutscher (1907–1967) found in Zionism "the paradoxical consummation of the Jewish tragedy. … The world had compelled the Jew to adopt the nation-state and to make it his pride and hope just at a time when there is little hope or pride left in it."[87] Deutscher was conveying his views in 1958 to the Canadian Jewish Congress, today an improbable audience for such introspection.

In 1938, alluding to Nazism, Albert Einstein warned an audience of Zionist activists against the temptation to create a state imbued with "a narrow nationalism within our own ranks against which we have already had to fight strongly, even without a Jewish state."[88] Another world-renowned German Jew, the philosopher Martin Buber (1878–1965), a cultural Zionist, spoke out in 1942 against the "aim of the minority to 'conquer' territory by means of international maneuvers."[89] From Jerusalem, in the midst of the hostilities that broke out after Israel unilaterally declared independence in May 1948, Buber cried with despair, "This sort of 'Zionism' blasphemes the name of Zion; it is nothing more than one of the crude forms of nationalism."[90]

One of the objects of the humanist critique of Zionism is Zionism's discrimination against non-Jews. This is particularly evident in the portable citizens' rights that the settlers carry with them irrespective of their actual physical location. They were able to exercise their right to vote in national elections from the Occupied Territories in 1967, while the conquered local population was deprived of this political right. Several observers, including Meron Benvenisti, former deputy mayor of Jerusalem, characterized this system as "*Herrenvolk* [master race] democracy."[91]

Marxist critics are likewise universalists, but more ideological than their humanist counterparts. Leon Trotsky (1879–1940), "an observer at the Sixth Zionist Congress in Basel in 1903, branded Herzl a 'shameless adventurer' who had the impudence and 'devilish perfidy' to seek a fatherland for the Jews."[92]

Marxists, like humanists, did not accept the basic postulates of political Zionism, particularly the notion that hatred of the Jews is endemic and eternal. But the Marxists went further still, attributing it to class interests, pointing out that Zionism—which is conceptually similar to anti-Semitism—is a movement of the Jewish bourgeoisie and as such opposed to the interests of Jewish workers. They note that the Zionist project was, from its inception, financed by the capital of the high bourgeoisie, people such as the Rothschilds. It would thus be impossible to see it as being in the interests of the working class. The Bund, the most widespread Jewish Marxist movement in Eastern Europe before the Second World War, was critical of Zionism but accepted the legitimacy of a Jewish cultural autonomy that should, however, be exercised within the framework of existing states. Georgi Plekhanov (1856–1918), Russian Marxist theoretician and translator of Marx and Engels's *Manifesto of the Communist Party*, described the Bundists in ironical terms as "Zionists who suffer from sea-sickness."[93]

Another aspect of Zionism, its links with imperialism, was also a source of sustained Marxist criticism. The critics point out the dependence of the Zionist project on at least one major imperialist power. Nor was that dependence ever concealed: Herzl's initiatives were addressed solely to the Great Powers of the day. In fact, the support of the United Kingdom proved crucial during the Mandate period, of the Soviet Union at the time of the partition of Palestine, of France for the production of nuclear weapons, and of the United States throughout Israel's history.

Political and social criticism focused on the treatment of the Palestinians, the fate of non-Europeans in Israeli society, and the symbiosis of Zionist interests and anti-Semitic projects. But what drove Jewish opposition was the chronic violence attributed to Zionism, which explains the relatively substantial number of Jews in pro-Palestinian organizations around the world.

The Use of Force and Its Critics

The use of force by the Zionists, which may lead to a gamut of reactions in Jews, from boundless pride to embarrassment and even revulsion, is no stranger to the Torah. The Pentateuch and several of the books of the Prophets, such as Joshua and Judges, teem with violent images when read literally. Biblical Israel was conquered under conditions that could hardly be described as peaceful. But far from glorifying war, Jewish tradition identifies allegiance to God, and not military prowess, as the principal reason for the victories mentioned in the Bible. The Torah cautions: "He that is slow to anger is better than the mighty; and he that ruleth his spirit is better than he that taketh a city [Proverbs 16:32]." The metamorphosis in Jewish life that followed the destruction of the Second Temple of Jerusalem reinforced that sensibility.

For almost two millennia, Jewish tradition has emphasized a predominantly pacifist approach.[94] The Lubavitch Rebbe Shalom Dov Ber Schneerson confirmed that he regretted nothing of the Jewish tradition of political docility, which he judged to be a positive value. Not only does it guarantee survival; it is above all an act of devotion directed toward final redemption.[95]

The sense of revulsion toward war is clear and repeatedly uttered: "God did not send us into exile because we did not have an army, but because we had sinned."[96] The oral tradition interprets allegorically the biblical verses that speak of the instruments of war. Thus do the sword and the bow used by the Patriarch Jacob against his enemies [Genesis 48:22] become prayer and supplication [Bereshit Rabbah 97:6]. Tradition locates Jewish heroism in the study halls rather than on the battlefields.

From the Zionist standpoint, which reproduces and reinforces European nationalist values often in quite violent terms, it is better to choose an honorable death on the battlefield, or even collective suicide such as Masada and Gamla, rather than compromise with the invader. However, Jewish law allows people to expose themselves to mortal danger in only three situations: if forced, under threat of death, to practice idolatry, to kill another human being, or to engage in sexual relations forbidden by the Torah.

Many atheist Jews, primarily in the Russian Empire at the turn of the 20th century, found Jewish law, rather than violence, revolting. Religious Jews who remained patient in the face of injustice and persecution filled them with shame and impelled them to take fate into their own hands. The new sensibility first triumphed in imperial Russia and then spread, though to a lesser extent, to other Jewish communities. But the older tradition, the source of inspiration for those who oppose Zionism in the name of the Torah, has endured.

In Jewish tradition, two outstanding figures are credited with transforming Temple-centered Judaism into a Judaism that was at once more personal and more cosmopolitan. The first is Yohanan Ben Zakkai, a Torah scholar who, while trapped in Roman-besieged Jerusalem, first sent a note to the Romans that he was "an admirer of the Emperor," and then contrived to flee hidden in a coffin from the defenders of the city who had refused to permit anyone to leave. Tradition holds that he gained permission from the Romans to teach the Torah at Yavne, a small town southwest of Jerusalem. He thus became an emblematic figure in the emphasis on Torah study, as opposed to the struggle for political independence. The Torah replaced the land in its physical sense and became, to use the expression of Rabbi Weinberg, "the national territory."[97] Henceforth, the Jews were to be known as the "people of the Book"; their standard-bearer would be the scholar, the wise man, the *talmid hakham*, rather than the conquering general or the military hero. In today's nationalistic context, a figure like Yohanan Ben Zakkai would likely be seen as a "traitor" who abandoned his brethren in their struggle against the foreign invader. But Ben Zakkai's attitude toward military might continues to inspire many of the Judaic critics of Zionism.

The second outstanding figure was Judah the Prince, revered by Jews as the compiler of the Mishna. According to tradition, he had the clairvoyance to write down the oral Torah in the conditions that arose after the destruction of the Temple, when geographical dispersion of the Jews threatened to disrupt word-of-mouth transmission. A signal aspect of the life of Judas the Prince, as preserved in the Talmud, was his friendship, even intimacy, with Marcus Aurelius Antoninus, the Roman emperor of the day.

Both figures, Yohanan Ben Zakkai and Judah the Prince, embody a conciliatory attitude toward any occupying power and point up the sharp difference between the patriots who perished in armed or collective struggle (Masada, Gamla) and the rabbis who fled confrontation, preoccupied as they were by the survival and development of Judaism, and by extension of the Jews. There can be little doubt that the survival of the Jewish community owes much to these two "collaborationist" rabbis who hold such a prominent place in tradition.

Should the inhabitants of a town populated by Jews be endangered, however, Jewish law allows for self-defense, even on the Sabbath. It draws on the Talmud, which enjoins the Jews, "He that comes to kill you, rise up and kill him."[98] But tradition remains far removed from violence in any form, laying down the three character traits that must distinguish the Jews: they must be bashful, compassionate, and charitable.[99] The Talmud accords supreme value to peace, while downplaying the use of force.[100] Interpreters of the verse "seek peace and pursue it" [Psalms 34:15] postulate that it is the only precept that obliges Jews to "pursue the commandment"[101] in order to discharge it. However, if peace is not present it must be sought, with no regard for the effort to be made or the distance to be traveled. This tradition remained dominant until the 20th century, when National Judaism rehabilitated military heroism and political intransigence.

The radicals insisted that the Jews who for centuries had remained prostrate must be righted, both before their oppressors and before their volumes of the Talmud; they must be freed of the yoke of exile but also of the yoke of Jewish tradition, described as the "yoke of the heavenly kingdom": that is, allegiance to the Torah. It was a liberation that implied, among other things, greater recourse to the use of force. At the Second Zionist Congress, held in 1898, Max Nordau (1849–1923), one of the founding fathers of Zionism, called for the transformation of the Jews, who for him were "degenerates," into a *muskuljudentum*, a "muscular Jewry." He left no doubt about the origins of his inspiration. It was with the music of Richard Wagner, famous both as a composer and as an anti-Semite, that he chose to open his speech to the Congress.

From the outset, the pioneering Zionists projected onto Palestinian reality the clichés inherited from the Russia of old: the Arab threat was often likened to the murderous shadow of the pogroms. But they also behaved as colonialist groups in a foreign land in obtaining arms and assuming responsibility for the defense of their colonies. The mass arrival of European Jews after the Second World War and the Zionist interpretation of the Nazi massacres produced a cultural mix of great power: a self-image of the just victim.

The actual work of providing religious legitimacy for the use of force was left to the partisans of National Judaism. But the task was not a simple one: two of the precursors enlisted by religious Zionism—Rabbis Avi Hirsch Kalischer and Yehuda Salomon Hai Alkalai—proved to be more inspired by the heady atmosphere of 19th-century European nationalism than by the Jewish tradition. Avineri notes that the call to arms that reverberates in the writings of the two rabbis is based explicitly on the experience of the European countries that had recently won their independence.[102] Even among those rabbis who supported the Zionist enterprise we find lasting traces of Jewish pacifism. They continued to refer to one of the three oaths, not to "rebel against the nations,"[103] and affirmed that the return to Israel would not imply military force: "neither shall the sword go through your land" [Leviticus, 26:6].

The Israeli sensibility is quite different. According to the legendary general Moshe Dayan:

> Death in combat is not the end of the fight but its peak. And since combat is a part and at times the sum total of life, death, which is the peak of combat, is not the destruction of life but its fullest, most powerful expression.[104]

The Zionist mobilization of youth contrasted with the pacifist self-image of

the Jews, practicing or not, and quite naturally led to hostile reactions. Albert
Einstein, along with other Jewish humanists, in 1935 denounced the Betar
youth movement founded by Jabotinsky, calling it "as much of a danger to
our youth as Hitlerism is to German youth."[105] Einstein, who was close to
cultural and humanist Zionism, was openly opposed to the establishment
of a Zionist state in Palestine, and repeatedly criticized the rightward drift
of the Zionist movement in the 1940s.[106] Irving Reichert (1895–1968), a
Reform rabbi, pointed to a dangerous "parallel between the insistence of
some Zionist spokesmen upon nationality and race and blood and similar
pronouncements by fascist leaders in certain European dictatorships."[107]
Such parallels can be found in a memoir of life in a Lithuanian town between
the two world wars: "In Biliunas Street, a member of the Young Lithuania
movement wearing a green uniform met a member of Betar, in gray-brown;
they greeted each other raising their arms in the fascist salute."[108]

A substantial gap opened up between traditional Jewish sensibilities,
which placed a premium on conciliation, and the new value system that
called for total victory. Most rabbis also reacted with revulsion at the militarization of the Jews: rabbinical authorities, in their great majority, stood
against political violence. They warned that to defy the local population
could only lead to new disasters, and remained faithful to the tradition
that favored compromise, and even emigration, rather than confrontation
with local populations and governments.[109]

The political and military positions of National Judaism came under
sustained attack from Haredi critics. Worst of all, the critics claimed,
National Judaism was complicit in murder, as it had fomented wars in
which thousands had died. Aguda's participation in successive Israeli governments, including the one that launched the war against Lebanon, drew
similar accusations. No one, the religious critics thundered, had the right
to send Jews off to war, both because of the prohibition against the use of
force, and for humanitarian reasons: "They decided irresponsibly to send
thousands of Jews to war without considering the anguish and sorrow of
the mothers and fathers whose children would be killed."[110]

At the height of the war triggered by the unilateral proclamation of
the state in 1948, which Ben-Gurion saw as "a revolutionary act devoid
of formal authority,"[111] several old-stock inhabitants of Jerusalem proclaimed, "We will not allow you to drag us, our wives and our children,
off to die, God forfend, in the name of Zionist idolatry."[112] Absent from
their attitude was the slightest trace of patriotism or ethnic solidarity,

but quite clearly not the survival instinct. Against prevailing opinion, the anti-Zionist Haredim understood that the danger came from the Zionists and from the insolence of those impious Jews who took themselves for masters of the world.

Israel's military victories naturally posed serious questions for those who condemned Zionism. How could such wicked people enjoy such military success? Contrary to the proponents of National Judaism who saw those successes as miracles and thus as a sign of divine benevolence, the anti-Zionist Haredim attributed victory to Satan's work. They could not imagine how God could possibly have assisted those who they considered idolaters.[113] The lines were clearly drawn: the victory of 1967 was a work of either divine providence or Satan, who created mirages of redemption in order to misguide the innocents. Between the two extremes of this polarized vision there remained no room for a compromise interpretation. For the detractors of Zionism, victory formed a part of a continuum of destruction that came into being with the rise of Zionism, by way of the Nazi massacres, and must inevitably end with its decline and fall.

The partisans of National Judaism have on occasion deplored the cult of force, which was often tinged with racism and intolerance. Yitzhak Blau, a rabbi in a nationalist *yeshiva* on the West Bank, demonstrated how religious sources had been systematically deformed in order to extract from them warlike teachings.[114] He showed that many rabbis used the Torah to denigrate the value of compassion, to promote xenophobia and to make the occupation of the land a supreme value. Rabbi Blau has since returned to the United States.

The better to illustrate the cruelty of the Jewish national liberation movement, the critics of Zionism often cite the first Jewish political assassination in the land of Israel for centuries, the murder of Jacob Israel de Haan, spokesperson for Agudat Israel.[115] One of the first Dutch Jews to immigrate to Palestine for Zionist reasons, he was lionized by Jerusalem high society and quickly gained entry to the most influential circles. His dispatches, published in the Netherlands at that time, reflected his boundless confidence in Zionism. Gifted and creative as a barrister, in 1920 he organized a spectacular defense of Vladimir Jabotinsky, who had been accused of anti-Arab violence. However, his acquaintance with Jabotinsky and other leaders of the future Israeli right wing, quite a few of whom were fascinated by European fascist movements,[116] rapidly distanced de Haan from Zionism.

He became aware of the threat inherent in the violent side of Zionism, for both the pious Jews and the Arabs. De Haan openly deplored the aggressive nature of the Zionist enterprise and allied with Agudat Israel, becoming shortly thereafter a spokesperson for religious anti-Zionism. He took due note of the conflict with the Arabs that Zionist activists were fomenting through discriminatory hiring policies, moral laxity, and nationalist aspirations which had until then been foreign to the region.

De Haan's dispatches, published in Europe, began to assume an anti-Zionist tone. He laid bare the financial machinations of the Zionist organizations, and held their leaders up to ridicule before their Western financial supporters. De Haan was well acquainted with Zionist circles, and with the Western audience to which his reports were addressed. His articles set forth an alternative to the Zionist movement, and articulated visions of harmony between religious Jews and Arabs under the benevolent tutelage of the United Kingdom. He had begun to think seriously about setting up an anti-Zionist coalition that would have included Agudat Israel and other religious Jewish groups, as well as Arab notables. An alliance of Jews, Muslims and Christians for peace stood poised to discredit the minority Zionists who, imbued with a sense of mission, insisted that they alone could speak for the Jewish people. They ostracized, demeaned and insulted de Haan.

De Haan began to receive death threats, but he refused either to leave Palestine or to abandon his anti-Zionist activities. Finally, when a newspaper drew attention to his intention to establish an anti-Zionist movement on his return from a trip to London, agents of the Haganah gunned him down as he came out into the street after prayers. A Haganah historian gave this account of the assassination and its motives:

> Agudat Israel had thrust itself into the midst of a communal struggle. Until the First World War, the Old Yishuv was in control. They had comprised the majority of the Jewish population and now felt like prisoners in their own home. The Old Yishuv refused to surrender and submit to secular domination. ... When they broke away and formed an independent community ... no one disturbed them. Were it not for de Haan, they would have organized their own small community devoid of any political or communal significance. De Haan used his connections to move the struggle into the realm of international politics. He aspired to establish a political organization to rival the Zionist movement, which was still in its infancy and not yet fully established—this was the danger of de Haan.[117]

The Zionists feared that de Haan would succeed in setting up a rival organization comprised of leading rabbis who would reject the nationalist ambitions of the Zionist movement and establish cooperative relations with Arab leaders. Such an eventuality struck fear into the Zionists who, in demographic terms, were still a minority in Palestine.

David Tidhar (1897–1970), the British police officer in charge of the de Haan murder investigation, was also a Haganah agent. Only 40 years later were the accomplices to admit the organization's role in what had been a political assassination. Tidhar ultimately revealed his participation in a radio interview:

> After he [de Haan] had done so much damage, it was decided in the Haganah to remove him and not allow him to travel to London. If he would have continued to live, he would have caused trouble. I regret that I was not chosen to liquidate him. My job was to protect those who did. De Haan would come to *daven Minchah* [pray in the afternoon] in Shaarei Zedek's synagogue. I was the officer in charge of the Machane Yehuda precinct, most of whose policemen were Arabs. I was asked to insure that no Arab officers would be present in the station between three and five in the afternoon. I replaced the Arab officers with Jewish ones and informed them that if they heard gunfire they were not to move until receiving orders from me. After thus arranging matters with the police officers, I moved into the area and waited for the shots.[118]

The order to "eliminate the traitor" may well have come from the highest echelons of the Zionist movement, most probably from the future president of Israel, Itzhak Ben-Zvi (1884–1963), who was at the time intimately involved in Zionist paramilitary activities.

The description of de Haan as a "traitor" shed light once more on the influence of the Russian terrorist movements, much of whose rhetoric was adopted by the Zionists. Like the Bolsheviks, the Zionists considered all opposition to their political goals as illegitimate. Though they might tolerate tactical divergences within the movement, they could not countenance principled opposition to the Zionist project. Intolerance necessarily legitimized violence.

For today's critics of Zionism, the sad tale of de Haan stands as a reminder that the terrorism the Zionists brought with them from Russia to Palestine in the early years of the 20th century would ultimately be turned against their descendants in the closing decades of that century. Indeed, aside from the Haganah, which was responsible for the assassination of de Haan, several other armed organizations—such as Lehi and Irgun—perpetrated terrorist acts. Their leaders, Itzhak Shamir and Menahem Begin, went on to become prime ministers of Israel. What united these military organizations was the conviction that it was necessary to inculcate fear: in other words, to terrorize the adversary to ensure the triumph of the national ideal.[119] Ironically, terrorism boomeranged later to plague Israel as part of Palestinian resistance.

The assassination of de Haan achieved its aim: it brought contacts established between the anti-Zionist majority in the Holy Land in the 1920s and the world's great powers to a halt. In both cases, terrorism bore bitter fruit: discord among Jews and Arabs. Today the Haredim venerate de Haan as a martyr and as a Jew locked in the ongoing struggle for moral perfection. In the synagogues of the Masorti (Conservative) movement in Great Britain, recitation of his poetry is part of the Yom Kippur ritual.[120]

The rabbinical critique of the violence inherent in Zionism is often difficult to distinguish from that formulated by secularists, Jews and Arabs alike. Rabbi Amram Blau of Neturei Karta in Jerusalem accuses the Zionists of having no respect for human life: "they have proven to be irresponsible, extended their rule over parts of the Holy Land, which had been inhabited by Arabs, and thereby brought the entire Arab world into conflict with the Jewish community."[121] The analysis of Hannah Arendt, a secular German Jew assimilated into Western culture, barely differs:

> And even if the Jews were to win the war... [t]he "victorious" Jews would live surrounded by an entirely hostile Arab population, secluded inside ever-threatened borders, absorbed with physical self-defense.... And all this would be the fate of a nation that—no matter how many immigrants it could still absorb and how far it extended its boundaries (the whole of Palestine and Transjordan is the insane Revisionist demand)—would still remain a very small people greatly outnumbered by hostile neighbors.[122]

Criticisms of the use of force by the Zionists from rabbinical thinkers and secular Jewish intellectuals frequently resemble each other. Reform Jews and the Haredi Neturei Karta movement both reacted in like manner to Israeli military operations in Gaza.[123] When the chief Ashkenazi rabbi of Israel suggested placing Gaza's Palestinians in a town to be built in the Sinai desert, Neturei Karta, denouncing the government-appointed rabbi as a "Zionist stooge" and an "emissary of evil," demanded that he himself "be deported from the Holy Land."[124]

Zionism has undermined traditional Jewish attitudes to war. Scholarly historical research and historical novels have pointed up the contrast between the values of romantic virility embodied by the Christian royalty and aristocracy, and the deep-seated pacifism of their Jewish counselors.[125] But many modern-day leaders of Jewish organizations, as well as prominent Jewish public figures, are clear, albeit armchair, incarnations of the muscular Jewry sought by Nordau, who call on Israel and the United States to be tough with the Arabs. Many are former leftists, like the ex-Trotskyist and founder of neo-conservatism Irving Kristol (1920–2009) in the United States, and the ex-Maoist Alexandre Adler in France, who today espouse shrill right-wing positions.

It is not at all clear, however, that such leaders represent a real trend toward pugnacity among the Jews, particularly among the young.[126] Revulsion at the use of force continues to be dominant in Jewish life despite the incontestable impact of Zionism and the state of Israel on Jews for more than a century. The Jewish adversaries of Zionism remain, in their commitment to peace, quite close to the Jewish mainstream in the United States, and perhaps in many other communities.

Jewish anti-Zionists and New Historians are not alone in facing ostracism and accusations of washing Israel's dirty linen in public. Steven Spielberg, in his film *Munich*, pointed at the moral cost of the permanent use of force. He also showed the European nature of the Zionist project: all the protagonists are Ashkenazim. The film underscores the incompatibility of the Zionist project and the Jewish moral values. When one of the protagonists, a member of the commando team assigned to assassinate the Palestinian suspects in Europe, refuses to continue, he argues that "the Jew's vocation is to be just and not to behave like his enemies."

Unsurprisingly, the Israel lobby viciously attacked the director even before the film's release. It is easy to understand why Spielberg, a world-renowned figure and icon of the American Jewish establishment, shot his film in conditions of extreme secrecy, concealing the scenario even from the actors themselves, each one being privy only to their individual role.[127]

In his commentary on Zionist religious activism, Rabbi Sober, a graduate of Zionist schools and one of the translators of the Talmud into English, lashes out at the usurpation of divine will that he attributes to

National Judaism, where the Jewish concept of providence is employed to justify any Israeli action:

> The notion that we can do whatever we please, succumb to any kind of temptation, or engage in any form of foolish self-aggrandizement without fear of penalty because we have an inside track to the Almighty is the plain opposite of religious faith. It is in fact an affront to the Divine, whose authority to determine the course of history we are usurping. The traditional penalty for this sin is to be sent to face a hostile world with no lucky breaks, no Divine assistance whatsoever, until we learn that only those who are performing God's will can count on Him for assistance. Such blind faith is not really a faith in God at all, but rather faith in ourselves. It makes a tool out of the Almighty. It turns him into a kind of "secret weapon" whose purpose is to guarantee our success at whatever we fancy. It is an idolatrous concept that masks what is actually an irrational belief in our own invincibility.[128]

His warning came as a reaction to the growing tendency to "enlist God" for military service, particularly among the settlers in the West Bank who continue, as I write these lines, to defy the Arab population and to expand their settlements in the name of their version of Judaism. The settlers even turned on the Israeli army when it attempted to restrain them, attacking an IDF base in the West Bank, causing material damage and wounding an officer.[129]

In the course of the Israeli operation against Gaza in 2009–10, the press revealed a new tactic by the military rabbinate: to use Judaic texts to lend weight to calls for merciless repression of the Palestinian population.[130] One year later, a rabbi from Itzhar in the West Bank affirmed, in a book entitled *Torat ha-melekh* (*The King's Torah*) that the prohibition "Thou shalt not kill" (just like "You shall love your neighbor") applies only to Jews.[131] The 230-page volume consists of commentaries on the conduct of war, and promotes acts that the Israeli press described as terrorist in nature. For example, it is described as permitted, and even obligatory, to kill all those—Jews or non-Jews—who oppose Israeli military operations. By identifying the modern state of Israel with the realms of biblical Israel, the book advocates murder to children "who will grow up to hurt us." As on previous occasions, calls for murder by rabbis in the West Bank settlements have been followed by brief arrests of their authors. The book has been widely distributed, while neither its authors, nor its promoter, most of who are affiliated with National Judaism, have been reprimanded or fired from their positions as state-salaried rabbis. The counterpart of National Judaism in the United States, Modern Orthodoxy, particularly the Rabbinical Council of America, echoes the same line of argument, insisting that it is "incorrect to risk the lives of our soldiers in order to minimize civilian deaths on the other side."[132] It should also be noted that harnessing Judaism for political and military purposes intensified in the 1970s, well before the emergence of Islamism, which has attracted much more attention of late.

The direct link established by followers of National Judaism between the biblical texts and the challenges facing Israel tends to encourage violence. Unsurprisingly, Rabin's assassin Igal Amir was convinced that his victim had become a danger to Israel and that he should be killed without hesitation. Another assassin who emerged from the same camp, Baruch Goldstein (1956–1994), massacred dozens of Muslims praying in Hebron on the day of Purim before he himself was killed on the spot. He would have been influenced by the biblical readings associated with Purim, calling for the extermination of Amalek, whom he associated with Muslims and Arabs. The association of the Arabs with Amalek seems to have become common in Israel.[133]

Amir had studied at Bar-Ilan University, affiliated with National Judaism in Israel. Goldstein received his degree in medicine from Yeshiva University in New York, the training ground for the Modern Orthodox elites who often join the ranks of National Judaism in Israel. In these circles, the Jewish tradition that interprets and moderates the text of the Torah is often set aside to the profit of a direct, even literal application of the biblical words to the modern world: a phenomenon that reveals an additional affinity between National Judaism and Protestant Zionism, long close political allies.

As we have seen, in *Munich* Spielberg projected onto movie screens his doubts about Zionism and its relationship with Jewish continuity. It would not be wrong to see in it "a validation of Jewish anti-Zionism."[134] Is Zionism the culmination of Jewish history, the accomplishment of its messianic dream, or is it instead a sterile and immoral episode? The film positions itself as the successor to *Schindler's List*; it shows that the latent violence unleashed by the Nazi regime was carried over into the Israel–Palestinian conflict. While *Schindler's List* concentrates on the physical survival of the Jews, *Munich* deals primarily with threats to their moral survival. In recent years several books have been published—all written by Jews—on this very conflict between Zionism and Jewish moral values.[135]

The moral justification of Zionism, and of the state that embodies it, remains central to Jewish concerns.

But what exactly do the various anti-Zionist thinkers propose at this, the beginning of the 21st century? Without attributing the slightest value to the perpetuation of the Zionist character (often called the "Jewish character") of the state, the anti-Zionists put forward reconciliation strategies that range from recognition and reparation of the injustices committed against the Palestinians to the search for stability, and even friendship, in the Holy Land. Though neither unified nor of one voice, the adversaries of Zionism invite the Jews to find the courage to break the cycle of violence that these thinkers attribute to Zionism. A Haredi-authored document, in question and answer form, provides an insight into anti-Zionist thinking on the issue:

> A. Today, Zionism stands revealed before the Jewish people and, indeed, all mankind, as a failed enterprise. Zionism's founders (all Jews who had rejected their ancestral faith) claimed that it was going to solve the problem of Jewish exile and suffering. It would offer a safe haven for all of world Jewry. Over half a century later, it has proven itself incapable of the far less grandiose task of so much as protecting the Jews already living in the Holy Land.
>
> Q. But the state has survived, hasn't it?
>
> A. It is farcical to call a government that has subjected its citizens to five wars and endless suffering a desirable "survival." How much blood must be shed till Jewry shakes off the shackles of world Zionism's domination and begins to rethink this ideology's root assumptions?[136]

This assessment of Zionist efforts to build and maintain a state closely resembles that of Rabbi Blau's widow, in the late 1970s:

> To what end have all these transgressions of the Torah benefited the leaders of the Israeli state? They promised non-religious Jews a state that would be like all the world's other states. But in this small state, military service lasts longer, taxes are more onerous, wars more frequent, and physical and moral poverty are more acute than in any other Western country .... Ah, but the Jews must be saved in the state of Israel, they said, the very state that would bring to an end the misfortunes of the sons of Jacob! What are we to expect after the next war, which threatens not only this state, but the entire world?[137]

Anti-Zionist literature regularly evokes the apocalyptic danger that the state of Israel represents for the whole world. The emergence of suicide bombing in the Middle East and around the world, the destruction of several Arab states by Israel's indefectible ally the United States and the presence of Israel's nuclear arsenal, together reinforce premonitions of doom. Some Haredi rabbis are keenly aware of the Israeli threat to the entire world, which only confirms their conviction that the creation of Israel—for them, an arrogant revolt against God—will ultimately lead to a catastrophe of worldwide and cataclysmic proportions. Their vision is reflected in the perception of the state of Israel as a danger to the entire world, revealed in public opinion polls carried out in several countries.[138]

Some voices, most of them emanating from Haredi anti-Zionist circles, have taken on an openly apocalyptic tone, employing arguments that recall classical anti-Semitism. Not only do they posit a link between the suicide attacks in the West and the Israel–Palestine crisis, they see in those attacks the beginning of divine punishment for Israel's transgressions. For these voices, the state of Israel stands condemned as a violator of the global order, and all attempts to oppose God's will can only lead to an equally global disaster.[139]

Defined in these terms, Zionism appears as a universal evil, transcending the bounds of Jewish history. In this sense, the anti-Zionist declaration issued several decades earlier at Meah Shearim has now taken on prophetic proportions: "The independence of the Zionists was the last straw and it broke the back of the Middle East peace and that of the entire world as well."[140] The universal scope the anti-Zionist rabbis attribute to punishment for the sin of Zionism fully conforms to their vision of Judaism as a religion that goes beyond the purely Jewish framework.

Certain opponents of Zionism have already begun to prepare for a "post-Israel" dispensation, which explains their ongoing contacts with the Palestinians. More often than not, these contacts are more symbol than substance, such as the nomination of Rabbi Moshe Hirsch (1923–2010) of Neturei Karta as minister for Jewish affairs of the Palestinian Authority. Still, an official letter written under the letterhead of the Palestinian Authority and signed by Arafat would indicate that the work of the anti-Zionists had begun to bear fruit. After thanking the Haredim for demonstrating against the state of Israel and exhibiting their compassion for the sufferings of the Palestinian people during the Intifada, he concludes:

These expressions are priceless examples of the long-standing and abiding relationship between Jews and Arabs reaching back hundreds of years, and enable the entire world to see the stark contrast between the eternal and beautiful values of Judaism and those embodied in aggressive Zionism. These demonstrations and expressions are of critical importance in enabling the Palestinian people and Arabs worldwide to see this crucial difference so that everybody understands that the actions of the Israeli state do not reflect anything rooted in the traditions, beliefs, and laws of Judaism. This is vital in emphasizing that there is no conflict between Jew and Arab.[141]

Their overtures to the Arabs and their continuing insistence on compromise and negotiation have won for the anti-Zionist Haredim the scorn of the Zionists, who feel nothing but disdain for "this tradition of the weak" and insist on the values of courage and pride. But for the critics of Zionism from among both the Haredi and the non-Orthodox Jews alike, such values not only contradict traditional Jewish sensibility, but represent a veritable danger for the Jewish people as well. They point out that the Jews constitute a truly minuscule group when measured against the whole of humanity: 0.2 percent of the world's population (approximately 14 million against a total of 7 billion). The time has come, the anti-Zionists warn, to abandon delusions of grandeur and omnipotence. While opposition to Zionism has known ebb and flow, it is certainly a permanent feature of the contemporary Jewish scene.

Chapter Eight

Israeli Society and Jewish Communities

Distinctions between "left" and "right" within the Zionist movement have become increasingly blurred. The two terms, though employed in Israel and throughout the world, lack clarity. True, the "left" electorate is better off and more educated than that of the "right." But it would surely be more useful to speak of a division between liberal cosmopolitanism and ethnic nationalism. Zionism, meanwhile, is fundamentally hostile to liberal cosmopolitanism, which explains why the Zionist "left," in Israel and elsewhere, has gone largely over to the "right." What unites the two camps—their conviction of the legitimacy of Zionism—is more substantial that the tactical or stylistic differences that divide them. For the Labor Party has been no less active than its Likud adversaries in encouraging settlement in the West Bank.

"The state of Israel is in danger." This mindset, which is usually articulated by the most hard-core Zionists, points to a paradox: Israel, often held up as a place of refuge, and even as the ultimate refuge, may well have become the most precarious places of all for the Jews. More than a few Israelis feel as if they have been caught in a "bloody trap," despite Israel's overwhelming military superiority in the Middle East. As perceptions go, this one is increasingly widespread, even though many refuse to admit it.

We have already seen how such a mindset crystalizes when the traditional ways of explaining the persecutions suffered by Jews begin to lose their power of conviction. Now, in contrast to the early years of Zionism, the sense of victimhood has become, over the last few decades, an integral part of Israeli Jewish identity.[1] The role of victimhood in shaping Israeli identity and that of suffering for the Jews in general have both commonalities and differences.[2]

Even though nationalism in other countries is also often rooted in a sense of victimhood,[3] this sense has been institutionalized and has actively been cultivated as an effective form of Zionist education ever since the Israeli victory in June 1967. Zionist pioneers laid strong emphasis on the intrepid and valiant New Hebrew Man who had broken with the victimhood of the past. It was only later, faced with resistance kindled by the Zionist settler movement, that Israelis assumed the role of innocent victims, forced to defend themselves. The use of the expression *ein berera* ("we have no choice") has become as frequent as it is instructive. The museum of Yad Vashem, which commemorates the Jewish victims of the Nazi regime, the visits to the Nazi extermination camps, and the day dedicated to the soldiers who died for Israel, are all essential components of a didactic arsenal. The sense of victimhood also draws on the history of exile that followed the destruction of the Second Temple of Jerusalem, an episode that, as we have seen, was never associated with victim status in Jewish tradition, which sees in it a well-deserved instance of divine punishment.

Many Israeli Jews, whatever their origins, see themselves as the innocent heirs of the victims of Nazi violence, and now confronted by an Arab violence that appears to them as constant and irrational. Post-Zionist studies in both history and sociology have since called into question this historical interpretation, and along with it at a more popular level, a substantial number of films, novels, and plays that depict the Israelis transform immigrants, the poor, women, and even survivors of the Nazi genocide into victims of the Palestinians, who are permanently cast in the role of victimizers.[4] Some of those who have persisted in seeing themselves as victims have come to realize that they are actually victims of the Zionist enterprise, which has subjected them to interminable wars and, in the case of the Arab Jews, chronic social and economic inferiority.[5]

For many Israelis, the image of Zionism as a national liberation movement has been transformed into that of an oppressive state that stifles the national aspirations of the Palestinians. Zionism as a symbol of the struggle against racism and for human rights has acquired the characteristics of an ideology that produces Jewish racism and an institutional system that has much in common with South African-style apartheid. By way of example, Israel has developed a system involving more than 100 kinds of permit designed to control the daily lives of Palestinians in the territories.[6] The Zionist state, which was to have been an instrument of national liberation, has in reality become a skilled manipulator that has attempted to monopolize control of the land, the water, and the country's other resources. Finally, Zionism, which was to have transformed the Jews into

productive laborers, has spawned an economic system in which both cap-
ital and the means of production are concentrated in the hands of Israeli
Jews while productive labor is performed primarily by non-Jews, often
Palestinians and foreign workers who toil in deplorable conditions.

Non-Arab Israeli society remains ethnically, religiously, and culturally fragmented. A kind of solidarity in the face of the "Arab threat" has
become the common denominator of identity. But as perceptions of this
threat weaken, old tensions resurface, as acute as they ever were, between
the settlers and their adversaries, between "Russians" and long-time
Israelis, as well as between the Haredim and the rest of society. The cultural references—musical, culinary, or literary—of each of these groups
remain largely segregated: they hardly ever read the same books, listen
to the same music, or buy the same food. It must also be remembered
that the Haredi Jews are exempt from obligatory military service, which
functions as a crucible of social integration.

Indeed, by invoking the tragedy of the European Jews or the deep-seated
insecurity of the Israeli population, the state of Israel has more often than
not contrived to sidestep moral scrutiny.[7] This is hardly surprising, for
"whereas Judaism places man's obligations to God at the center of its value
system, inferring his obligations to the community from his relationship
to God, the new civil religion places the individual's obligations to the
nation at its center."[8] This is the reason why the civic religion provides no
answers to questions of ultimate meaning, while at the same time obliging
its practitioners to accept the ultimate sacrifice. Civic space in Israel has
become associated above all with "death for the fatherland,"[9] a linkage that
harks back to the beginning of Zionist colonization when the first "memory
books" commemorating the settlement guards killed in the line of duty were
published in Palestine in 1911.[10]

Even though the Zionist civic religion remains in force among a significant portion of the population, the Haredim have never accepted it, since
it was intended to replace Judaism. Meanwhile, more and more atheist
Israelis see in the civic religion an anachronistic embodiment of European ideologies of the "blood and soil" variety decorated with selective
interpretations of the Jewish tradition.

Any society founded upon an ideological project or premise must,
sooner or later, compare the project as it has been applied and the results
obtained. Israeli society is no exception, even though comparisons of this
kind may well further enfeeble it. When violence against Israelis flares

up they may wonder aloud if the state of Israel is not rushing headlong toward collective suicide. Indicative of this mindset is a sarcastic article comparing Sharon with Caesar, published in the Israeli daily *Haaretz* during the second Intifada:

> We start to wonder whether, for the sake of your goals, you have made a strategic decision to move the battlefield not into enemy territory, as is normally done, but into a completely different dimension of reality—into the realm of utter absurdity, into the realm of utter self-obliteration, in which we will get nothing and neither will they. A big fat zero .... One way or another, when we finally discover what those motives and reasons are, which are currently beyond us, we will understand why we have had to spend decades living in a world parallel to the one we were meant to live in, and why we agreed to live our one and only life in a kind of latent death. Until then, we will continue to support you with all our heart. We, who are about to die—in the dozens, the hundreds and the thousands—salute thee. Hail, Caesar![11]

Tragically, the author of the article lost his son in the war against Lebanon instigated by Sharon in 2006.

Immigration has long been a feature of Israeli society. For decades, to leave the Zionist state was considered a badge of shame. Today, however, the children and grandchildren of refugees from Germany, Poland, and other European countries obtain European Union passports; as a result the number of German passports actually issued in Israel has increased radically over the last few years.[12] Avraham Burg views the future of the Zionist state as perilous, and openly calls on all who are able to acquire a foreign passport to do so. An estimated two-thirds of the Israeli population have either taken the step or intend to follow suit. If during the Second World War the Jews could only dream of a document that would allow them to leave Europe for Palestine, in our day many Israelis obtain European passports the better to leave Israel. Similarly, more than half a million Israelis hold U.S. passports. Emigration affects primarily the best-educated strata of the population. An estimated 25 percent of Israeli academics work in the United States.[13]

The questioning of Zionism's basic postulates, a process often associated with the term "post-Zionism," has polarized Israeli society for a least two decades.[14] Of course, there had been other, well-known protagonists and activists such as Lova Eliav and Simha Flappan, who were pioneers, or better still precursors. But today it is no longer a question of individuals, but of an entire gamut of critical approaches that hundreds of students first master then apply in their own professional lives.

Post-Zionism has made its mark in the literary, theatrical, and film worlds: in the national culture as a whole, in fact. Diverse trends can be identified.[15] Thus the transition of Israeli society from the ideological to the post-ideological stage (in the manner of Daniel Bell's "end of ideologies") represents, in its own way, a post-Zionist development that bypasses rather than rejects, Zionism. On the other hand, the post-modernist trend presages the collapse of Zionism, in which nationalism is perceived as a form of oppression that must give way to the affirmation of otherness and multiculturalism. Zionism and the state of Israel are by no means a satisfactory response—and even less a necessary one—to the Jewish condition. As a trend, this affirms the multiplicity of Jewish identities that in no way revolve around the centrality of Israel.

In this way the postcolonial approach is articulated, which calls into question the modes of perception and the representations of which the colonized were the literary and political subject. Its founders, thinkers like Frantz Fanon (1925–1961) and Edward Said (1935–2003), turned their attention to the way that the formerly colonized restructured nationalism in reaction to dominant European values. Postcolonial writing lavishes great attention on the history of Zionist thought and practice, integrating questions of both identity and international relations. It suggests the existence of a common fate that Zionism, a European settler movement, reserves for all Arabs, whatever their present or former religion. All of them share the same fault, in the Zionist worldview: that of not being European.[16]

The postcolonial approach continues to inspire post-Zionist discourse. In contrast the Palestinian Arabs, who do not have the privilege of criticizing "their" institutionalized state, remain for the most part in the nationalist register. We can therefore conclude that post-Zionism remains largely a Jewish phenomenon. It draws attacks that hark back to the conflict between the partisans of the Enlightenment and those of romantic nationalism in Europe, between the universalist perspective and that which affirms the primacy of the nation.

The dominant political currents in Israeli politics are, however, running against post-Zionism. According to polls, over two-thirds of Israeli Jews would prefer not to have Arabs as neighbors.[17] Several bills submitted to the Knesset have been designed to strengthen segregation and discourage all forms of dissidence. Post-Zionism likewise throws light on the conflict between the Jewish and the democratic dimensions of Israeli society. While for many anti-Zionists the Zionist era is far from ended and thus warrants determined opposition, many post-Zionists consider Zionism to be a vestige of the past that hinders society from moving forward toward a democratic and multinational future, toward a state of all its citizens.

Although relatively few Israeli intellectuals dare term themselves post-Zionists, critical studies of Israeli society continue to undercut its founding myths, attack its institutions and the ideology on which they are founded: the authors do what intellectuals do in most countries around the world. They "de-ideologize" official discourse, and refer to immigrants rather than *olim* (those who ascend)—except that in Israel this kind of intellectual dissidence generates severe anxiety about the future of the state, and reinvigorates the Israeli self-image as victim.

At the critical moment experienced by Jews at the beginning of the 21st century, the temptation to fall into line behind Zionist ideology is apparent. Over the centuries, the Jews were accused of being too cerebral. Has Zionism made them too impassioned and visceral to debate its ideological underpinnings? Has asking hard questions about Zionism truly become a taboo subject? Were not only the thinkers of rabbinical anti-Zionism but also personalities as notable as the philosopher Martin Buber and the president of the Hebrew University of Israel Judah Magnes, or Albert Einstein and Hannah Arendt in the United States, opposed to the idea of a separate state for the Jews? Their efforts, however, came to naught. Magnes, in his farewell address to the Hebrew University in 1947, deplored the fact that Jews from around the world, but primarily from the United States, would be forced "to yield to that Zionist totalitarianism which seeks to subject to its discipline the entire Jewish people and every individual therein, and if necessary by force and violence."[18] The wife of his grandson would not live in Israel because, in her words, "the fascism had gotten to be too overwhelming."[19]

Indeed, the totalitarian current gives no sign of abating. If probing questions about certain Israeli policies are sometimes tolerated, not only are all fundamental critiques of Zionism delegitimized, but likewise any individual who might have dared to formulate such criticisms in the past. Such people are systematically excluded from community activities.[20]

As for the Haredi anti-Zionists, Zionist intellectuals ignore their public demonstrations, and they are called "enemies of the Jewish people" by a substantial number of Jews. Let us recall that the leaders of socialist Zionism made the decision to assassinate Jacob de Haan above all because he "spoke ill of the movement to the outside world," and because of his capacity to discredit, and even to publicly mock, their enterprise.[21]

The apprehension that many Jews feel about the future of the state of Israel impedes frank discussion. Such sensitivity to any criticism of Israel can easily be explained by the fact that for many people allegiance to Israel has long replaced Judaism as the anchoring principle of Jewish identity. But in the diaspora, this allegiance extends to an ideal, even imaginary, state rather than to the real and existing state of Israel, that economic and military power that dominates the region. Still, there also exists a Jewish identity whose sole content is to criticize and even to denounce the state of Israel, just as there exists a Jewish identity that is grounded mostly in solidarity with the Palestinians and their insistence on reparative justice for the misfortune that the establishment of the state of Israel represents for them.[22]

The overwhelming majority of Jewish communities prefer not to listen to dissident Israelis. Centralized efforts are undertaken to marginalize any argument that might threaten to raise doubts among Jews about the legitimacy of the cause of Israel and of Zionist ideology. The Jewish press is reluctant to allow such arguments to be expressed. The historian Jack Ross observes that "the totalitarian impulse of Zionist ideology to brand any opposition as illegitimate and intolerable was alive and well."[23] There is concern that "any society that does not tolerate moral questioning of its policies is necessarily corrupt. In contemporary Israel too many strident and influential religious voices can be heard proposing exactly such a society."[24] These voices continue to dominate public debate.

Harassment of dissidents and their families is likewise on the upswing. Adam Shapiro is an American Jew who, by visiting Yasser Arafat in Ramallah in 2002, sought by his presence to protect the Palestinian leader from being assassinated by Israeli troops.[25] A reporter for the *New York Post* nicknamed him the "Jewish Taliban" despite his commitment to nonviolence; his ageing parents were threatened and obliged to leave their residence in Brooklyn.[26] Equally visible is the growing intolerance toward those Jews who dare to criticize and denounce Zionism and the state that practices it.

Many Jews around the world identify with Israel, attend concerts by Israeli singers, and defend Israel's image. For the last three decades,

Zionist organizations have inculcated the idea of Israel's centrality in the majority of non-Haredi Jewish schools around the world. The existence of a state boasting a national flag, a powerful army, and a prosperous economy confers a certain sense of security.

What could be termed "vicarious Israelism" has replaced for many the traditional Jewish identity, a shift that has been all the easier given the less demanding nature of the new identity. As traditional Jewish identity is founded upon obedience to the Torah and to the precepts that it articulates, it impinges on both the private domain, such as food and intimate relations, and public conduct, such as non-use of automobiles on the Sabbath and dressing in a modest manner. At the same time "Israelism" carries with it no particular obligation, though it does impart a sense of belonging. The new identity breaks as cleanly as does the new Israeli one with the traditional ways of being Jewish, including compassion toward the poor and the downtrodden. Boaz Evron asserts that "moral identification with power politics is equivalent to idolatry,"[27] while Marc Ellis considers that this same identification constitutes a "disaster" and reminds his readers that "collective pride implies collective guilt."[28]

Seven decades after the Nazi genocide, world Jewish organizations are numerous and present in most of the industrialized countries, and span a wide range of professional disciplines: politics, law, journalism, student life, and so on. The principle of the centrality of the state of Israel that these organizations have adopted, whether de facto or de jure, binds their activities to Israeli policies and interests. Several governmental and para-governmental agencies try to coordinate and direct the activities of these ostensibly Jewish organizations.[29]

But the incontestable majority of Zionists can today be found among the Christians, certain of whom are prepared to take up arms to defend the Zionist state.[30] Evangelical churches make up the strongest pillar of the support enjoyed by the state of Israel, and have done so for years. The commitment to facilitate the return of the Jews to Israel touches off flutters of ecstasy among Zionist Christians at the four corners of the world, who provide aid that is as massive as it is unconditional to the Zionist state and its most intransigent nationalist groups.

Jeffrey Wiesenfeld, an American Zionist activist, admits, "It's a tragedy to tell you that we could do without 80 percent of the Jews. It's the good Christians who stand up for Israel and for us."[31] The sentiment is widespread among Zionist Jews who find Jewish support for the state of Israel too conditional for their taste, and thus lacking in resolve. In a speech transmitted by satellite to the annual convention of Christians United for Israel in 2011, Israeli prime minister Binyamin Netanyahu asserted, "When you support Israel, you don't have to choose between your interests and your values; you get both. Our enemies think that we are you and that you are us. And you know something? They are absolutely right."[32] Public opinion polls confirm that perception. In October 2013, 82 percent of white Christian evangelicals in the United States agreed with the statement that God has given the land of Israel to the Jews, a conviction far less widespread among American Jews, barely reaching 40 percent.[33]

Israel is not faced with religious conflicts rooted in centuries of Jewish history. Instead, it harks back to an era in which colonialism and the right of Westerners to settle among indigenous populations was taken for granted. In affirming its right to act as it does, the state of Israel finds itself in the vanguard of the international community as constituted by Western elites. But even though nowadays it is well positioned, it remains fundamentally fragile, as testified by the violent reaction of the Israeli government to pro-Palestinian pacifists barred from access to Gaza in 2010.[34] The international Boycott, Divestment and Sanctions (BDS) campaign directed against Israeli products has also had an effect in delegitimizing "the democratic and Jewish State." In Israel BDS, an admittedly peaceful tactic, has been branded as another "existential threat."

The supporters of the state of Israel, who style themselves as the ultimate defenders of the Jews, are quick to conflate all criticism of political Zionism with the promotion of a second Shoah. In responding to suggestions that the territory between the Jordan and the Mediterranean be transformed into an inclusive state of all its citizens, an Israeli apologist wrote:

> Behind the one-state solution lurks something truly monstrous. If Israel as a Jewish state is the centre of the Jewish people, the legatee of the Holocaust, then what we are facing here is not only the liquidation of a state but, functionally, the destruction of a people.[35]

We can understand Israeli leaders when they purport, as did Herzl, to be acting on behalf of the world's Jews: they need to legitimize the continuing existence of an explicitly ethnic state and its policies. Their allies in the diaspora, who proclaim to one and all that the Jewish community is united in its allegiance to Israel, must deal with a rather more ambiguous situation since such declarations may feed resentment, and even violence, against Jews.

A call to emancipate the Jews from the state of Israel erased a few old divisions while at the same time creating new ones. The extent to which the Israel question has become divisive was apparent in a controversy at Brandeis University, Massachusetts, whose student body is primarily Jewish. American universities regularly invite a leading personality each year to address the new graduates as they receive their diplomas. In 2010, faculty and students objected to an invitation to the Israeli ambassador to give the graduation speech, lest his participation "polarized the audience." Israel is no longer a rallying point, but a point of discord.[36]

It remains to be seen whether the chasm between those who hark back to the Jewish moral tradition and those who have converted to Jewish nationalism can be bridged. No matter how fateful it may be for the Jews and for Judaism, this chasm should not affect Israel, which as we now know relies far more upon Christian evangelicals than Jews for unconditional support.

While many are concerned about the parting of the ways between Jews and Israel, Israeli intellectual Boaz Evron defuses the tension by reminding them that:

> The state of Israel, and all the states of the world, appear and disappear. The state of Israel, clearly, will disappear in one hundred, three hundred, five hundred years. But I suppose that the Jewish people will exist as long as the Jewish religion exists, perhaps for thousands more years. The existence of this state is of no importance for that of the Jewish people . ... Jews throughout the world can live quite well without it.[37]

Chapter Nine

Israel in the International Arena

Israel's position in its region appears, at first glance, at odds with its position in the Western world. Largely abhorred among its neighbors, Israel seems to enjoy support in Europe and North America. But in fact, with only a few exceptions, public opinion around the world is critical with regard to the Zionist state. Those who look upon Israel as a negative factor in the world are far more numerous that those who hold a positive view (49 percent versus 21 percent). Even in the United States and the United Kingdom, two countries where Christian Zionism is historically deep-rooted, a deterioration in public perceptions of Israel can be observed.[1] These findings are all the more significant in that Zionist organizations in those countries bring substantial resources to bear to bolster Israel's image. One of their most recent strategies consists of pointing to Israel's modern, "trendy" side ("rebranding Israel") in an attempt to downplay the effects of its policies on Palestinian lives. At the same time, a world campaign of Boycott, Divestment, and Sanctions (BDS), a non-violent means of so far very limited economic pressure, has been cast as another "existential threat" facing Israel.[2] Prime minister Netanyahu invoked Nazi discrimination against Jewish businesses in Hitler's Germany as he denounced the guidelines of the European Commission to identify products that come from the Occupied Territories.[3] This kind of emotional response not only plays the guilt card against the Europeans, but above all fuels the sentiment of "all the world is against us" that is the hallmark of Zionism.

At the same time, Israel appears as a enclave of peace and prosperity in its region. Syria, Libya, and Iraq are rent by violence in the wake of Western interventions. While Israel seems an impassive observer of the tragedy, it has benefited greatly from the disintegration of the most modernized Arab-majority countries.

The idea to reshape the map of the Middle East belongs to a group of "Israel firsters" in the United States, neo-conservative journalists and politicians, mostly Jewish, with a strong commitment to Israel's right wing.[4] In 1996 they drafted a comprehensive plan titled "A Clean Break: A New Strategy for Securing the Realm" for Binyamin Netanyahu. He carried out its first recommendation, to transform Israel's economy from a mildly socialist into a neoliberal one. However, he balked at the rest, namely a regime change in Syria and a plan to "redefine Iraq." The report:

> called for Israel to take steps to reorder the entire Middle East. Netanyahu did not follow its advice, but Feith, Perle and Wurmser [among the authors of the report] were soon urging the Bush administration to pursue those same goals. ... There is little doubt that Israel and the Lobby were key factors in the decision to go to war. It's a decision the US would have been far less likely to take without their efforts. And the war itself was intended to be only the first step. A front-page headline in the *Wall Street Journal* shortly after the war began says it all: "President's Dream: Changing Not Just Regime but a Region: A Pro-US, Democratic Area Is a Goal that Has Israeli and Neo-Conservative Roots."[5]

This lengthy quote outlines the origins of Western, mostly U.S., intervention in the region which profoundly destabilized it, causing the death of hundreds of thousands of people and the displacement of millions. Besides the military-industrial complex, Israel appears to be the sole beneficiary of this intervention. The most educated and secular societies in the Arab world have been destroyed, unleashing an orgy of demodernization. National identities have degenerated to tribal and confessional ones, and all the three countries (Syria, Libya, and Iraq) face the prospect of disintegration. The Western intervention facilitated the emergence of extremist military formations, such as Daesh, the so-called "Islamic State," which has so far not confronted Israel, albeit it has voiced occasional threats.[6] At the same time, there have been reports that Israel buys oil from Daesh and otherwise provides it with covert assistance.[7]

Even though Daesh attracts more limelight at the time of this writing, Israel has consistently been perceived as a source of chronic conflict, and has been the focus of intense diplomatic activity, learned analysis, and media attention. Indeed, the territorial expansion of the Zionist settlements and the ongoing dispossession of the Palestinians have continued apace for more than a century. Israel plays a key role as a bridgehead of Western influence, even though some influential voices suggest that it constitutes an obstacle to American and European interests in the region.[8]

The question of Israel goes well beyond the narrow confines of foreign policy and has assumed domestic political relevance, especially in countries with significant Christian or Jewish Zionist constituencies. Zionism and Israel have galvanized these activists for decades, and their commitment does not seem to wane. That commitment takes a variety of forms, from financial contributions, to political lobbying, all the way to running tours of Israel for prospective supporters, and volunteering in the IDF. The Israeli government is involved in coordinating these activities, but the human and monetary resources needed for their implementation come from private sources in the countries involved. Anti-Zionist and pro-Palestinian activists are yet to match this degree of dedication and professionalism. Netanyahu's speech at the U.S. Congress in May 2015, attempting to torpedo the arms control agreement with Iran, was remarkable not only because Iran's "nuclear threat" had largely been fabricated by the Israel lobby,[9] but also because it constituted an apparent intervention in the U.S. political process, even though Israel has been so much of a domestic issue in the United States that the borders are blurred. Here again, Israel's situation on the international chessboard is an exceptional one.

Another factor in Israel's global standing is the dynamism of its high-tech—and particularly military—industries. Israeli exports as well as cooperation agreements for the production of military materiel help consolidate relations with the elites of several countries, even those where public opinion views Israel negatively. Arms sales not only ensure the viability of the Israeli military industry, but also facilitate the country's international relations.[10]

Israel also maintains multifaceted relations with the post-Soviet countries.[11] The USSR, after having supported the creation and expansion of Zionist settlement in 1947–49, went on to become a formidable adversary in the context of the cold war. The Soviet Union and its allies made sure that the Arab countries were kept supplied with arms, and steadfastly defended their diplomatic positions. At the same time, and over the protests of several Arab governments, hundreds of thousands of highly educated Soviet Jews were permitted to leave for Israel. Perestroika and the subsequent dismemberment of the USSR led to a considerable increase in migration, strengthening both the country's radical right and its defense industries. This immigration has also contributed to the improvement of attitudes toward Israel on the part of Russia and other post-Soviet republics. Israel is today home to the largest Russian-speaking diaspora in the world, and several former Soviet citizens have served as key ministers in Israeli governments.

Given current trends, these prominent immigrants' influence can be expected to grow in the near future. Structures for long-term collaboration between Russia and Israel have been established in sectors such as defense, security, arms production, and high-tech industry. Israeli agricultural products have carved out significant niches in post-Soviet markets, including Russia, affected by sanctions imposed in the context of the confrontation in Eastern Ukraine. The struggle against resistance movements in the Caucasus has created substantial opportunities for cooperation between the two armies and intelligence services. Before the flare-up in Eastern Ukraine and the ensuing depreciation of the Russian and Ukrainian currencies, citizens of the former Soviet countries made up the largest European contingent of visitors to Israel.[12] Relations between Russia and Israel are so cordial, even intimate, that Vladimir Putin has remarked, "Israel is, in fact, a special state to us. It is practically a Russian-speaking country. Israel is one of the few foreign countries that can be called Russian-speaking."[13]

At the same time, Russia attends to its strategic interests in the region, where it maintains close relations with Iran and Syria. Despite Israeli opposition, Russia deployed substantial efforts to bring about a final agreement on the Iranian nuclear issue in 2015. Later in the year, high-level contacts between the two countries were held prior to the deployment of Russia's air force in Syria.[14] As 2015 was coming to an end, Israelis named Russia's President Putin "the man of the year."[15]

Israeli security know-how is exported to the four corners of the world, including major supplies to China and India.[16] Israel has helped to train the armed forces of several countries, including the United States and Colombia. Canada, whose recently defeated Conservative government was Israel's most dedicated ally on the international scene, has signed several military and police collaboration agreements between the two countries. Some 30 Canadian police chiefs travelled to Israel to learn new techniques of crowd control and prison management. Aerospace is another aspect of Canada–Israel cooperation.[17] Similar cooperation, sometimes initiated and funded by local Zionists, has been established with several other countries. Israeli fighter aircraft participated in military maneuvers in Alberta, the two countries' intelligence agencies trade information on individuals, while Canada does not seem overly concerned about the use of Canadian passports by Israeli secret service agents, even when they are employed on assassination missions. Israel agents outfitted with false Canadian documents shot and killed a Moroccan in Norway, taking him for a Palestinian militant. In Jordan, counterfeit Canadian passports were used in an attempt on the life of a Hamas leader.[18]

An Alien Presence in the Region

The Arab League, in the name of its members, has already offered Israel peace and the normalization of diplomatic relations in exchange for withdrawal from the territories occupied in June 1967. Even though the offer has been on the table for more than a decade, Israel continues to ignore it as it continues to colonize these same territories. Behind the apparent indifference lies the constant of Israeli policy, which is often obscured by the rhetoric of peace-seeking that Israel has systematically deployed ever since its creation. The disjunction between words and deeds is by no means rare in the foreign policy of the great powers, but it is more unusual for a small country like Israel, which enjoys impunity and is often portrayed as a victim entitled to defend itself.

Still and withal, the Zionist state remains culturally and economically isolated from neighboring countries; its dominant position in the Middle East depends on its military superiority and a robust weapons industry. Until the beginning of the first Intifada in 1987, the existence of the state seemed natural, and for some, eternal. Not long before the end of the 20th century the Knesset proclaimed, "United Jerusalem the eternal capital of Israel." But since then, a sense of fragility has emerged, even if the state does not appear to be in any danger, and no regional army can match the IDF in the "dangerous neighborhood" so frequently invoked by Israeli politicians. However, no amount of military hardware and know-how can protect citizens from random acts of violence perpetrated by Palestinians frustrated by the hopelessness of their predicament, whom Israel imprisons by the thousand without trial, including minors.[19]

The sense of fragility is fed by awareness of Palestinian hostility, and of the hostility of the region's population as a whole, a hostility often attributed to so-called "essentialist" causes—Islamic religion and irrational Jew-hatred—rather than to perfectly understandable social and political ones such as the anger generated by discrimination, dispossession, and deportation of the indigenous population. David Ben-Gurion well understood this challenge when he declared, "Peace without justice cannot be a lasting law."[20] Yet, it was Ben-Gurion who ordered the Zionist armed forces to drive hundreds of thousands of Palestinians from their homes.[21]

Even in the eyes of a number of its supporters, the state of Israel stands as the last colonial state, founded precisely at the moment when the worldwide process of decolonization was getting underway. Its image as a Western foothold in the Middle East underlines its character as a state implanted and maintained in the region by force. The prospective democratization of the neighboring Arab countries is of substantial concern to Israel. Their oppressive regimes such as that of former Egyptian President Hosni Mubarak and his current successors cooperate with the Israeli army, but public opinion in these countries is largely anti-Israel and continues to favor the Palestinian cause. The autocratic Saudi Arabia has also warmed up to Israel in the context of their common hostility toward Iran.[22]

Non-Arab Israeli society, which was forged in circumstances of enemy encirclement, today looks with anxiety upon the Palestinian civilian population, whose growth is widely viewed as "a demographic time-bomb." Convinced that a non-Arab majority is an essential condition of their survival, an ever-increasing number of Israeli Jews are calling for the deportation of the Palestinians to the nearby Arab countries and the formal annexation of the territories occupied in 1967.[23] At the same time, such a prospect repels many Jews, both in Israel and throughout the world, some of whom have come to realize that sustaining the Zionist identity of the state calls for measures that, from their inception, have been unacceptable in terms of both the Jewish moral tradition and elementary human decency. Yet current Israeli political trends seem to suggest the growing popularity of such plans.[24] Nearly half of non-Arab Israelis want their Arab compatriots to be stripped of citizenship rights, and 69 percent are against giving the right to vote to the Palestinians when their territories are annexed to Israel; most people advocate official discrimination against Arabs and do not want their children to attend the same school as them.[25] There is little wonder that indignant segregationists have torched one of a handful of mixed Arab–Jewish schools existent in Israel.[26] Segregated Zionist settlements continue to expand, while the settlers continue to produce radicals who resort to violence against Israeli peace activists and Palestinians.[27]

At the same time, disappointment with Zionism is also in evidence. A former speaker of the Knesset, Avraham Burg, believes that converting Israel into a state of all its citizens, and erasing its distinct Jewish nature, is "our only hope for survival."[28] Prominent poet and intellectual Yitzhak Laor argues, "We don't have to leave this place or give up our lives. ... we have to get rid of Zionism."[29] These Jews, many of whom are veterans of Israel's many wars, today feel that they are being held hostage to a situation over which they have no control. They are seeking a more peaceful outcome, one compatible with their sense of decency; despair has sensitized them to the arguments put forward for more than a century detailing the dangers that the Zionist nature of the state represents first of all for the Jews.

However, neither Zionism itself nor the Zionist structure of the state appear negotiable at this time. The Israeli government and its Western allies have begun, in recent years, to insist on recognition of Israel as a "Jewish state" as a precondition to any negotiations with the Palestinians. The Zionists who advocate greater use of force and the anti-Zionists who suggest that the state be dismantled before it is too late find themselves in curious agreement: both groups believe that the region will never accept the presence of a Zionist state in its midst. They even agree that the Jews in the land of Israel face eventual collective massacre. For the Zionists, only the state can prevent such a massacre; for their adversaries, the state would be its single and unique cause.

In accepting the idea that the structures of Zionism could simply be dismantled, Rabbi Moshe Sober emphasizes its psychological aspect—and expresses guarded optimism about its practicality:

> A solution is not impossible; it is not even particularly costly. But it will never be achieved unless we can allow ourselves to forget for a moment our cherished beliefs for which we have sacrificed so many lives, and look instead at the actual realities of the situation. We must stop treating Israel as a romantic dream and learn to see her as a heterogeneous country in which two fiercely proud ethnic populations of similar size are struggling for control .... We, the people who gave the world the words of the prophets, must find the humility to admit that we were wrong, and the courage to do that which is right.[30]

All discussion of the occupation simply conceals another reality, he concludes. Israel has in fact become a binational state that denies political rights to one of the two nations.

Those who propose a return to Muslim sovereignty in the Holy Land, like those who advocate the transformation of Israel into a binational state, agree that the hatred of the Jews now prevalent in many Arab societies is a recent—and therefore reversible—development. Several Jewish historians in and outside of Israel share their vision, which is also supported by foreign sources who were *a priori* neutral with regard to the Zionist enterprise.

The idea of a binational state between the Jordan and the Mediterranean has continued to gain ground, in both Israel and the diaspora. Meron Benvenisti, the eminent specialist in Palestinian affairs and former vice-mayor of Jerusalem, articulates the concept as the only remaining solution.[31] Elsewhere in the world, the idea is likewise presented as the "last hope."[32] A publication as conservative as the *Economist* has seriously discussed the binational solution.[33] Many Israeli leaders, however, see it not as an opportunity but as an existential threat.[34] Obviously, such proposals are interpreted as undercutting the legitimacy of the Zionist project. But the perspective itself becomes all the more realistic, particularly as Israeli intellectuals have begun to question the concept of the Jewish people, which underlies Zionist ideology.[35]

From Left to Right

Between 1948 and 1967 most of the world's leftists backed Israel as a symbol of human progress. The Labor Party in Israel, which held power without interruption from 1948 to 1977, became a member of the Socialist International.[36] Today, however, it is those on the right wing of the political spectrum who lavish admiration and support upon Israel, and view it as a bulwark against the alleged "Muslim onslaught."

At its beginnings, Israel enjoyed broad sympathy within the international left. Jean-Paul Sartre was "constant in his fundamental pro-Zionism."[37] Bertrand Russell endorsed the Zionist cause, arguing in 1943 that "the Zionist State, if it is enlightened and liberal, can make contributions which will be of inestimable value and will command the respect of the world."[38] Even Leon Trotsky, though rather tepidly and opposed in principle to ethnic nationalism, sympathized with the Zionist vision in the context of Nazi persecution. He attended the sixth Zionist Congress in 1903 but found the project unworkable. However, in 1937 the Zionist idea reportedly "found an echo in his heart."[39] Zionists were then seen as representatives of Jewish victims, which won them the sympathy of people on the left.

The left also appreciated the new forms of social organization created by the Zionists, such as the kibbutz. Although Israeli-style socialism served in the first instance the imperative of settling the land, it stimulated true interest and sincere admiration among millions of progressives around the world. Jews and non-Jews by the thousands volunteered to work in the kibbutzim and to contribute to the construction of the country.

Conversely, the Arab countries were seen then as retrograde and reactionary, which made it possible to conceal the fate reserved for the Palestinians in 1947–49, the reprisal operations carried out against entire Palestinian villages in the 1950s, and other actions directed against the indigenous population. In certain cases, the left justified the expulsion of the Palestinians. The executive of the British Labour Party proposed, in 1944, to "let the Arabs be encouraged to move out as the Jews move in."[40]

The Six Day War, and above all the colonization of the Occupied Territories that followed the Israeli pre-emptive attack, signaled the beginning of a new awareness that modified left-wing Israeli attitudes and nourished sympathy for the Palestinians, despite the fact that their suffering since 1967 has been less acute than the military rule imposed on the Arabs in Israel's borders in the wake of the establishment of the state. If, in 1947–49, more than 500 Palestinian villages were stricken from the map and their population driven into exile, the Zionist settlement that has continued since 1967 consists generally of the annexation of ostensibly uninhabited—but usually cultivated—land.

Ever since the 1967 war, the left in many countries has mobilized against the occupation and supported the Palestinian resistance. Certain left-wing extremist groups, from as far afield as Japan,[41] even participated in armed operations against Israeli targets. The Soviet Union and its allies, which, with the exception of Romania, severed diplomatic relations with Israel in 1967, trained Palestinian fighters and offered them material assistance. In the context of the cold war, the conflict in Israel/Palestine became polarized between left and right, a polarization that continues down to the present day, even though the cold war has long ended with the dismemberment of the USSR.

Israel continues to enjoy support among the wealthier segments of society in many countries, and among the political and economic elites irrespective of religious denomination or ethnic origin. Non-Jewish chief executives of major companies are regularly honored at pro-Israel functions. The right looks on Israel as a source of emulation: after all, the country's leadership was successful in transforming what was once a relatively egalitarian society into a neoliberal economy. The absence of tangible civil resistance to such a transformation, which has impoverished hundreds of thousands of citizens, reflects the intensity of the fear of the Arabs that distracts Israeli citizens from questions of social justice and the economy.

The unfettered Zionism that underlies the state of Israel likewise inspired that part of the right that prizes ethnic nationalism. For example, the White nationalists of South Africa have identified with Israel and lent it their support since 1948, while their National Party did not admit Jews. The close collaboration established between the Zionist state in Asia and the Apartheid state in Africa reflected not only a confluence of interests but equally, ideological affinities.[42]

Once again, anti-Semitism combines admiration for the valiant and intrepid New Hebrew Man and the Zionism that had shaped this image. Several right-wing groups known for their anti-Semitic past—the Dutch Freedom Party, Vlaams Belang in Belgium, the English Defence League in the United Kingdom, and the Bündnis Zukunft Österreich in Austria—have rallied enthusiastically to the cause of Israel in recent years.[43]

Not surprisingly, a European anti-Muslim terrorist found inspiration in the example of Israel. Anders Breivik, the perpetrator of the massacre of dozens of people in Norway in the summer of 2011, in his manifesto cited the Zionist state 359 times as a rampart against Islam and an example of armed resolve.[44] For the extreme right, Israel embodies the ideology of superiority, an idea popular at the dawn of Zionism when colonialism appeared natural. In Europe this ideology, which had gone into temporary eclipse between 1960 and 1980, is gaining ground once more, particularly since the end of the cold war.[45] The right likewise appreciates the dominant role played by former military officers in Israeli economic and political life, which makes explicit and legitimate the link—usually more discreet in other countries—between politics and the military-industrial complex. The state of Israel remains vital to understanding not only today's world but also the way its history is manipulated and used.

The leaders of a fascist-leaning group, the Russian Democratic National Alliance, were welcomed at the Knesset, including by a member of the government, during their visit to Israel in the summer of 2011. They expressed their admiration for Israel, a state overtly founded on ethnic nationalism, which inspired them as a model in their effort to create a "Russia for the Russians."[46] The common denominator of these right-wing movements is Islamophobia; it is hardly surprising that they strongly endorse Israeli military action, including attacks on Gaza.

Wedded to assertive nationalism, Israel, which some deem to be "the most racist state in the industrialized world,"[47] thus preserves the European tradition of the use of force to ensure colonial settlement. This tradition is certainly not of Jewish origin. But it reflects the historical role of which the state of Israel is proud: the affirmation of European values, and in the event, assertive military behavior. Following the Nazi period and during the decolonization undertaken in the context of the cold war, the principles of racial equality, aversion for war, and a kind of internationalism prevailed in European societies. The use of force as a matter of course against "the Other" in far-off countries fell into temporary discredit. Nowadays, shootings of African-Americans by police officers in the United States are no longer glorified but portrayed as transgressions rather than policy.[48] Meanwhile, however, Israel kept that tradition alive in its relations with its neighboring countries and the Palestinians of Gaza and the West Bank. It is highly symbolic that Israeli specialists have provided a wealth of "anti-terrorist" expertise, which the European countries as well as the United States and Canada draw upon when they prepare their troops for operations in Afghanistan, Libya, Iraq, and other Muslim-majority countries.[49]

At the same time, Israeli society and its elites adopted, from the very inception of the Zionist enterprise, a reductionist vision of the "Arab" identical to racial anti-Semitism, a vision fundamentally opposed to the political liberalism that prevailed in Europe during the post-war years. On the ground, it made possible discrimination against Palestinian Arabs, Jews from Muslim countries, and immigrant workers from Asia. It is in this light that we can best understand the somewhat counter-intuitive observation of the British-Israeli historian Ilan Pappe, for whom "Zionism is far more dangerous to the safety of the Middle East than Islam."[50]

As already mentioned, public opinion in Israel tends to interpret the animosity of the region's peoples as prompted by their religion, and even their innate nature, rather than by their response to the way the Palestinians are treated. Only this colonialist vision, in fact, warrants legitimacy. As a result Israel, irrespective of the government in power, has become one of the main sources of the anti-Arab, and later anti-Muslim, discourse that is now broadcast to the four corners of the planet. It is a discourse perfectly integrated into the dominant Western rhetoric, which seeks to depict other peoples and cultures as inferior under the pretext that they resist Western democracy which was brought to them on the tip of the sword. What the rhetoric really signals, however, is a return to the dichotomy between the "civilized" and the "backward" that Europe employed to justify its colonial conquests. For all his socialist appearances, Ben-Gurion himself proudly proclaimed that those who built the state of Israel belonged to "one of those few civilized peoples that have returned to their ancient Homeland."[51] It is hardly surprising, then, that the partisans of Israel, Jews and non-Jews alike, are today playing a leading role in the recolonization of the world, a tendency to reverse the process of decolonization that was energized by the defeat of Nazism and the ensuing competition in less developed regions between the United States and the Soviet Union. The right to self-determination is no longer seen as self-evident, and establishing the hegemony of the West, including military intervention, has once again become a legitimate policy.

Israel's justification of the use of force may well have influenced American behavior in the wakes of the attacks of September 11, 2001. Rather than identifying the root causes of the hostility as Muslims' perceptions of U.S. foreign policy, the government, the media, and consequently public opinion, quickly adopted an explanation as intransigent as it was single-minded: "They hate our values." So it was that the United States, following Israel's example and on occasion surpassing it, unleashed a "War on Terror" that ignored the sovereignty of states, the Geneva Conventions, and a host of other accords codified in international law with regard to war and to human rights. Attacks against other countries, the kidnapping of suspects on foreign soil, and a world-spanning prison system where torture was institutionalized, became the rule that simply ignored international law and replaced it with the principle "might makes right." Just as some banks in the 21st-century financial crisis had become "too big to fail," some countries are too strong to prosecute in court. Quite like Israel since the beginning of the Zionist settlement in Palestine, the United States treats the symptoms of the problem without being able to recognize that its own policies might have engendered armed resistance.

This "Israelization" of American foreign policy spares Israel the consequences when the American government expresses occasional reservations about Israeli actions. In fact, those actions have become models. Thus the Israeli attack on a nuclear reactor in Iraq in 1981, condemned by most countries—including the United States—became in the new circumstances a model to be applied to Iran.[52] Although both Israel and the United States possess nuclear weapons, they deny Iran the right to acquire similar weapons, arguing that its rulers are irrational religious fanatics. Clearly the principle of double standards is at work, reflecting the revival of the concept of so-called civilized countries that, against empirical evidence, are claimed to possess a monopoly on rationality in international politics.

References to Judaism and to Jewish tradition are of little help in understanding contemporary Israel; quite the contrary, they are more likely to mislead, for Zionism and the state that incarnates it are revolutionary phenomena. It is easier, in fact, to understand that state's politics, structure, and laws without reference to either the Jews or their history. To interpret the conduct of the state of Israel in a positive or negative manner by associating it with Judaism can only skew and obscure the outcome. It is thus imprecise to speak of a "Jewish state" or a "Jewish lobby": "Zionist state" and "Zionist lobby" would be more appropriate.

As the founders of the country dreamed, the state of Israel should be treated like any other modern political configuration, without the fear of accusations of anti-Semitism: that is, by its acts and words, and not as the culmination of biblical history or a miraculous revival after the Nazi genocide. The reader's time would be far better spent in analyzing it within the context of international politics and Western interests and actions toward the Middle East and its resources. The state of Israel has been a vanguard and a barometer of changes that have taken place in international relations, in warfare, and in "the war on terror" in the 21st century.

Conclusion: A State Without Borders

The state of Israel and Zionism, which forms the official ideology of the state, give every appearance of having triumphed. As the dominant power in the Middle East, Israel looms invincible over its adversaries. The Zionist state has developed strategic ties not only with the Western powers, but also with Russia, China, and India, and rather more discreetly, with the Saudi elites as well as those of other Arab countries. Shortly after attacking Gaza in 2009, and over sharp criticism of its treatment of the Palestinians, Israel was unanimously accepted into the Organization for Economic Cooperation and Development (OECD), made up of some 30 countries that boast democratic structures of governance. A wide range of scientific and technical cooperation programs enables Israeli experts to profit from grants and other forms of research and development assistance set up by the Western countries.

Israel has also succeeded in making the Zionist outlook—by definition anti-liberal—acceptable to the general public as well as in the media and the academic world, even in countries with a long liberal tradition where the state, rather than confessional or "tribal" solidarity, theoretically ensures the rights of the citizen. In these countries, Jews who have adopted such an outlook face a challenge: how to reconcile Zionist ideology with the liberal values that enabled them to join the mainstream. The same kind of cognitive dissonance also characterizes Israel's non-Jewish supporters. In Canada, for instance, racial, religious, and ethnic discrimination is formally prohibited. But the JNF, which for a century has been establishing segregated settlements that are out of bounds to Arabs, enjoys not only Canadian fiscal benefits, but the personal participation of top federal officials in the organization's fund-raising efforts.[1]

The leaders of major Jewish organizations in the United States and elsewhere routinely act on behalf of Israel, even though more and more ordinary Jews feel uncomfortable with political activism of this kind. Their discomfort is even more intense when the activism in question is directed against the policies of their government, as happened in July 2015 when Israel called on Jewish leaders to wage a campaign against the nuclear agreement concluded between Iran and the world powers, including the United States.[2] Those leaders appear to have bypassed the limits of the "double loyalty" Jews are often accused of harboring, insisting that loyalty to the state of Israel must prevail over all others, including that toward their own country. By conflating Jews and Zionists they forget that, in the words of veteran Israeli scholar and diplomat Shlomo Avineri, "the anti-Zionist position has accompanied Zionism from the very outset, and it is a legitimate position even if one does not agree with it."[3]

That such conflation may fuel anti-Semitism hardly seems to concern the Zionists: an increase of anti-Semitism would only confirm the validity of Zionism and encourage still more Jews to migrate to Israel. It is truly a win–win situation. Paradoxically, Israel styles itself as the defender of the Jews wherever they may be, in imitation of the role played, for primarily political reasons, by the European powers who in preceding centuries claimed to protect the Christians of the Holy Land, then under Ottoman sovereignty. By affirming that the Jews automatically "belong" to it, Israel does not hesitate to pressure other states to deny access to Jews leaving their country of origin, the better to redirect them to the Zionist state.

Israel's anti-Iranian activism and the atrocities committed by Daesh have all but succeeded in erasing the Palestinian question from the international agenda. Israel enjoys solid backing from right-wing movements in Europe and North America riding on the wave of anti-Arab and Islamophobic sentiments, which further undermine the legitimacy of pro-Palestinian activism. Systematic support for Israel has become a right-wing rallying cry and an ideological principle, even when the right holds power and should be constrained by the broader interests of the state. For right-wing Christians it is also an article of faith. For example, former Canadian prime minister Stephen Harper, while still in office, placed solidarity with Israel above Canada's interests to the point of claiming that his government would support Israel "whatever the cost."[4]

Indeed, Harper's words seem rooted in religious commitment, rather than in rational policy. Far more numerous than the world's entire Jewish population, Christian Zionists wield a growing influence on Western policies toward Israel. In their haste to accelerate the Second Coming of Christ through the "ingathering of the Hebrews" in the Holy Land, the Christian Zionists are helping Israel cope with the fact that Jews have become a minority between the River Jordan and the Mediterranean.[5] To this end, Zionist activists, Christians and Jews alike, are mobilizing considerable human, political, and financial resources, a testimonial to their solid and ongoing allegiance. No comparable dedication can be seen on the Palestinian side, even though the populations of Western countries, not to mention those of the Arab and/or Muslim majority countries, sympathize with the Palestinians and their predicament.

The official Zionist ideology has made Israel a state without borders. In geographical terms, it can be extended with military conquest or colonization. The Zionist movement and successive Israeli governments have taken great pains never to define the borders they envisage for their state. This borderless character is also embodied by Israel's claim that it belongs to the world's Jews rather than to its citizens. This leads to the increasingly overt transformation of Jewish organizations around the world into Israeli vassals. Moreover, by emphasizing the primacy of an ethnically and denominationally defined "Jewish nationality", the state of Israel turns its back on the idea of an "Israeli nationality" that would reflect the multicultural society that has taken shape on this land in the Eastern Mediterranean over the last century.

Israeli society is multifaceted, made up of a secular majority, several dozen different Jewish communities, Druze, Muslim, and Christian Palestinians, Christians from the former Soviet Union, thousands of foreign workers, and still more indigenous or immigrant groups. The demand that the Palestinians recognize Israel as a "Jewish and democratic" simply affirms the Zionist nature of the state in the face of the "de-Zionization" naturally brought about by social and demographic realities.

The Arab citizens of Israel (who make up more than 20 percent of all Israelis and are represented by the third largest bloc in the Knesset in 2015[6]) are by definition excluded from governing the country, a fact that can only stoke the fires of conflict in the Holy Land. Israeli society, even were we to set aside this indigenous group, suffers from the effect of diverse centrifugal forces. According to the Israeli philosopher Joseph Agassi, Israeli governments have behaved like community functionaries still living in a ghetto, sweeping aside the interests of Israel's non-Jews and thus stoking the fires of perpetual war, for a ghetto equipped with a powerful army is dangerous.[7]

Israel's Jews do not even agree among themselves on the nature of the state, for many of them have rejected the Zionist project from the earliest days. Haredi circles have an entirely different vision of the state than do their putative co-religionists who adhere to National Judaism. The secular majority also remains divided. What sustains the fragile unity of the non-Arab majority is fear: a siege mentality that most frequently takes the form of a victim-centered nationalism meant to prevent a repetition of the Nazi genocide. The memory of that European tragedy has become one of the rallying points for Israelis to the Zionist cause, if not the principal one. Its political utility is still far from exhausted. As if to underscore the point, it was at Yad Vashem, the memorial to the Nazi genocide in Jerusalem, that the Israeli prime minister chose to condemn any agreement with Iran alongside French President François Hollande during the latter's visit to Israel in November 2013. (Hollande changed his mind and signed a deal with Iran a few days later.) Fear, actively maintained, seems still to be the cement that holds Israeli society together, however tenuously.

But fear, in turn, can touch off an entire gamut of reactions. Many Israelis prefer to emigrate and rebuild their lives somewhere else, most often in Europe.[8] This trend contradicts the Zionist media, which, harping on "the eternal hatred of the Jew," brandish the specter of resurgent anti-Semitism on the European continent.

At the same time, for a growing number of young Jews, the concept of a "Jewish state" appears increasingly incongruous and foreign. The question of Israel divides Jews far more than any other. The idea that Israel embodies God's promise to the Jewish people is today far more widespread in American society as a whole than among Jewish Americans. Among the white Evangelicals the proportion reaches 82 percent while among the Jews it is only 40 percent.[9] This brings us back to the fact that Zionism has Protestant origins.

These factors combine to make Israel a country without borders in more ways than one. Its ideology ignores borders, affirming that it is the state of the world's Jews, and expressions such as "Jewish state" and "Hebrew state" are widely used in the media, so much so that they have entered into everyday language. Israeli leaders ignore borders, intervening in the political process of other countries, particularly in the United States where Israel often plays Congress against the White House. In the Middle East, the IDF pays no heed to borders, striking targets in its neighboring countries, interventions carried out with impunity. Israel has thus placed itself above the constraints of international law and, *a fortiori*, beyond the moral limitations of the Jewish tradition that the founders of the state expressly—and scornfully—rejected. Israel, for all its embrace of modernity, remains bound by the Zionist ideology, which ensures that in spite of its respectable age it remains a daring frontier experience rife with conflict within and without.

Notes

Introduction

1 www.ynetnews.com/articles/0,7340,L-4625937,00.html
2 http://unctad.org/en/Pages/DIAE/World%20Investment%20Report/ Country-Fact-Sheets.aspx
3 André Chouraqui, *L'État d'Israël* [*The State of Israel*], Paris: PUF, 1962, p. 126.
4 http://data.worldbank.org/country/west-bank-gaza
5 Roee Nahmias, "GDP per capita of Arab Israelis third of that of Jews," Ynet News, January 18, 2007, www.ynetnews.com/articles/0,7340,L-3354260,00. html
6 Donald MacIntyre, "Secret paper reveals EU broadside over plight of Israel's Arabs," *Independent*, December 27, 2011.
7 Colin Shindler, *A History of Modern Israel*, Cambridge: Cambridge University Press, 2008, p. 7.
8 "China becomes the world's third largest arms exporter," BBC, March 16, 2015, www.bbc.com/news/technology-31901493
9 www.btselem.org/press_releases/20090909
10 www.globescan.com/news-and-analysis/press-releases/press-releases-2013/277-views-of-china-and-india-slide-while-uks-ratings-climb.html
11 See Benedict Anderson, *Imagined Communities: Reflections on the Origin and Spread of Nationalism*, London: Verso, 1991.
12 Other versions of Zionism existed, particularly cultural Zionism, some of whose advocates are discussed in this book. But Zionism without a qualifier refers here to political Zionism as it has been understood since 1942.
13 http://news.bbc.co.uk/2/hi/in_depth/middle_east/israel_and_the_ palestinians/key_documents/1682961.stm
14 This movement in known in Israel as *dati-leumi*, "national-religious" or National Judaism. For an analysis of its rise since 1967, see Charles Enderlin, *Au nom du Temple: Israël et l'irrésistible ascension du messianisme juif (1967–2013)* [*In the Name of the Temple: Israel and the Irresistible Ascension of Jewish Messianism (1967–2013)*], Paris: Seuil, 2013.
15 F. M. Dostoevsky, *Notes from the Underground and The Gambler*, trans. J. Kentish, Oxford: Oxford University Press, 2008, p. 10.
16 M. B. Otradin (ed.), Петербург в русской поэзии, XVIII–XX века [*Petersburg in Russian Poetry, 18th–20th centuries*], Leningrad: Leningrad University Press, 1988, pp. 148–50.
17 George E. Munro, *The Most Intentional City: St. Petersburg in the Reign of Catherine the Great*, Cranbury, N.J.: Associated University Presses, 2008, p. 267.
18 David Ben Gurion (1886–1973) was founder and first prime minister of the state of Israel.
19 Quoted in Georges Bensoussan, *Un nom impérissable. Israël, le sionisme et la destruction des Juifs d'Europe (1933–2007)* [*An Imperishable Name: Israel,*

Zionism and the Destruction of the Jews of Europe(1933–2007)], Paris: Seuil, 2008, pp. 151–2.

1 The Land of Israel and its Place in Jewish Tradition

1   Shlomo Avineri, *The Making of Modern Zionism: The Intellectual Origins of the Jewish State*, New York: Basic Books, 1981, p. 13.

2   Jehiel Jacob Weinberg, quoted in Marc Shapiro, *Between the Yeshiva World and Modern Orthodoxy*, London: Littman Library of Jewish Civilization, 1999, pp. 98–9.

3   Biblical quotations are taken from *The Torah: the Five Books of Moses*, Philadelphia: Jewish Publication Society of America, 1962; *The Prophets: Nevi'im*, Philadelphia: Jewish Publication Society of America, 1978, and *The Writings: Kethubim*, Philadelphia: Jewish Publication Society of America, 1982.

4   Aviezer Ravitzky, *Messianism, Zionism, and Jewish Religious Radicalism*, Chicago, Ill.: University of Chicago Press, 1996, p. 46; see e.g. the comment on Deuteronomy 11:10 by Rashbam (Samuel ben Meir, 1085–1158): "this land is the best of all the lands for those who keep His commandments, and the worst of all lands for those who do not."

5   Yeshayahu Leibowitz, *Peuple, Terre, État* [*People, Land, State*], Paris: Plon, 1995, pp. 95–6.

6   Israel Domb, *Transformation. The Case of the Neturei Karta*, Brooklyn, N.Y.: Hachomo, 1989, p. 20.

7   See Yakov Rabkin, *A Threat from Within: A Century of Jewish Opposition to Zionism*, London: Zed, 2006, ch. 3.

8   *Babylonian Talmud: Talmud Bavli*, Kesubos [Ketubot], Brooklyn, N.Y.: Mesorah, 2000 (bilingual edition), p. 111a.

9   Leibowitz, *Peuple, Terre, État*, p. 171.

10 *Babylonian Talmud*, p. 110b1–2 note 15.

11 Aviezer Ravitzky, *Messianism, Zionism, and Jewish Religious Radicalism*, p. 18.

12 The Artscroll edition of the *Babylonian Talmud* (p. 111a2, note 13) details a series of rabbinical references to the three oaths and the danger of their transgression: Bahiya on Genesis 32, 7; Abarbanel, Yeshouoth Meshiho part 1, p. 11b; Kaftor ve-ferah, Jérusalem, 5657, p. 197; Yefe Toar on Vayikra rabba 19, 5; Yefe Kol on Shir ha-shirim rabba 2, 7.

13 *Yedei Haim*, Jerusalem: Yehudiof, 1988, p. 47

14 Joseph Haim Sonnenfeld, quoted in Aharon Rosenberg (ed.), *Mishkenoth ha-ro'yim* [*Shepherds' Tents*], New York: Nechmod, 1984–87 (3 vols.), vol. 2, p. 441.

15 *The Complete ArtScroll Siddur, Nusach Ashkenaz*, Brooklyn, N.Y.: Mesorah, 2002, p. 189.

16 In some versions, "May you rebuild Jerusalem, the holy city ...."

17 *Complete ArtScroll Siddur*, p. 191.

18 Shlomo Avineri, *The Making of Modern Zionism*, p. 3.

19 *Complete Art Scroll Siddur*, p. 679.

20   David Hartman, *The God Who Hates Lies*, Woodstock, Vt.: Jewish Lights, 2011, p. 160.

21   Quoted in Paul Johnson, *A History of the Jews*, New York: Harper & Row, 1987, p. 582.

22   As Jewish practice is often described in traditional terms.

23   Simon Schwab, *Heimkehr ins Judentums* [*Return to Judaism*], New York: n.p., 1978 (1st edition published in Frankfurt, 1934).

24   *Pirkei Avor* (Ethics of the Fathers), 4, 2.

25   Michel Brunet, "Qu'est-ce que l'assimilation?" ["What is assimilation?"], *Action nationale*, vol. 45, no. 5, January 1956, pp. 388–93.

26   Leibowitz, *Peuple, Terre, État*, p. 44.

27   Jacob Neusner, "Jew and Judaist, ethnic and religious: how they mix in America," *Issues of the American Council for Judaism*, Spring 2002, pp. 3–4, 10–14.

28   Neusner, "Jew and Judaist."

29   Yosef Hayim Yerushalmi, *Zakhor: Jewish History and Jewish Memory*. Seattle, Wa.: University of Washington Press, 1996.

30   *Babylonian Talmud*, Tractate Yoma, p. 9b. It appears that the term "gratuitous hatred" relates exclusively to the Jews. An Internet search produces some 100 references, all to Jewish texts.

31   *Babylonian Talmud*, Tractate Gittin, pp. 55, 56.

32   Yerushalmi, *Zakhor*, p. 38.

33   Yerushalmi, *Zakhor*, p. 103. Underlined in the original.

34   For further details, see Yakov M. Rabkin, "Christian and Jewish roots of Zionism," *Ukrainian Orientalistics*, Special Issue on Jewish Studies, Kiev: Kiev-Mohyla Academy, 2011, pp. 304–24.

35   Lionel Kochan, *The Jew and his History*, New York: Shocken, 1977, p. 3.

36   See e.g. Julius Guttman, *Histoire des philosophies juives*, Paris: Gallimard, 1994; Jacob Breuer, (ed.), *Fundamentals of Judaism: Selections from the works of Rabbi Samson, Raphael Hirsch and outstanding Torah-true thinkers*, New York: Feldman, 1949; Léon Ashkenazi, *La parole et l'écrit* [*Speech and Writing*], Paris: Albin Michel, 1999.

37   Quoted in Lionel Kochan, *The Jew and his History*, p. 105.

38   This group of historians includes among others Baruch Kimmerling, Benny Morris, Ilan Pappe, Tom Segev, and Avi Shlaim. For a scholarly debate on the New Historians see the special issue of *History and Memory*, vol. 7, no. 1, 1995.

39   Ilan Pappe, "The Post-Zionist discourse in Israel: 1990–2001," *Journal of Holy Land Studies*, vol. 1, no.1, 2002, pp. 9–35.

40   See Moshe Idel, *Kabbalah: New Perspectives*, New Haven, Conn.: Yale University Press, 1998.

41   Michel Abitbol, "Introduction" in Florence Heymann and Michel Abtibol (eds.), *L'historiographie israélienne aujourd'hui* [*Israeli Historiography Today*], Paris: CNRS, 1998.

42   Moshe Schonfeld, *Genocide in the Holy Land*, Brooklyn, N.Y.: NK of USA, 1980; Esther Meir-Glitzenstein, *Yetsiat yehoudei taïman…* Tel-Aviv: Resling, 2012.

43   Ella Shohat, "Rupture and return: Zionist discourse and the study of Arab
     Jews," *Social Text*, vol. 21, no. 2, 2003, pp. 49–74.
44   Efraim Karsch, *Fabricating Israeli History: The "New Historians"* London:
     Frank Cass, 1997; Nur Masalha, "New history, post-zionism and neo-
     colonialism: a critique of the Israeli 'New Historians'," *Holy Land Studies*, vol.
     1, no. 1, pp. 1–53.
45   Abitbol, "Introduction," pp. 21–2.
46   Romi Sofer, "Knesset passes Nakba law," Ynet, March 23, 2011, www.ynet-
     ?news.com/articles/0,7340,L-4046440,00.html
47   Akiva Eldar, "A softer touch on the Nakba," *Haaretz*, January 24, 2012.
48   Yakov Rabkin, "Nakba in narratives about Zionism," *Kyoto Bulletin of Islamic
     Area Studies*, vol. 3, no. 1, July 2009, pp. 21–36. On the question of expul-
     sions, see Ilan Pappe, *The Ethnic Cleansing of Palestine*, Oxford: Oneworld,
     2006.
49   For example, in the Haifa City Museum: www.hcm.org.il/eng/Exhibitions/
     1559/Palestinian_Arab_Houses%3A_Haifa_%281860%E2%80%931930%29
50   Rima Peled, *"Ha-adam ha-hadash" shel ha-maapekha ha-tsionit* [*The New
     Man of the Zionist Revolution*], Tel-Aviv: Am Oved, 2002.
51   *Haredi* refers to Jews often described as ultra-orthodox in Western-language
     sources.
52   Yerushalmi, *Zakhor*, p. 116.
53   For a study of the relations between the socialist and nationalist dimensions
     of Zionist ideology, see Zeev Sternhell, *The Founding Myths of Israel: Nation-
     alism, Socialism and the Making of the Jewish State,* Princeton, N.J.: Princeton
     University Press, 1998.
54   See Shlomo Sand, *The Invention of the Jewish People*, London: Verso, 2009.
55   Israel Bartal, "Inventing an invention," *Haaretz*, July 6, 2008.

2 The Jews of Europe

1   Howard Morley Sachar, *A History of the Jews in the Modern World*, New York:
     Vintage, 2005, p. 47.
2   Franz Kobler, *Napoleon and the Jews,* New York: Schocken, 1976, pp. 55–7.
3   Arthur Hertzberg, *The French Enlightenment and the Jews*, New York:
     Columbia University Press, 1968.
4   Sternhell, *The Founding Myths of Israel*, p. 11.
5   See Robert Liberles, *Religious Conflict in Social Context: The Resurgence of Or-
     thodox Judaism in Frankfurt am Main*, Westport, Conn.: Greenwood Press, 1985;
     and Noah Rosenbloom, *Tradition in an Age of Reform: The Religious Philosophy
     of Samson Raphael Hirsch*, Philadelphia, Pa.: Jewish Publication Society, 1976.
6   Yaakov Zur, "German Jewish Orthodoxy's attitude toward Zionism," in
     Shmuel Almog, Jehuda Reinharz and Anita Shapira (eds.), *Zionism and
     Religion*, Hanover, N.H.: University Press of New England, 1998, p. 111.
7   Samson Raphael Hirsch, *Horev: A Philosophy of Jewish Laws and
     Observances*, New York: Soncino Press, 1981, p. 461.

8   Jehiel Jacob Weinberg, quoted in Shapiro, *Between the Yeshiva World and Modern Orthodoxy*, pp. 98–9.
9   Zvi Gitelman and Ken Goldstein, "The 'Russian' revolution in Israeli politics," pp. 141–61 in Asher Arian and Michal Samir, *The Elections in Israel 1999*, Albany, N.Y.: SUNY Press, 2002.
10   Zvi Gitelman, *A Century of Ambivalence: The Jews of Russian and the Soviet Union, 1881 to the Present*, Bloomington, Ind.: Indiana University Press, 1998.
11   The basic work on the question is without doubt Leon Poliakov, *The History of Anti-Semitism*, 4 vols., Philadelphia, Pa.: University of Pennsylvania Press, 2003.
12   Alex Bein, *The Jewish Question: Biography of a World Problem*, Madison, N.J.: Farleigh Dickinson University Press, 1990, p. 594.
13   Gil Anidjar, *Semites, Race, Religion, Literature*, Stanford, Calif.: Stanford University Press, 2007.
14   Sternhell, *The Founding Myths of Israel*, p. 55.
15   www.historyplace.com/worldwar2/holocaust/h-statistics.htm
16   www.jewishvirtuallibrary.org/jsource/Immigration/First_Aliyah.html
17   Nathaniel Popper, "Germany is moving to end mass immigration of Jews from Russia," *Forward*, December 24, 2004.
18   Gabriel Piterberg, *The Returns of Zionism*, London: Verso, 2008, p. 247.
19   Ari Shavit, "Leaving the Zionist ghetto," *Haaretz*, June 7, 2007 (interview with Avraham Burg).
20   Robert S. Wistrich "Zionism and its religious critics in Vienna," in Almog et al., *Zionism and Religion*, p. 145.

3 A Return to the Promised Land as a Return to History

1   Regina Sharif, *Non-Jewish Zionism: Its Roots in Western History*, London: Zed, 1986, p. 39.
2   Tim LaHaye and Jerry Jenkins, *Left Behind*, www.imdb.com/title/tt2467046/
3   Immanuel Kant, quoted in Sharif, *Non-Jewish Zionism*, p. 37.
4   J. G. Fichte, quoted in Sharif, *Non-Jewish Zionism*, p. 38.
5   Isaiah Friedman, The *Question of Palestine: British-Jewish-Arab Relations 1914–1918*, Brunswick, N.J.: Transaction, 1992, p. xvi.
6   Sharif, *Non-Jewish Zionism*, p. 58.
7   Sharif, *Non-Jewish Zionism*, p. 58.
8   Laurence Oliphant, *The Land of Gilead, with Excursions in the Lebanon*, Edinburgh and London: W. Blackwood & Sons, 1880, pp. 285–6.
9   Oliphant, *The Land of Gilead,* p. 317.
10   Claude Duvernoy, *The Prince and the Prophet*] (n.p.), Land of Promise Productions, 1973.
11   André Chouraqui, "Preface," in Duvernoy, *Le prince et le prophête*, p. 4 (my translation).
12   Chouraqui, "Preface," pp. 3–4.

13   Colin Schindler, *A History of Modern Israel,* Cambridge: Cambridge University Press, 2008, p. 92.
14   David Ben-Gurion, *Israel: Years of Challenge,* New York: Holt, Reinhart & Winston, 1964, p. 49.
15   Ben-Gurion, *Israel: Years of Challenge,* p. 60.
16   James Hider, "A tragic misunderstanding," *The Times,* January 13, 2009.
17   Shlomo Sand, *The Invention of the Jewish People,* London: Verso, 2008, pp. 185–6.
18   Ben-Gurion, *Israel: Years of Challenge,* p. 65.
19   Netanyahu's speech to AIPAC Conference (www.haaretz.com/news/prime- minister-benjamin-netanyahu-s-speech-to-aipac-conference-1.265227).
20   www.nytimes.com/2012/05/01/world/middleeast/benzion-netanyahu-dpininies-at-102.html
21   Amnon Raz-Krakotzkin, "I feel responsible for the victims of Zionism," https://en.qantara.de/content/interview-amnon-raz-krakotzkin-i-feel-responsible-for-the-victims-of-zionism
22   The Peel Commission, or Palestine Royal Commission, was a royal commission set up in 1936 to modify the British Mandate and to control the situation in Palestine, then in the throes of the Arab revolt.
23   John Hagee, "Christians united for Israel," www.pbs.org/moyers/journal/10052007/profile.html
24   Tom Segev, "On the third thought," *Haaretz Magazine,* August 5, 2005.

4 The Zionist Enterprise

1   For more details see Rabkin, *A Threat from Within.*
2   Ella Shohat, "Sephardim in Israel: Zionism from the standpoint of its Jewish victims," *Social Text,* 1988, pp.19–20.
3   Ben-Gurion, quoted in Élie Barnavi, "Sionismes," in Élie Barnavi and Saul Friedländer, *Les Juifs et le XXe siècle* [*The Jews and the 20th Century*], Paris: Calmann-Lévy, 2000, p. 219.
4   Shlomo Avineri, *The Making of Modern Zionism,* p. 13.
5   Avineri, *The Making of Modern Zionism,* p. 26.
6   Barnavi, "Sionismes," p. 218.
7   Jacques Kornberg, *Theodor Herzl: From Assimilation to Zionism,* Bloomington, Ind.: Indiana University Press 1993, p. 116.
8   Edwin Black, *The Transfer Agreement: The Dramatic Story of a Pact between the Third Reich and Jewish Palestine,* New York: Macmillan, 1984.
9   Joshua Joseph Preil, quoted by Yosef Salmon in Almog et al., *Zionism and Religion,* p. 30.
10   Jonathan Adelman, *The Rise of Israel: A History of a Revolutionary State,* New York: Routledge, 2008, p. 200.
11   Sue Fishkoff, "Israeli population in U.S. surges, but exact figures hard to determine," *JTA,* December 22, 2010, www.jta.org/news/article/ 2010/12/22/2742296/israeli-population-jumps-in-the-us-but-is-still-hard-to-count
12   Sharif, *Non-Jewish Zionism,* p. 62.

13   Yossi Gurwitz, "Yedioth: Soviet Jews were cheated into immigrating to Israel," +972, April 16, 2011, http://972mag.com/how-israel- swindled-soviet-jews/13381/; Fred A. Lazin, *The Struggle for Soviet Jewry in American Politics: Israel Versus the American Jewish Establishment*, Lanham, Md.: Lexington, 2005; Nathaniel Popper, "Germany is moving to end mass immigration of Jews from Russia," *Forward*, December 24, 2004, http://forward.com/news/4029/germany-is-moving-to-end-mass-immigration-of-jews/

14   Yakov (Yasha) Kedmi, *Hopeless Wars*, New York: Contento Now, 2015.

15   Barak Ravid, "Hoenlein criticizes Netanyahu's call on American Jews to oppose Iran deal," *Haaretz*, August 6, 2015, www.haaretz.com/beta/. premium-1.669986

16   I. M. Rabinowitch, "Political Zionists and the state of Israel," *Jewish Guardian*, no. 1, April 1974, p. 10.

17   Barnavi, "Sionismes," p. 228.

18   Lucian Heichler, "Israel: an insoluble problem," *Issues of the American Council for Judaism*, Summer 2002, pp. 5–6.

19   Ralph Peters in the *New York Post*, September 3, 2003, quoted in "Pollard seeks new hearing: Jewish groups are criticized for seeking his release," Allan C. Brownfield (ed.), *American Council for Judaism Special Interest Report*, vol. 32, no. 5, 2003, p. 2.

20   "Poll: 50% in U.K. think Jews more loyal to Israel than to home nation," *Haaretz*, July 17, 2007, p. 2.

21   Hanoch Marmari, "In France, cause for real anxiety," *Haaretz*, May 10, 2002.

22   Ben-Gurion, *Israel: Years of Challenge*, p. 160.

23   Uri Avnery, "Manufacturing anti-Semites," September 28, 2002, www.gush-shalom.org/archives/article213.html

24   Interview by the author with Rabbi Menashe Fullop, November 11, 2002, Williamsburg, N.Y.

25   Alan Hart, *Zionism: The Real Enemy of the Jews*, 3 vols, Atlanta, Ga.: Clarity Press, 2009–11.

26   http://news.reformjudaism.org.uk/press-releases/update-from-the-new-israel-fund.html

27   Avineri, *The Making of Modern Zionism*, p. 221.

28   "Why are so many French Jews voting for Front National?" *Forward*, September 14, 2014.

29   Jeffrey Simpson, "How the political shift among Jewish voters plays in Canada," *Globe & Mail*, September 28, 2011.

30   Jay Michaelson, "What are Jewish issues?" *Forward*, August 22, 2008, www.forward.com/articles/14029

31   David Eugene Blank, "The *New York Times*' strange attack on classical Reform Judaism," *Issues of the American Council for Judaism*, Washington DC, Fall 2002, pp. 5–14.

32   See "Tikkun," www.tikkun.org

33   Rabbi David Goldberg, "Let us have a sense of proportion," *Guardian*, January 31, 2002.

34 Henry Siegman, "Separating spiritual and political, he pays a price," *New York Times*, June 13, 2002.

35 Alisa Solomon, "Intifada dyptich," Jewish in America, special issue, *Michigan Quarterly Review*, vol. 41, no. 4, 2002, p. 650.

36 "Yehuda Bauer: Israel's genocidal nationalists," interview on Al-Jazeera, January 8, 2012, www.aljazeera.com/programme/talktojazeera/2012/01/20121774 656322518.html

37 Joseph B. Schechtman, *Fighter and Prophet*, New York: Thomas Yoseloff, 1961, p. 411.

38 Hayyim Nahman Bialik, *Songs from Bialik*, Syracuse, N.Y.: Syracuse University Press, 2000, p. 35.

39 Schechtman, *Fighter and Prophet*, p. 410.

40 Avineri in Almog et al., *Zionism and Religion*, p. 6.

41 Eliezer Don Yehiya and Charles S. Liebman, "The symbol system of Zionist socialism: an aspect of Israeli civil religion," *Modern Judaism*, vol. 1, no. 2, September 1981, pp. 121–48.

42 Sternhell, *The Founding Myths of Israel*, p. 56.

43 Quoted in Anita Shapira, *Land and Power: The Zionist Resort to Force*, New York: Oxford University Press, 1992, p. 102.

44 "IDF to remove 'God' from memorial text," *Forward*, May 17, 2012.

45 Avishai Ben Hayim, *Ish ha-hashkafa. Ha-ideologiya ha-haredit al-pi ha-rav shakh* [*A Man of Perspective: Haredi Ideology According to Rav Shakh*], Jerusalem: Mozaika, 2004.

46 Yehuda Reinharz, "Zionism and Orthodoxy: a marriage of convenience," in Almog et al., *Zionism and Religion*, pp. 116–39.

47 Leibowitz, *Peuple, Terre, État*, p. 176.

48 Reinharz, "Zionism and Orthodoxy," p. 125.

49 Michael Neumann, *The Case Against Israel*, Petrolia/Oakland, Calif.: CounterPunch/AK Press, 2005.

50 Shapira, quoted in Gershon Shafer, "Origins of the Israeli-Palestinian conflict," in Laurence J. Silberstein (ed.), *Postzionism: A Reader*, New Brunswick, N.J.: Rutgers University Press, 2008, p. 47.

51 Shapira, *Land and Power*, p. 355.

52 Benny Morris, *Righteous Victims*, New York: Vintage, 2001, p. 676.

53 Yaron Ezrahi, *Rubber Bullets: Power and Conscience in Modern Israel*, Berkeley, Calif.: University of California Press, 1998.

54 Oren Yiftachel, "Ethnocracy: the politics of Judaising Israel/Palestine," in Silberstein, *Postzionism*, p. 141.

55 Yiftachel, "Ethnocracy," pp. 120–30.

56 Yiftachel, "Ethnocracy," p. 131.

57 Susan Nathan, *The Other Side of Israel: My Journey Across the Jewish/Arab Divide*, New York: Doubleday, 2005, pp. 148–56.

58 Amram Blau, "A call from Jerusalem," *Jewish Guardian*, no. 1 (April 1974), pp. 2–3.

59 David Ben-Gurion, quoted in Sternhell, *The Founding Myths of Israel*, pp. 20–1.

60 Ben-Gurion, quoted in Sternhell, *The Founding Myths of Israel*, p. 21.

61 Sternhell goes to great lengths to invent the term "nationalist Socialism" to avoid calling Ben-Gurion's political outlook National Socialism: "Introduction: Socialism, nationalism and nationalist socialism," in *The Founding Myths of Israel.*

62 Vladimir Jabotinsky, "О железной стене" [*About the Iron Wall*] *Razsviet* (Paris), November 4, 1923.

63 Sharif, *Non-Jewish Zionism*, p. 78.

64 Shapira, *Land and Power*, pp. 366–7.

65 Tikva Honig-Parnass, *False Prophets of Peace: Liberal Zionism and the Struggle for Palestine*, Chicago, Ill.: Haymarket, 2001.

66 Avineri, in Almog et al., *Zionism and Religion*, p. 3.

67 Ivan Berend, *History Derailed: Central and Eastern Europe in the Long Nineteenth Century*, Berkeley, Calif.: University of California Press, 2003, ch. 3.

68 To understand the context in which this literature arose, see David Aberbach, *Revolutionary Hebrew, Empire and Crisis: Four Peaks in Hebrew Literature and Jewish Survival*, New York.: New York University Press, 1998.

69 Paul R. Mendes-Flohr and Jehuda Reinharz (eds.), *The Jew in the Modern World: A Documentary History*, New York: Oxford University Press, 1995, p. 83.

70 The neologism *galuti*—or "exilic"—reflects disdain for life in the diaspora, presented as a life with neither roots nor vigor: the term was introduced into Modern Hebrew by two nationalist authors, Itamar Ben-Avi (son of Eliezer Ben-Yehuda) and Uri Tzevi Greenberg. It can be compared to "rootless cosmopolitan" introduced into the Russian language during Stalin's anti-Semitic persecutions, which also had a pejorative connotation .

71 Arieh Bruce Saposnik, *Becoming Hebrew: The Creation of Jewish National Culture in the Ottoman Palestine*, Oxford: Oxford University Press, 2008, p. 269.

72 Ernest Renan, *Qu'est ce que c'est une nation?* [*What is a Nation?*], Paris: Mille et une nuits, 2009, p. 15 (quoted from the English translation: http://ucparis.fr/files/9313/6549/9943/What_is_a_Nation.pdf).

73 Yael Chaver, *What Must be Forgotten: The Survival of Yiddish in Zionist Palestine*, Syracuse, N.Y.: Syracuse University Press, 2004, pp. 16–17.

74 Nur Masalha, *The Bible and Zionism: Archeology and Post-Colonialism in Palestine-Israel*, London: Zed, 2007.

75 Tuvya Yoel Steiner, *Peduyoth Tuvya* [*Tuvya's Distinctions*], Bnei-Brak (n.p.), 1996, p. 37.

76 "Parsha pearls from the words of the Gedolim," *True Torah Jews*, Brooklyn, N.Y., May 2009.

77 Leslie Stein, *Hope Fulfilled: The Rise of Modern Israel*, Westport, Conn.: Praeger, 2003, p. 35.

78 Marc H. Ellis, *Out of the Ashes: The Search for Jewish Identity in the Twenty-first Century*, London: Pluto, 2002, p. 6.

79 Elyakim Shlomo Shapira quoted in Ravitzky, *Messianism*, p. 4.

80 Rav Kook quoted in Ravitzky, *Messianism*, pp. 131–7.

81   Ben-Gurion, *Israel: Years of Challenge*, p. 240.

82   Israel Bartal, "Responses to modernity," in Almog et al., *Zionism and Religion*, p. 21.

83   David Roach, "Modern Hebrew Bible translation reaches out to Israeli youth," *Baptist Press*, April 7, 2006.

84   David Ben-Gurion, *Israel: Years of Challenge*, p. 114.

85   Albert Swissa quoted in Gil Z. Hochberg, *In Spite of Partition: Jews, Arabs and the Limits of Separatist Imagination*, Princeton, N.J.: Princeton University Press, 2007, p. 93.

86   Ghil'ad Zuckerman, *Yisraelit safa yafa* [*Israeli is a Fine Language*], Tel-Aviv: Am Oved, 2009.

87   The Jerusalem Talmud, Tractate "Berakhot" (2:8) contains one reference to the land of Israel as mother: "The mother of a man degrades him while the wife of his father honors him: where should he turn?" The story is about a rabbi badly treated in Israel but highly respected in Babylonia. Despite its ironic context, this maternal reference is used in the Hebrew title *Em Ha-banin semeha* [*The Mother of the Children is Happy*], a passionate plea for the *aliya* composed during the Shoah: Yissakhar Shlomo Teichtal, *Restoration of Zion as a Response during the Holocaust*, Hoboken, N.J.: Ktav, 1999, pp. 33–6 and 192–203; it pleads to "leave the land of exile and return to the bosom of the mother that is Eretz Israel" (p. 229).

88   "For us, Eretz Israel is not a homeland .... It is inconceivable that the simple possession of the land of Israel might make of us a nation," stated Rabbi Wasserman (quoted in Aharon Sorasky, *Reb Elchonon* [*Rabbi Elchonon*], New York: Menora, 1996, p. 224).

89   Chaver, *What Must be Forgotten*, p. 40.

90   Arieh Bruce Saposnik, *Becoming Hebrew: The Creation of Jewish National Culture in the Ottoman Palestine*, Oxford: Oxford University Press, 2008, p. 252.

91   Circular letter dispatched to the rabbis of Russia by the Jerusalem Rabbinical Court, quoted by Yosef Salomon in *Zionism and Religion*, p. 28.

92   For more details on this conflict see my *A Threat from Within*.

93   Bat-Zion Eraqui-Klorman, "Yemen," in Reeva S. Simon, Michael M. Laskier, and Sara Reguer (eds.), *The Jews of the Middle East and North Africa in Modern Times*, New York: Columbia University Press, 2003, p. 406.

94   Shimon Peres and David Landau, *Ben-Gurion: A Political Life*, New York: Schocken, 2011, p. 83.

95   "BBC Poll: Israel's global image plummets" Ynet, July 17, 2012, www.ynetnews.com/articles/0,7340,L-4230395,00.html

96   Sternhell, *The Founding Myths of Israel*, p. 27.

97   Mikhail Heller, *Cogs in the Wheel: The Formation of Soviet Man*, New York: Knopf, 1988.

98   See e.g. Nahum Menahem, *Israël: tensions et discriminations communautaires* [*Israel: Community Tensions and Discrimination*], Paris: l'Harmattan, 1986.

99   Tamar Ruth Horowitz (ed.), *Children of Perestroika in Israel*, Lanham, Md.: University Press of America, 1999.

100 Noah Efron, "Trembling with fear: how secular Israelis see the ultra-Orthodox and why," *Tikkun*, vol. 6, no. 5, 1991, pp.15–22 and 88–90.

101 Efron, "Trembling with fear," pp. 16, 18–19.

102 *Haaretz* editorial, "Mousaf," Elul 5703 (1941).

103 André Malraux, "Préface," in Nicolas Lazar, Izis, and André Neher, *Israël*, Lausanne, Switzerland: la Guilde du livre, 1955, p. 9.

104 Jacqueline Rose, *The Question of Zion*, Princeton, N.J.: Princeton University Press, 2005, pp. 91–2.

105 Raphael Falk, "Zionism, race and eugenics," in Geoffrey Cantor and Marc Swetlitz (eds.), *Jewish Tradition and the Challenge of Darwinism*, Chicago, Ill.: Chicago University Press, 2006, p. 150.

106 Falk, "Zionism, race and eugenics," p. 155.

107 Shlomo Sand, *The Invention of the Jewish People*, London: Verso, 2010, p. 265.

108 Bensoussan, *Un nom impérissable*, pp. 76–7.

109 Efron, *Trembling with Fear*, p. 16.

110 Efron, *Trembling with Fear*, p. 16.

111 Efron, *Trembling with Fear*, p. 16. For a more detailed treatment of the subject, see *Noah Efron, Real Jews: Secular versus Ultra-Orthodox and the Struggle for Jewish Identity in Israel*, New York: Basic Books, 2003.

112 Yehonatan Geffen, "Trading Anna Karenina for Golda Meir," *Lilith*, vol. 27, no. 1, 2002, pp. 13–15.

113 Barnavi, "Sionismes," p. 220.

114 Yuval Avivi, "Secular Jews rediscover Jewish heritage," *Al-Monitor*, May 24, 2015, www.al-monitor.com/pulse/originals/2015/05/mickey-gitzin-tel-aviv-feast-of-weeks-secular-orthodox.html#

115 Haim Ha-Levi Soloveitschik, quoted in Rosenberg, *Mishkenoth ha-ro'yim*, vol. 1, p. 269.

116 Vered Levi-Barzilai, "Divine Secrets of the Basia sisterhood," *Haaretz*, February 13, 2002.

117 Leibowitz, *Peuple, Terre, État*, p. 111.

118 Elhanan Bunim Wasserman, *Yalkout maamarim u-mikhtavim* [*Collected Articles and Letters*], Brooklyn (n.p.), 1986, p. 7.

119 Quoted in Schindler, *A History of Modern Israel*, p. 16.

120 Judah Leon Magnes, quoted in Elmer Berger, *Judaism or Jewish Nationalism: The Alternative to Judaism*, New York: Bookman Associates, 1957, p. 32.

121 Adin Steinsaltz, "Interviu," *Vremia I my*, no. 1468, 2000.

122 Jay Y. Gonen, *A Psychohistory of Zionism*, New York: Mason Charter, 1975, p. 334.

123 Rabbi Shalom Baer Schneerson, "Three questions and answers on Zionism and Zionists," *Jewish Guardian*, vol. 2, no. 8, Spring 1984, pp. 19–24.

124 Shaul Stempfer, *Ha-yeshiva ha-litait ba-me'ah ha-tesh'a-'esreh* [*Lithuanian Yeshiva in the 19th Century*], Jerusalem: Merkaz Zalman Shazar le-toldor Yisrael, 1995, p. 224.

125 Boaz Evron, quoted in Leibowitz, *Peuple, Terre, État*, p. 132.

126 *Jewish Chronicle* (January 9, 1880) quoted in Catherine Delmas et al., *Science and*

Empire in the Nineteenth Century: A Journey of Imperial Conquest and Scientific Progress, Newcastle upon Tyne: Cambridge Scholars Publishing, 2010, p. 195.

127 *Encyclopaedia Judaica,* 1971, vol. 8, cols. 729–30.

128 See K. C.Tessendorf, *Kill the Tsar: Youth and Terrorism in Old Russia,* New York: Atheneum, 1986.

129 See Tristan Landry, *La valeur de la vie humaine en Russie (1836–1946)* [*The Value of Human Life in Russia, 1836–1946*], Québec,Canada: Les Presses de l'Université Laval, 2001.

130 Maurice Kriegel, "La societé israélienne et le passé juif" ["Israeli society and the Jewish past"], *Le Débat,* no. 82, 1994, p. 104.

131 Kornberg, *Theodor Herzl,* pp. 124–6.

132 Sorrel Kerbel (ed.), *The Routledge Encyclopedia of Jewish Writers of the Twentieth Century,* New York: Fitzroy Dearborn, 2003, p. 444.

133 Haim Nahman Bialik, "On the slaughter," www.poemhunter.com/ hayyim-nahman-bialik/

134 Sternhell, *The Founding Myths of Israel,* p. 52.

135 Rosenheim, quoted in Yaakov Zur, "German Jewish Orthodoxy's attitude toward Zionism," in Almog et al., *Zionism and Religion,* p. 111.

136 Schechtman, *Fighter and Prophet,* p. 297.

137 Drawn from *Who is Who in Israel 1960,* quoted in Martin Gilbert, *The Atlas of Jewish History,* New York: William Morrow, 1992, p. 115.

138 Mohammed Kenbib, *Juifs et musulmans au Maroc, 1859–1948* [*Jews and Muslims in Morocco, 1859–1948*], Rabat: Université Mohammed V, 1994, p. 478.

139 Jonathan Adelman, *The Rise of Israel: A History of a Revolutionary State,* New York: Routledge, 2008, p. 37.

140 "Poll: Israel viewed negatively around the world," *Jerusalem Post,* May 17, 2012.

141 Dmitry Fuhrman "Нас объединяет жестокость" ["It is cruelty that unites us"], *Moscow News,* November 20, 2002.

142 Dmitry Radyshevskiy, "Русские спасут Израиль" ["The Russians will save Israel"], *Moscow News,* November 20, 2002.

143 http://jerusalem-temple-today.com/for/viewtopic.php?f=80&t=5065

144 http://izrus.co.il/wfre/index.php?articleid=18695

5 The Nazi Genocide, Its Memory and Its Lessons

1 Bensoussan, *Un nom impérisssable,* p. 63.

2 Quoted in I. M. Rabinowitch, "Political Zionists and the state of Israel," *Jewish Guardian,* no. 1, April 1974, p. 10.

3 Boaz Evron, *Jewish State or Jewish Nation,* Bloomington, Ind.: Indiana University Press, 1995, pp. 259–61.

4 Rabinowitch, "Political Zionists," p. 11.

5 Rabinowitch, "Political Zionists," p. 10.

6 Claude Duvernay, *Le prince et le prophète* [*The Prince and the Prophet*], Vannes, France: Keren Israël, 1996, p. 193.

7   Bensoussan, *Un nom impérisssable*, p. 19.

8   Quoted in Dina Porat, "Une question d'historiographie: l'attitude de Ben Gourion à l'égard des juifs d'Europe à l'époque du genocide" ["A question of historiography: the attitude of Ben-Gurion to the Jews of Europe in the time of genocide"], in Florence Heymann and Michel Abitbol (eds.), *L'historiographie israélienne aujourd'hui* [*Israeli Historiography Today*], Paris: CNRS éditions, 1998, p. 120.

9   Hartglass, quoted in Michael R. Marrus (ed.), *Bystanders to the Holocaust*, Vol. 2, Westport, Conn.: Meckler, 1989, p. 591.

10   Bensoussan, *Un nom impérisssable*, p. 71.

11   Ben-Gurion, quoted in Porat, "Une question d'historiographie," p. 128.

12   Sternhell, *The Founding Myths of Israel*, p. 51.

13   Jack Ross, *Rabbi Outcast: Elmer Berger and American Jewish Anti-Zionism*, Washington DC: Potomac, 2011, p. 76.

14   Ernst, quoted in Elmer Berger, *Judaism or Jewish Nationalism*, p. 57.

15   Barnet Litvinoff (ed.), *The Letters and Papers of Chaim Weizmann*, Vol. 2, series B, New Brunswick, N.J.: Transaction, 1984, p. 286.

16   Leonard R. Sussman, "Judaism for all seasons," *The Christian Century*, April 3, 1963, p. 428.

17   Marrus, *Bystanders to the Holocaust*.

18   See e.g. Tom Segev, *The Seventh Million: The Israelis and the Holocaust*, New York: Hill & Wang, 1993.

19   Howard R. Greenstein, *Turning Point: Zionism and Reform Judaism*, Chico, Calif.: Scholars Press, 1981, p. 79.

20   Sternhell, *The Founding Myths of Israel*, p. 50.

21   Ross, *Rabbi Outcast*, p. 141.

22   Joachim Prinz, "Zionism under the Nazi government," *Young Zionist*, London, November, 1937, p. 18.

23   Jacob Boas, "A Nazi travels to Palestine," *History Today*, vol. 30, no. 1, 1980, pp. 33–9.

24   Boas, "A Nazi travels."

25   This story is illustrated in the Israeli-German documentary *The Flat*: Nirit Anderman, "'When to tell, how to tell, whether to tell,'" *Haaretz*, September 5, 2011, www.haaretz.com/culture/leisure-when-to-tell-how-to-tell-whether-to-tell-1.382573

26   Edwin Black, *The Transfer Agreement: The Dramatic Story of a Pact between the Third Reich and Jewish Palestine*, New York: Macmillan, 1984.

27   Moshe Zimmerman, quoted in Leibowitz, *Peuple, Terre, État*, p. 61.

28   Bensoussan, *Un nom impérisssable*, p. 230.

29   Orna Kennan, *Between Memory and History: The Evolution of Israeli Historiography of the Holocaust*, New York: Peter Lang, 2005, p. 31.

30   Kennan, *Between Memory and History*, p. 15.

31   Idith Zertal, *Israel's Holocaust and the Politics of Nationhood*, Cambridge: Cambridge University Press, 2005, p. 95.

32   Jean-Michel Chaumont, *La concurrence des victimes: génocide, identité,*

reconnaissance [*The Accord Between the Victims: Genocide, Identity, Memory*], Paris: La Découverte, 1997, p. 32.

33 David Cesarini, *After Eichmann: Collective Memory and the Holocaust since 1961,* London: Routledge, 2005, p. 23.

34 Quoted in Charles S. Liebman and Eliezer Don Yehiya, "The symbol system of Zionist-Socialism: an aspect of Israeli civil religion," *Modern Judaism*, vol. 1, no. 2, September 1981, p. 178.

35 Words of the poet Haim Gouri quoted in Bensoussan, *Un nom impérissable*, p. 165.

36 Katarzyna Mala, "Israeli warplanes over Auschwitz," Reuters, September 4, 2003.

37 "ADL survey finds vast majority of Israeli teenagers aware of global anti-Semitism," http://archive.adl.org/presrele/islme_62/5014_62.html#.VnCFKuJN-p4

38 www.science.co.il/Ilan-Ramon/Moon-Landscape.php

39 Quoted in Liebman and Don Yehiya, "The symbol system," p. 184.

40 Irena Klepfisz, *Dreams of an Insomniac*, Portland, Ore.: Eighth Mountain, 1990, pp. 130–1.

41 Paul Foot, "Palestine's partisans," *Guardian*, August 21, 2002.

42 Steven F. Aschheim, *Hannah Arendt in Jerusalem*, Berkeley, Calif.: University of California Press, 2001.

43 Reuven Hammer quoted in Liebman and Don Yehiya, "The symbol system," p. 184.

44 Yair Auron, Jack Katzenell, and David Silberklang, "The Holocaust and the Israeli teacher," *Holocaust and Genocide Studies*, vol. 8, no. 2, 1994, pp. 225–57.

45   Moshe Sober, *Beyond the Jewish State*, Toronto, Ont.: Summerhill Press, 1990, p. 49.

46 The belief in reward and punishment is recited daily at the end of the traditional morning prayer in the list of Thirteen Tenets of Faith, formulated by Maimonides: www.chabad.org/library/article_cdo/aid/332555/jewish/Maimonides-13-Principles-of-Faith.htm

47 See, *inter alia*, BT Meggila 14a, Sanhedrin 47a as well as Rashi's commentary on Exodus 14:10; see also Menasse Ben-Israel, *De la fragilité humaine et de l'inclinaison de l'homme au péché* [*Of Human Frailty and the Human Inclination to Sin*], Paris: Éditions du Cerf, 1996.

48 "Rav Elchonon Wasserman," *Jewish Guardian*, no. 12, July, 1977.

49 Elchonon Wasserman, *Epoch of the Messiah*, Brooklyn, N.Y.: Ohr Elchonon, n.d.

50 Simon Schwab, *Homecoming to Judaism*, New York, unpub., 1978, p. 5. (The German-language original, *Heimkehr ins Judendums*, was published in Frankfurt in 1934.)

51 Schwab, *Homecoming to Judaism*, pp. 15–16.

52 Wasserman, *Epoch*, p. 23.

53 Moshe Hirsch, "Reb Amrom's last demonstration," *Jewish Guardian*, no. 2, July 1974, pp. 5–6.

54 Greer Fay Cashman, "No stranger to controversy," *Jerusalem Post*, May 24, 2000.

55 "Statement to UN Special Committee on Palestine," *Jewish Guardian*, no. 3, November 1974, p. 4.

56 Judah Magnes, "Palestine peace seen in Arab-Jewish agreements," *New York Times*, July 18, 1937.

57 Matthew Wagner, "Exclusive: No shuls, please, we're atheists," *Jerusalem Post*, November 3, 2006.

58 Benoussan, *Un nom impérissable*, pp. 139–40.

59 "'Palestinian mufti convinced Hitler to massacre Europe's Jews,' Netanyahu says," *Jerusalem Post*, October 21, 2015.

60 Quoted in Liebman and Don Yehiya, "The symbol system," p. 184.

61 Amos Oz, *The Slopes of Lebanon*, San Diego, Calif.: Harcourt, Brace & Jovanovitch, 1989, p. 40.

62 Liebman and Don Yehiya, "The symbol system," p. 237.

63 Liebman and Don Yehiya, "The symbol system," pp. 237–8.

64 Ross, *Rabbi Outcast*, p. 181.

65 Enzo Traverso, *La fin de la modernité juive* [*The End of Jewish Modernity*], Paris: La Découverte, 2013, p. 132.

66 Babylonian Talmud, Tractate Baba-Kama, p. 60a.

67 Babylonian Talmud, Tractate Shevuoth, p. 39a.

68 Wasserman, *Epoch of the Messiah*, pp. 44–5.

69 Wasserman, *Epoch of the Messiah*, pp.44–5.

70 Wasserman, *Epoch of the Messiah*, p. 46

71 Ruth Blau, *Les gardiens de la cité: histoire d'une guerre sainte* [*The Guardians of the City: Story of a Holy War*], Paris: Flammarion, 1978, p. 296.

72 Wasserman, *Epoch of the Messiah*, p. 24.

73 Yaffa Eliach, *Hassidic Tales of the Holocaust*, New York: Vintage, 1982, pp. 160–1.

74 Eliach, *Hassidic Tales*, p. 19.

75 Eliach, *Hassidic Tales*, p. xxxii.

76 Interview with Rabbi Moshe Dov Beck, Monsey, N.Y., November 11, 2002.

77 "Warsaw Ghetto revolt: true or fiction? The Torah view," *Jewish Guardian*, vol. 2, no. 8, Spring 1984, pp. 5–7.

78 "Warsaw Ghetto revolt," p. 6.

6 The Making and Maintaining of the Zionist State

1 www.jewishvirtuallibrary.org/jsource/History/balfour.html

2 Tom Segev, *One Palestine, Complete*, New York: Metropolitan, 2000, p. 43.

3 Rafael Medoff and Chaim I. Waxman, *Historical Dictionary of Zionism*, New York: Routledge, 2000, p. 7.

4 Shindler, *A History of Modern Israel*, p. 19.

5 Boas, "A Nazi travels," p. 34.

6 Francis R. Nicosia, *Zionism and Anti-Semitism in Nazi Germany*, Cambridge: Cambridge University Press, 2008, p. 125.

7 Medoff and Waxman, *Historical Dictionary of Zionism*, p. 9.

8 Quoted from Ruth Gavison (ed.), *The Two-State Solution: The UN*

Partition Resolution of Mandatory Palestine – Analysis and Sources, New York: Bloomsbury, 2013, p. 23.

9   Ilan Pappe, *The Ethnic Cleansing of Palestine*, London: Oneworld, 2006.

10   Benny Morris, *Israel's Border Wars, 1949–1956: Arab Infiltration, Israeli Retaliation, and the Countdown to the Suez War*, Cambridge: Clarendon Press, 1997, pp. 431–2.

11   Leibowitz, *Peuple, Terre, État*, pp. 95–6.

12   Benny Morris, "The new historiography," in Silberstein, *Postzionism*, pp. 31–45.

13   Avi Shlaim, *The Politics of Partition: King Abdullah, the Zionists, and Palestine, 1921–1951*, Oxford: Clarendon Press, 1999.

14   Quoted from Eve Spangler, *Understanding Israel/Palestine: Race, Nation, and Human Rights in the Conflict*, New York: Springer, 2015, p. 91.

15   Ari Shavit, "Survival of the fittest," *Haaretz*, January 8, 2004, www.haaretz.com/survival-of-the-fittest-1.61345

16   Morris, *Israel's Border Wars*, pp. 431–2.

17   Guy Rolnik, "Who is benefitting from a never-ending peace 'process'?" *Haaretz*, June 28, 2015, www.haaretz.com/peace/1.601471; Edward Said, *Peace and its Discontents: Essays on Palestine in the Middle East Peace Process*, New York: Vintage, 1995.

18   Lesley Terris, "It's time to revisit the Arab peace initiative," *Jerusalem Post*, January 12, 2014; "Lost moments: the Arab peace initiative, 10 years later," *Atlantic*, March 29, 2012.

19   Schindler, *A History of Modern Israel*, p. 93.

20   Schindler, *A History of Modern Israel*, p. 95.

21   Celina Mashiach, "Children's literature in Hebrew," *Jewish Women's Archive*, http://jwa.org/encyclopedia/article/childrens-literature-in-hebrew

22   On Iraq: Abbas Shiblak, *The Lure of Zion*, Atlantic Highlands, N.J.: Humanities Press, 1986; Moshe Gat, "The connection between the bombings in Baghdad and the emigration of the Jews from Iraq: 1950–51," *Middle Eastern Studies*, vol. 24, no. 3, 1988, pp. 312–29; on Morocco: Asher Ben-Haim, *The Zionist Illusion*, Bloomington, Ind.: iUniverse, 2010, p. 19; Igal Bin-Nun, *Les relations secrètes entre le Maroc et Israël… [Secret Relations Between Morocco and Israel …]*, Paris: PUF, 2002.

23   Rough estimate by Élie Barnavi, apparently valid even for the most ideological period of Zionist colonization: see Gur Alroey, "Aliya to America? A comparative look at Jewish mass migration, 1881–1914," *Modern Judaism*, vol. 28, no. 2, 2008, pp. 109–33.

24   Shohat, "Rupture and return," p. 248.

25   Shohat, "Rupture and return," p. 251.

26   Quoted by Yehuda Shenhav, "History begins at home," in Silberstein, *Postzionism*, p. 264.

27   Michel Abitbol, "Introduction," in Heymann and Abitbol, *L'historiographie israélienne aujourd'hui*, pp. 15–16.

28   A detailed account of this chapter of the history of Zionism can be found in Schonfeld, *Genocide in the Holy Land*, which levels accusations that

were later confirmed by several academics. See also Shohat, "Sephardim in Israel."

29 Ruth Blau, *Les gardiens de la cité*, p. 275.

30 Ruth Blau, *Les gardiens de la cité*, pp. 187–8.

31 Meira Weiss, *The Chosen Body: The Politics of the Body in Israeli Society*, Stanford, Calif.: Stanford University Press, 2002, p. 61; Yossi Klein Halevi, "Where are our children?" *Jerusalem Report*, March 21, 1996, pp. 14–19.

32 Quoted in Ruth Blau, *Les gardiens de la cité*, p. 271

33 Quoted in Ruth Blau, *Les gardiens de la cité*, p. 273.

7 Jewish Opposition to Zionism

1   Yosef Salmon, "Zionism and anti-Zionism in traditional Judaism in Eastern Europe," in Almog et al., *Zionism and Religion*, p. 25; for a detailed treatment of Jewish opposition to Zionism see Rabkin, *A Threat From Within*.

2   Leibowitz, *Peuple, Terre, État*, p. 133.

3   Central Rabbinical Council, "A clarification of Torah doctrine," *New York Times,* January 8, 2008.

4   Leibowitz, *Peuple, Terre,* État, p. 144.

5   Emile Marmorstein, "Religious opposition to nationalism in the Middle East," *International Affairs*, vol. 28, no. 3, July 1952, pp. 344–59.

6   Shmuel Almog, in *Zionism and Religion*; Ravitzky, *Messianism, Zionism, and Jewish Religious Radicalism*; Ehud Luz, *Parallels Meet: Religion and Nationalism in the Early Zionist Movement, 1882–1904*, Philadelphia, Pa.: Jewish Publication Society, 1988; Yosef Salmon, *Religion and Zionism: First Encounters*, Jerusalem: Magnes Press, 2002.

7   The most complete source for Haredi anti-Zionist thought is the anthology edited by Aharon Rosenberg, *Mishkenoth ha-ro'yim*.

8   Avineri, *The Making of Modern Zionism,* p. 13.

9   Yosef Salmon, in Almog et al., *Zionism and Religion*, p. 32.

10 Alexander Lapidos to Mordecai Eliasberg; letter quoted by Yosef Salmon in Almog et al., *Zionism and Religion*, p. 25.

11 Israel Domb, *Transformation: The Case of the Neturei Karta*, Brooklyn, N.Y.: Hachomo, 1989, pp. 14–15.

12 Güdemann, quoted in Robert S. Wistrich, "Zionism and its religious critics in Vienna," in Almog et al., *Zionism and Religion*, p. 151.

13 Shelomo Zalman Landau (ed.), *Or la-yesharim* [*Light for the Righteous*], Warsaw: Heller, 1900.

14 Ephraim Weingott, *Orah le-Tsion* [*Light unto Zion*], Warsaw, n.p., 1902; Abraham Baruch Steinberg (ed.), *Daath Harabanim* [*The Judgment of the Rabbis*], Warsaw: Unterhendler, 1902.

15 Avraham Baruch Steinberg, quoted in Emmanuel Lévyne, *Judaïsme contre Sionisme* [*Judaism against Zionism*], Paris: Clerc, 1969, p. 226.

16 The name consists of the last words from Ecclesiastes 7:3: "by the sadness of the face the heart is made good."

17 Israel Rubin, *Satmar: An Island in the City*, Chicago, Ill.: Quadrangle, 1972, p. 40.

18 Hillel Danziger, *Guardian of Jerusalem*, Brooklyn, N.Y.: Mesorah, 1983, p. 450.

19 Menachem Friedman, "The state of Israel as a theological dilemma," in Baruch Kimmerling (ed.), *The Israeli State and Society: Boundaries and Frontiers*, Albany, N.Y.: SUNY Press, 1989, pp. 165–215.

20 Ben Hayim, *Ish ha-hashkafa.*, p. 172.

21 Shindler, *A History of Modern Israel*, p. 26.

22 Omar Kamil, "The synagogue, civil society, and Israel's Shas party," *Critique: Critical Middle Eastern Studies*, vol. 10, no.18, 2001, pp. 47–66.

23 www.mfa.gov.il/mfa/aboutisrael/history/pages/results%20of%20 elections%20to%20the%2016th%20knesset%20-%20jan%2028-.aspx

24 William B. Helmreich, *The World of the Yeshiva: An Intimate Portrait of Orthodox Jewry*, New Haven, Conn.: Yale University Press, 1986.

25 Anthony Weiss, "Ultra-Orthodox break from tradition," *Forward*, November 28, 2007.

26 For a selection of documents opposing participation in Israeli elections, see *Milhamoth Hashem* [*God's Wars*], Monroe, N.Y., 1983.

27 Aharaon Shalom ben-Itzhak Naimi (ed.), *Ari Ala mi-Bavel* [*A Lion Ascended from Babylonia*], Jerusalem: Shemesh Tsedaka, 1986, p. 109.

28 In reference to the biblical passage (Exodus 13:21): "And the Lord went before them by day in a pillar of cloud, to lead them the way; and by night in a pillar of fire, to give them light, to go by day and night."

29 David Yehudiof, *Hasabba Kadisha Baba Salé* [The Holy Old Man Baba Salé], vol. 2, Netivot, Israel: Barukh Abuhatsera, 1987, pp. 217–19.

30 Hofets Haïm, quoted in Rosenberg (ed.), *Mishkenoth ha-ro'yim*, vol. 2, p. 505.

31 Kenbib, *Juifs et musulmans au Maroc*, p. 557.

32 Yoel Teitelbaum, *Vayoel Moshe* [*And Moses Decided*; the title is a play on words which includes the names of the author and his grandfather], Brooklyn, N.Y.: Jerusalem Book Store, 1985, vol. 2, sect. 157.

33 Moshe Feinstein, *Iggueroth Moshe* [*Moshe's Epistles*], Brooklyn, N.Y.: Moriah Offset, 1959, part Orah Haim, siman (no.) 46, p. 105.

34 Ravitzky, *Messianism*, p. 35.

35 Pinhas Polonsky, *Рав Авраам-Ицхак ha-Коэн Кук. Личность и учение.* [*Rabbi Avraham Itzhak Hacohen Kook: Personality and Doctrine*], Jerusalem: Mahanaim – Beit Harav, 2006, p. 16.

36 Michael Oren, "Seven existential threats," *Commentary*, May 2009, www. commentarymagazine.com/article/seven-existential-threats/; soon after the publication of this article the author became Israel's ambassador to the United States.

37 Ian S. Lustic, "Israel as a non-Arab state: the political implications of mass immigration of non-Jews," *Middle East Journal*, vol. 53, no. 3, 1999, p. 417.

38 Chaim Levinson, "Dozens of top Israeli rabbis sign ruling to forbid rental of homes to Arabs," *Haaretz*, December 2, 2010.

39   Ravitzky, *Messianism,* p. 16.

40   Sholom Baer Schneerson, "Three questions and answers on Zionism and Zionists," *Jewish Guardian,* vol. 2, no. 8, Spring 1984, pp. 19–24.

41   Rosenberg, *Mishkenoth ha-ro'yim,* p. 379.

42   Babylonian Talmud, Tractate Megillah, p. 28a.

43   Ravitzky, *Messianism,* p. 60.

44   Solomon Breibart, *Explorations in Charleston's Jewish History,* Charleston, S.C.: History Press, 2005, p. 58.

45   Norton Mezvinsky, "Reform Judaism and Zionism: early history and change," in Roselle Tekner et al. (eds.), *Anti-Zionism: Analytical Reflections,* Brattleboro, Vt.: Amana , 1989, p. 315.

46   Mezvinsky, "Reform Judaism," p. 319.

47   Allan C. Brownfield, "Zionism at 100: remembering its often prophetic Jewish critics," *Issues of the American Council for Judaism,* Washington DC, Summer 1997, pp. 1–2 and 7–10.

48   Quoted in Brownfield, "Zionism at 100."

49   Morris Jastrow, Jr., *Zionism and the Future of Palestine: The Fallacies and Dangers of Political Zionism,* New York: Macmillan, 1919.

50   Ben Erenreich, "Zionism is the problem," *Los Angeles Times,* March 15, 2009.

51   Elmer Berger, *Memoirs of an Anti-Zionist Jew,* p. 57.

52   Berger, *Memoirs of an Anti-Zionist Jew,* p. 12.

53   Brownfield, "Zionism at 100," p. 9.

54   Barnavi, "Sionismes," p. 225.

55   See e.g. Alex Klaushofer, "The Unorthodox Orthodox," *Observer,* July 21, 2002 ; Agnès Gruda, "Un groupe de juifs ultrareligieux établi à Sainte-Agathe souhaite l'abolition d'Israël" ["A group of ultra-religious Jews settled at Sainte-Agathe seeks the abolition of Israel"], *La Presse,* May 26, 2002.

56   See e.g. www.nkusa.org; www.jewsagainstzionism.com; www.jato.org; www.jewishvoiceforpeace; www.counterpunch.org; www.tikkun.org; www.gush-shalom.org; www.palsolidarity.org; www.jcall.eu; www.thejc.com; www.ijsn.net

57   Rubin, *Satmar,* pp. 175–6.

58   Avner Cohen, *Israel and the Bomb,* New York: Columbia University Press, 1999.

59   Segev, *One Palestine, Complete,* p. 43.

60   Brian Klug, *Being Jewish and Doing Justice: Bringing Argument to Life,* London: Vallentine Mitchell, 2011, pp. 199–210.

61   Chemi Shalev, "When right-wing support for Israel clashes with liberal values of diaspora Jews," *Haaretz,* April 9, 2014, www.haaretz.com/blogs/west-of-eden/.premium-1.584838

62   Edwin Montagu, "Memorandum on the anti-Semitism of the present government—submitted to the British Cabinet," August 1919, www.zionism.israel.com/hdoc/Montagu|_balfour.htm

63   Sheila Stern Polishook, "The American Federation of Labor, Zionism and the First World War," *American Jewish Historical Quarterly,* vol. 65, no. 3, 1976, pp. 228–44.

64 Michel Abitbol, *Les deux terres promises. Les juifs de France et le sionisme ,
    1897–1945* [*Two Promised Lands: Jews of France and Zionism, 1897–1945*],
    Paris: Perrin, 2010, p. 43.

65 "Zionist Congresses," *Encyclopaedia Judaica*, vol. 16, p. 1164.

66 Sand, *The Invention of the Jewish People*, p. 21.

67 Alexander Keith, *The Land of Israel According to the Covenant with Abraham,
    with Isaac, and with Jacob*, Edinburgh: William Whyte, 1843.

68 Michael Berkowitz, "Rejecting Zion, embracing the Orient: the life and death
    of Jacob Israel de Haan," in Ivan Davidson Kalmar and Derek J. Penslar (eds.),
    Orientalism and the Jews, Waltham, Mass.: Brandeis University Press, 2005, pp.
    109–24.

69 Ruth Blau, *Les gardiens de la cité*, p. 276.

70 Martin Sicker, *Pangs of the Messsiah: The Troubled Birth of the Jewish State*,
    Westport, Conn.: Praeger, 2000, p. 62. The text of the petition is frequently re-
    produced in Neturei Karta publications; see "Memorandum to King Hussein,"
    Jewish Guardian, no. 3, November 1974, p. 5.

71 "Meeting with King Hussein by Rabbi Yosef Sonnenfeld," *Jewish Guardian*,
    vol. 2, no. 6, Autumn 1982.

72 For more information on the Histadrut, see Zachary Lockman, *Comrades
    and Enemies: Arab and Jewish Workers in Palestine, 1906–1994*, Berkeley,
    Calif.: University of California Press, 1996; Michel Shalev, *Labour and Polit-
    ical Economy in Israel*, Oxford: Oxford University Press, 1992; Getzel Karsal,
    Ha-histadrut. Arba'im Shenot Haim [*Forty Years of the Histadrut*], Tel Aviv:
    Tarbut ve Hinuch, 1960.

73 Joseph Haim Sonnenfeld quoted in Rosenberg, *Mishkenoth ha-ro'yim*, vol. 2,
    p. 440.

74 Hart, *Zionism*.

75 Wasserman, *Epoch*, p. 24.

76 See e.g. Moshe Ber Beck, *Kuntres Shav Shakad Shomer*, Monsey, NY (n.p.),
    1982.

77 *New York Times*, February 11, 2001 (emphasis in the original).

78 Interview by the author with David Weiss and Moses Katz, New York,
    November 2002.

79 Marc Ellis, *Judaism Does Not Equal Israel: The Rebirth of the Jewish Prophetic*,
    New York: New Press, 2009.

80 Ahad Ha'am (Asher Ginzberg), "Truth from Eretz Israel," in Adam Shatz
    (ed.), *Prophets Outcast*, New York: Nation, 2004, pp. 32–3.

81 Shatz, *Prophets Outcast*, p. 45.

82 Shatz, *Prophets Outcast*, p. 54.

83 Seth Farber, *Radicals, Rabbis and Peacemakers*, Monroe,Me.: Common
    Courage Press, 2005.

84 Peter Beinart, *The Crisis of Zionism*, New York : Henry Holt, 2012.

85 Shatz, *Prophets Outcast*, p. xii.

86 Walter Laqueur, *A History of Zionism*, London: Weidenfeld & Nicholson,
    1972, p. 596.

87 Isaac Deutscher, "The non-Jewish Jew," in Shatz, *Prophets Outcast*, p. 15.

88 Albert Einstein, "Three statements," in Shatz, *Prophets Outcast*, p. 64.

89 Quoted in Shatz, *Prophets Outcast*, p. 88.

90 Buber, in Shatz, *Prophets Outcast*, p. 57.

91 Benvenisti quoted in Bernard Avishai, *The Tragedy of Zionism: How its Revolutionary Past Haunts Israeli Democracy*, New York: Helios Press, 2002, p. 302.

92 Robert S. Wistrich, "Trotsky's Jewish Question," *Forward*, August 18, 2010, http://forward.com/opinion/130174/trotsky-s-jewish-question/

93 Elie Barnavi, *A Historical Atlas of the Jewish People*, New York: Schocken, 1992, p. 214.

94 For somewhat conflicting views on the subject see Ruth R. Wisse, *Jews and Power*, New York: Schocken, 2007; and David Biale, *Power and Powerlessness in Jewish History*, New York: Schocken, 1986.

95 Shalom Dov Ber Schneerson, "Three questions and answers on Zionists and Zionism," *Jewish Guardian*, vol. 2, no. 8, Spring 1984, p. 22.

96 Ruth Blau, *Gardiens de la cité*, p. 249.

97 Shapiro, *Between the Yeshiva World*, p. 99.

98 Babylonian Talmud, Tractate "Yoma," p. 85b.

99 Babylonian Talmud, Tractate "Yevamoth," p. 79a.

100 Babylonian Talmud, Perek Hashalom, Tractate "Derekh Erets."

101 Babylonian Talmud, Perek Hashalom, Tractate "Derekh Erets."

102 Avineri, *Zionism and Religion*, p. 4.

103 For a detailed analysis of the three oaths see Ravitzky, *Messianism*, pp. 211–34.

104 Moshe Dayan quoted in Shatz, *Prophets Outcast*, p. 26.

105 Peter A. Bucky, *The Private Albert Einstein*, Kansas City, Mo.: Andrews & McMeel, 1992, p. 64.

106 Fred Jerome, *Einstein on Israel and Zionism: His Provocative Ideas About the Middle East*, New York: St. Martin's Press, 2009.

107 Irving Reichert quoted in Ross, *Rabbi Outcast*, p. 37.

108 Rimantas Vanagas, *Nenusigrežk nuo saves: gyvieji tilta* [*Don't Turn Away From Yourself: Living Bridges*], Vilnius: Vyturys, 1995, pp. 69–70.

109 A more detailed treatment of this issue can be found in Rabkin, *A Threat From Within*, ch. 4.

110 "Torah comments during the Zionist war in Lebanon," *Jewish Guardian*, vol. 2, no. 8, Spring 1984, pp. 16–17.

111 David Ben-Gurion quoted in Schindler, *A History of Modern Israel*, p. 65.

112 *Torat Rabbi Amram*, Jerusalem (no. pub.), 1977, p. 17.

113 Ravitzky, *Messianism,* p. 75.

114 Yitzhak Blau, "Ploughshares into swords: contemporary religious Zionists and moral constraints," *Tradition,* vol, 34, no. 4, 2000, pp. 39–60.

115 For a Haredi account of this event, see Emil Marmorstein, *A Martyr's Message*, London, 1975, and Monsey, N.Y. (no publ.), 2000.

116 Colin Shindler, *Triumph of Military Zionism: Nationalism and the Origins of the Israeli Right*, London: Tauris, 2010, pp. 13 ff.

117 Yehuda Slutzki quoted in Danziger, *Guardian of Jerusalem*, p. 443.

118 David Tidhar quoted in Danziger, *Guardian of Jerusalem*, p. 444.

119 Nachman Ben Yehuda, *Political Assassination by Jews*, Albany, N.Y.: SUNY Press, 1993.

120 "Man has separated lust and sorrow/But God holds them together like day and night/I know lust; I know intense suffering./I praise God's one name." Quoted in Kalmar and Penslar, *Orientalism and the Jews*, p. 122.

121 Amrom Blau, "A call from Jerusalem," *Jewish Guardian*, no. 1, April 1974, p. 2.

122 Hannah Arendt, "To save the Jewish homeland," (published in May 1948), in *Jew as Pariah*, New York: Grove Press, 1978, p. 187.

123 "Orthodox Jews worldwide protest Zionist atrocities in Gaza," NK press release, February 8, 2008.

124 Saul Sadka, "Haredi sect brands Chief Rabbi Metzer 'Zionist stooge', wicked," *Haaretz*, February 5, 2008.

125 Lion Feuchtwanger, *Raquel, the Jewess of Toledo*, New York: Messner, 1956.

126 Steven M. Cohen, "The American Jewish community is fracturing. What's causing it?" *The New Republic,* March 16, 2015.

127 Ofer Shelah, "Saving *Munich*: Spielberg talks," Ynetnews, February 20, 2006, www.ynetnews.com/articles/0,7340,L-3219061,00.html

128 Moshe Sober, *Beyond the Jewish State*, pp. 30–1.

129 Barak Ravid, "Netanyahu calls urgent meeting after rightists attack IDF base," *Haaretz*, December 2011.

130 Amos Harel, "IDF rabbinate publication during Gaza war : We will show no mercy on the cruel," Haaretz, January 26, 2009.

131 http://torathamelech.blogspot.ca/; see also Daniel Estrin, "The King's Torah: a Rabbinic text or a call to terror?" *Forward,* January 20, 2010.

132 Matthew Wagner, "US rabbis urge change in IDF war code," *Jerusalem Post*, August 21, 2006.

133 Laurence J. Silberstein and Robert L. Cohn (eds.), *The Other in Jewish Thought and History,* New York: New York University Press, 1994, p. 274.

134 Isi Leibler, "The validation of Jewish anti-Zionism," *Jerusalem Post*, January 11, 2006.

135 Among them are Jack Ross, *Rabbi Outcast*; Adam Shatz, *Prophets Outcast*; Tony Kushner and Alisa Solomon (eds.), *Wresting with Zion*, New York: Grove Press, 2003; Jacqueline Rose, *The Question of Zion*, Princeton, N.J.: Princeton University Press, 2005; Ella Shohat, *Le sionisme du point de vue de ses victimes juives* [*Zionism from the Viewpoint of its Jewish Victims*], Paris: La Fabrique, 2006; David Landy, *Jewish Identity and Palestinian Rights*, London: Zed, 2011; Anthony Loewenstein, *My Israel Question*, Melbourne, Vic.: Melbourne University Publishing, 2006.

136 Central Rabbinical Council, *To Those Who May Wonder Why We Are Here Today*, February 7, 2002.

137 Ruth Blau, *Les gardiens de la cité*, pp. 279–80.

138 "BBC poll: Israel among world's least popular nations," *Haaretz*, May 25, 2013,

www.haaretz.com.world-news-bbc-poll-israel-among-world-s-least-popular-nations-1.525890

139 Interview with Rabbi Meyer Weberman, November 11, 2002, Williamsburg, N.Y.

140 "Meah Shearim Centennial hears call for Jerusalem internationalization," *Jewish Guardian*, no. 1, April 1974, pp. 9, 15.

141 Official letter from Yasser Arafat to Rabbi Moshe Hirsch, Ramallah, April 23, 2002.

8 Israeli Society and Jewish Communities

1   Adi Ophir, "Identity of the victims and victims of identity," in Laurence J. Silberstein (ed.), *Postzionism: A Reader*, New Brunswick, N.J.: Rutgers University Press, 2008, pp. 81–101.

2   Esther Benbassa, *La souffrance comme identité* [*Suffering As Identity*], Paris: Hachette, 2007.

3   Jie-Huyn Lim, "Victimhood nationalism in contested memories: national mourning and global responsibilities," in Aleida Assmann and Sebastien Conrad (eds.), *Memory in a Global Age: Discourses, Practices and Trajectories*, New York: Palgrave Macmillan, 2010, pp. 138–62.

4   Henriette Dahan Kalev "Fear of Arabness," in Stephen Hessel and Michèle Huppert (eds.), *Fear Itself: Reasoning the Unreasonable*, New York: Rodopi, 2010, pp. 151–62, http://works.bepress.com/henriettedahankalev/4

5   Shohat, "Sephardim in Israel."

6   Chaim Levinson, "Israel has 101 different types of permits governing Palestinian movement," *Haaretz*, December 23, 2011.

7   See the minutes of a symposium on morality and power held during the first Intifada: Daniel J. Elazar (ed.), *Morality and Power: Contemporary Jewish Views*, Lanham, Md.: Jerusalem Center for Public Affairs, 1990. The majority of participants accepted the principle of "*raison d'état*" and the imperative of state survival as priorities that should overcome individual moral scruples.

8   Don Yehiya and Liebman, "The symbol system," p. 229.

9   Yaron Ezrahi, *Rubber Bullets: Power and Conscience in Modern Israel*, Berkeley, Calif.: University of California Press, 1998, p. 47.

10 Bensoussan, *Un nom impérissable*, p. 35.

11 David Grossman, "Hail Caesar," *Haaretz*, February 22, 2002.

12 "Sharp rise in Israelis seeking German citizenship," Ynet, July 24, 2007, www.ynet.co.il/english/articles/0,7340,L-3429414,00.html

13 Matthew Kalman, "Report on Israeli academics in the United States fuels long-held concerns about brain drain," *Chronicle of Higher Education*, February 29, 2008. In comparison, only 12 percent of Canadian academics move south of the border to work, though Canada is far closer to the United States geographically and culturally.

14 The term itself has many meanings, which reflects an increasing sense among

many Israelis that the maps of meaning provided by Zionism are no longer adequate. Alongside the post-Zionism reader mentioned above (Silberstein, *Postzionism*), we find criticism of the intellectual phenomenon it denotes: Elhanan Yakira, *Post-Zionism, Post-Holocaust: Three Essays on Denial, Forgetting, and the Delegitimation of Israel*, Cambridge : Cambridge University Press, 2009; Shlomo Avineri, "Post-Zionism doesn't exist," *Haaretz*, July 6, 2007, www.haaretz.com/post-zionism-doesn-t-exist-1.224973

15   See Uri Ram, "Postcolonial studies in Israel," in Silberman, *Postzionism*, pp. 61–77.

16   Yehouda Shenhav, *Arab Jews: A Postcolonial Reading of Nationalism, Religion and Identity*, Stanford, Calif.: Stanford University Press, 2006.

17   Eli Ashkenazi, "Most Jews would refuse to live in a building with Arabs," *Haaretz*, March 23, 2006.

18   Ross, *Rabbi Outcast*, p. 81.

19   Max Blumenthal, *Goliath: Life and Loathing in Greater Israel*, New York: Nation, 2013, p. 409.

20   Among more recent cases: Benjamin Weinthal, "Inclusion of anti-Israel speaker at Berlin conference on ways to tackle anti-Semitism sparks uproar," *Jerusalem Post*, November 6, 2013; Vicky Tobianah, "Montréal Jewish festival cancels panel by anti-Birthright activist," *Haaretz*, November 3, 2013; see also a study dealing with the effects of this practice on academic freedom: Susan G. Drummond, *Unthinkable Thoughts: Academic Freedom and the One-State Model for Israel and Palestine*, Vancouver, BC: UBC Press, 2013.

21   Berkowitz, "Rejecting Zion," p. 115.

22   Landy, *Jewish Identity and Palestinian Rights*.

23   Ross, *Rabbi Outcast*, p. 167.

24   Yitzchak Blau, "Ploughshares into swords: contemporary religious Zionists and moral constraints," *Tradition*, vol. 34, no. 4, 2000, p. 57.

25   Susan Saulny, "A long night, and breakfast with Arafat," *New York Times*, March 31, 2002, www.nytimes.com/2002/03/31/nyregion/a-long-night-and-breakfast-with-arafat.html

26   Nicholas Blincoe, "A love under fire," *Guardian*, May 31, 2003, www.theguardian.com/world/2003/may/31/israelandthepalestinians.weekend7

27   Evron, *Jewish State or Israeli Nation*, p. 253.

28   Marc Ellis, *O Jerusalem: The Contested Future of the Jewish Covenant*, Minneapolis, Minn.: Fortress Press, 1999, p. 52.

29   Sam Sokol, "Jewish Agency accuses Diaspora Affairs Ministry of disinformation on diaspora initiative," *Jerusalem Post*, August 20, 2014, www.jpost.com/Diaspora/Jewish-Agency-accuses-Diaspora-Affairs-Ministry-of-disinformation-on-Diaspora-initiative-371662; Jay Ruderman, "Time for a strong Diaspora Affairs Ministry," *Times of Israel*, May 15, 2015,http://blogs.timesofisrael.com/time-for-a-strong-diaspora-affairs-ministry/

30   Yaakov Lappin, "Christians: We'll fight for Israel," Ynet, September 24, 2006.

31   Elliot Resnick, "'Tony Kushner is disingenuous and dissembling': an inter-

view with CUNY Board of Trustees member Jeffrey Wiesenfeld," *Jewish Press*, May 11, 2011.

32 Natasha Mozgovaya, "Christian Zionists unite in D.C. to express support for Israel," *Haaretz*, July 20, 2011.

33 Michael Lipka, "More white evangelicals than American Jews say God gave Israel to the Jewish people," Pew Research Center, October 3, 2013. www. pewresearch.org/fact-tank/2013/10/03/more-white-evangelicals-than-american-jews-say-god-gave-israel-to-the-jewish-people/#comments.

34 Robert Booth, "Israeli attack on Gaza flotilla sparks international outrage," *Guardian*, May 31, 2010, www.theguardian.com/world/2010/may/31/israeli-attacks-gaza-flotilla-activists.

35 Frederick Krantz, "One-state would mean the liquidation of Israel," *The Gazette*, November 14, 2003.

36 Josh Nathan-Kazis, "Oren speaking at Brandeis creates a commencement controversy," *Forward*, April 28, 2010, http://forward.com/news/127613/oren-speaking-at-brandeis-creates-a-commencement-c/

37 Leibowitz, *Peuple, Terre, État*, p. 154.

9 Israel in the International Arena

1 www.worldpublicopinion.org/pipa/pdf/mar11/BBCEvals_Mar11_rpt.pdf

2 Ryan Jones, "Israel increasingly sees boycotts as existential threat," *Israel Today*, June 4, 2015, www.israeltoday.co.il/NewsItem/tabid/178/nid/26722/Default.aspx

3 Peter Beaumont, "EU issues guidelines on labelling products from Israeli settlements," *Guardian*, November 11, 2015, www.theguardian.com/world/2015/nov/11/eu-sets-guidelines-on-labelling-products-from-israeli-settlements

4 M. J. Rosenberg, "Why the term "Israel first" matters," *Huffington Post*, February 3, 2012, www.huffingtonpost.com/mj-rosenberg/why-the-term-israel-first_b_1252789.html

5 John J. Mearsheimer and Stephen M. Walt, "The Israel lobby," *London Review of Books*, March 23, 2006,www.lrb.co.uk/v28/n06/john-mearsheimer/the-israel-lobby

6 "ISIS leader Baghdadi to Jews: Palestine will be your graveyard," *Jerusalem Post*, December 26, 2015, www.jpost.com/Arab-Israeli-Conflict/ISIS-leader-Baghdadi-to-Israel-We-havent-forgotten-about-you-438483

7 "Israel buys most oil smuggled from ISIS territory – report," *Globes: Israel's Business News*, November 30, 2015, www.globes.co.il/en/article.aspx?did=1001084873&from=iglobes

8 John J. Mearsheimer and Stephen M. Walt, *The Israel Lobby and U.S. Foreign Policy*, New York: Farrar, Strauss & Giroux, 2007.

9 Yakov M. Rabkin, "La campagne contre l'Iran: le lobby sioniste et l'opinion juive" [The campaign against Iran: the Zionist lobby and Jewish opinion"], "*Revue internationale et stratégique*, Paris: 70, 2008, pp. 195–208; for an English version see www.acjna.org/acjna/articles_detail.aspx?id=575

10 Jeff Halper, *War Against the People: Israel, the Palestinians and Global Pacification*, London: Pluto, 2015.

11 Evan Gottesman, "An Israeli pivot to Eurasia?" *The Diplomat* (Tokyo), December 2, 2015, http://thediplomat.com/2015/12-an-israeli-pivot-to-eurasia/

12 http://mfa.gov.il/MFA/PressRoom/2015/Pages/3-3-million-visitors-to-Israel-in-2014.aspx

13 http://eajc.org/page84/news24995.html

14 Peter Beaumont, "Netanyahu meets Putin to discuss concerns over Russian activity in Syria," *Guardian*, September 21, 2015, www.theguardian.com/world/2015/sep/21/netanyahu-meets-with-putin-over-concerns-of-russian-support-for-assad

15 Gil Hoffman, "The Israelis have spoken—Putin is their person of the year for 2015," *Jerusalem Post*, January 1, 2016, www.jpost.com/Israel-News/The-Israelis-have-spoken-Putin-is-their-person-of-the-year-for-2015-439074

16 Yaakov Lappin, "Israeli defense exports hit record high," *Jerusalem Post*, July 24, 2013, www.jpost.com/Defense/Israeli-defense-exports-hit-record-high-320850; Ben Lynfield, "Israeli arms exports under scrutiny amid claims they are 'helping to fuel conflict in South Sudan' despite EU embargo," *Independent*, August 12, 2015, www.independent.co.uk/news/world/middle-east/israeli-arms-exports-under-scrutiny-amid-claims-they-are-helping-to-fuel-conflict-in-south-sudan-10452399.html

17 Kole Kilibarda, *Canadian and Israeli Defense—Industrial and Homeland Security Ties: An Analysis*, 2008, www.sscqueens.org/sites/default/files/Canadian%?20and%20Israeli%20Defense%20Industrial%20and%20Homeland%20Security%20Ties.pdf.

18 "Canadian Passport Abuse," *Canadian Encyclopedia*, www.thecanadianencyclopedia.com/artikcles/macleans/canadian-passport-abuse

19 "Statistics on Palestinian minors in the custody of the Israeli security forces," Btselem, December 2, 2015, www.btselem.org/statistics/minors_in_custody.

20 Ben-Gurion, *Israel: Years of Challenge*, p.134.

21 Pappe, *The Ethnic Cleansing of Palestine*.

22 "Gold stresses common Israeli-Arab interests in unprecedented interview to Saudi paper," *Jerusalem Post*, December 28, 2015, www.jpost.com/Middle-East/Gold-stresses-common-Israeli-Arab-interests-in-unprecedented-interview-to-Saudi-paper-438689

23 Amnon Barzilai, "More Israelis favor transfer of Palestinians, Israeli Arabs—poll finds," *Haaretz*, March 12, 2002.

24 Ifat Maoz and Roy A. Eidelson, "Psychological bases of extreme policy preferences: how the personal beliefs of Israeli-Jews predict their support for population transfer in the Israeli-Palestinian conflict," *American Behavioral Scientist*, vol. 50 no. 11, July 2007, pp. 1476–97.

25 Catrina Stewart, "The new Israeli apartheid: poll reveals widespread Jewish support for policy of discrimination against Arab minority," *Indepen-*

dent, October 23, 2013, www.independent.co.uk/news/world/middle-east/the-new-israeli-apartheid-poll-reveals-widespread-jewish-support-for-policy-of-discrimination-8223548.html.

26 "Bilingual Jewish-Arab school in Jerusalem torched," *Times of Israel*, November 29, 2014, www.timesofisrael.com/bilingual-jewish-arab-school-in-jerusalem-torched/?fb_comment_id=656559981127345_656726707777339

27 Shira Rubin, "The new face of Jewish terror," *Foreign Policy*, August 20, 2015, http://foreignpolicy.com/2015/08/20/the-new-face-of-jewish-terror-hilltop-settlers-price-tag-attacks-israel/?utm_content=bufferec402&utm_medium=social&utm_source=twitter.com&utm_campaign=buffer

28 Quoted in Daniel Doron, "Avrum Burg and the demise of socialist Zionism," *Jerusalem Post*, February 8, 2015, www.jpost.com/Opinion/Avrum-Burg-and-the-demise-of-Socialist-Zionism-390415

29 Yitzhak Laor, "Get rid of Zionism," *Haaretz*, June 3, 2011.

30 Sober, *Beyond the Jewish State*, p. 26.

31 Meron Benvenisti, "The binational option," *Haaretz*, November 7, 2002; see also YairSheley, "The letters and a binational state," *Haaretz*, August 31, 2003.

32 Yakov M. Rabkin, "A glimmer of hope," *Tikkun*, July–August 2002, pp. 56–61; Virginia Q. Tilley, *The One-State Solution: A Breakthrough Plan for Peace in the Israeli-Palestinian Deadlock*, Ann Arbor, Mich.: University of Michigan Press, 2005; Ali Abunimah, *One Country: A Bold Proposal to End the Israeli-Palestinian Impasse*, New York, Metropolitan, 2006. For an overview of opinion in favor of a single state between the Jordan and the Mediterranean, see www.one-democratic-state.org

33 "The one state option," *Economist*, July 19, 2007.

34 Aluf Benn et al., "Olmert to Haaretz: two-state solution, or Israel is done for," *Haaretz*, November 29, 2007.

35 Sand, *The Invention of the Jewish People*.

36 Colin Shindler, *Israel and the European Left: between Solidarity and Deligitimation*, New York: Continuum, 2012.

37 Edward Said, "Diary," *London Review of Books*, vol. 22, no. 11, June 1, 2000.

38 Russell, quoted in Dina Porat, "Bertrand Russell on the Jewish state: 1943," *Studies in Zionism*, vol. 2, no. 1, 1981, pp. 125–31.

39 Shindler, *Israel and the European Left*, p. 168.

40 Quoted in Shindler, *A History of Modern Israel*, p. 57.

41 "1972: Japanese kill 26 at Tel Aviv airport," BBC On this day, http://news.bbc.co.uk/onthisday/hi/dates/stories/may/29/newsid_2542000/2542263.stm

42 Sasha Polakow-Suransky, *The Unspoken Alliance: Israel's Secret Relationship with Apartheid South Africa*, New York: Pantheon, 2010.

43 Adar Primor, "The unholy alliance between Israel's Right and Europe's anti-Semites," *Haaretz*, December 12, 2010.

44 Ben Hartman, "Norway attack suspect had anti-Muslim, pro-Israel views," *Jerusalem Post*, July 24, 2011.

45 Paul Hockenos, *Free to Hate: The Rise of the Right in Post-Communist Eastern Europe*, New York: Routledge, 1993; John Palmer, "The rise of far right parties across Europe is a chilling echo of the 1930s," *Guardian*, November 15, 2013, www.theguardian.com/commentisfree/2013/nov/15/far-right-threat-europe-integration; M. Golder, "Extreme right parties in Europe," *Annual Review of Political Science*, vol. 19, no. 1, 2015.

46 Alexey Shiropayev, "Моё открытие Израиля" ["My discovery of Israel"], http://nazdem.info/texts/256

47 This characterization belongs to Sami Michael, an acclaimed Israeli novelist and Nobel nominee: Lisa Goldman, "Sami Michael: 'Israel – Most racist state in the industrialized world,'" *+972*, August 2, 2009. http://972mag.com/author-sami-michael-israel-is-the-most-racist-state-in-the-industrialized-world/52602/

48 Dave McKinney, "Chicago mayor plans changes to police policy after deadly shootings," Reuters, December 30, 2015,www.reuters.com/article/us-usa-police-idUSKBN0UD18P20151231

49 Edmund Sanders and Batsheva Sobelman, "Israeli firms see a global market for their anti-terrorism know-how," *Los Angeles Times*, November 27, 2010, http://articles.latimes.com/2010/nov/27/world/la-fg-israel-homeland-security-20101128

50 Scott Wilson, "A shared history, a different conclusion," *Washington Post*, March 11, 2007.

51 Ben-Gurion, *Israel: Years of Challenge*, p. 198

52 Timothy Alexander Guzman, "Iran nuclear talks: remembering the Israeli attack on Iraq's peaceful nuclear reactor Osirak. Will history repeat itself?" www.globalresearch.ca/iran-nuclear-talks-remembering-the-israeli-attack-on-iraqs-peaceful-nuclear-reactor-osirak-will-history-repeat-itself/5358415

Conclusion

1 http://rabble.ca/news/2013/12/jnf-honors-stephen-harper-annual-gala-names-bird-sanctuary-after-pm

2 www.blog.standforisrael.org/articles/netanyahu-calls-on-american-jews-to-oppose-nuclear-deal-with-iran

3 Avineri, "Post-Zionism."

4 "Harper will defend Israel 'whatever the cost,'" CTV News, November 8, 2010, www.ctvnews.ca/harper-will-defend-israel-whatever-the-cost-1.572202

5 Gil Shefler, "Jews now a minority between the River and the Sea," *Jerusalem Post*, November 26, 2010, www.jpost.com/National-News/Jews-now-a-minority-between-the-River-and-the-Sea

6 Hassan Shaalan, "The Joint Arab List: seven new MKs, two women and a lot of hope," Ynet, www.ynetnews.com/articles/0,7340,L-4638619,00.html

7 Joseph Agassi, *Liberal Nationalism for Israel: Towards and Israeli National Identity,* Jerusalem and New York: Gefen, 2000.

8   Danièle Kriegel, "Les émigrés israéliens taxés de traîtrise à la cause sion-
    iste" ["Israeli emigrés accused of treachery to the Zionist cause"], *Le Point*,
    October 26, 2013.

9   Michael Lipka, "More white evangelicals than American Jews say God gave
    Israel to the Jewish people," Pew Research Center, October 3, 2013, www.
    pewresearch.org/fact-tank/2013/10/03/more-white-evangelicals-than-
    american-jews-say-god-gave-israel-to-the-jewish-people/

Index